PRAISE FOR
Faked Out: Tales for Lovers of Antiques and Art

"It is rare to come across eyewitness accounts of brushes with the antiques trade written by people who understand this unusual world. Arthur Cobin and Vivien Boniuk have compiled an amusing and well-written group of such stories, which are as educational as they are entertaining. *Faked Out* introduces you to the spectrum of characters that populate this world, and the fascinating situations you can find yourself in if you choose to enter it. I am confident seasoned antiquers and newcomers alike will find something of interest here."

> ~ Nick Dawes, Appraiser on Antiques Roadshow for PBS Television, produced by WGBH

"Collectors everywhere will discover something of themselves in these stories. They capture the emotions, from euphoria to anxiety, that every collector has experienced when faced with a great find."

> ~ Bruce Johnson, author of *Tales of the Grove Park Inn* and publisher of *ArtsAndCraftsCollector.com*

"Longtime antique collectors and dealers, Cobin and Boniuk have turned these sensibilities into skillfully written stories that are suspenseful, witty and provocative."

> ~ Thomas Hines, cultural, urban, and architectural historian, UCLA. Author of *Architecture of the Sun: Los Angeles Modernism, 1900-1970*

"If you love the quest for the perfect antique or flea market find, or if you just enjoy a good anecdote or story, this is the book for you. You will identify with the writers and it will bring back fond memories of treasures found and l

> ~ Alan M. Dersho

D1004690

"A fun and flavorful glimpse recalling the pre-internet world of antiquing — a series of musings from before the web-warriors dominated our game. Recollections from the days when you had to be there to touch, feel, smell and scrutinize the merchandise—and then compete with your cohorts to claim a treasured item. These short stories are captivating and entertaining—almost as cool as being there."

~ David S. Smith, Managing Editor, *Antiques and The Arts Weekly*

"In a market saturated with reality TV shows that glorify antiques and treasure hunting, it is delightful (and up until now visibly missing) to have a collection of short stories that capture the thrills, joys, intrigue, pitfalls and shenanigans of the antiques and art world. Although perhaps not true tales themselves, these stories resonate with the themes that we encounter in this business on a regular basis."

~ Nicholas D. Lowry, President. Swann Auction Galleries

FAKED OUT

Tales for Lovers of Antiques and Art

ARTHUR COBIN & VIVIEN BONIUK

Eyetooth
PRESS

Eyetooth Press LLC
New York

Filling Spaces and When It Snows in the Bronx and Rains in Hilton Head originally appeared in *Arts & Crafts Quarterly Magazine*.

Adirondack Camp and The Gift originally appeared in *Style 1900*.

Illustrations by Allison Constantine, alliconstantine@gmail.com
Design by Bobbi Benson, Wild Ginger Press, www.wildgingerpress.com

Publisher's Cataloging-in-Publication Data
Cobin, Arthur.
    Faked out : tales for lovers of antiques and art / Arthur Cobin and Vivien Boniuk.
    p. cm.
    ISBN: 978-0-9889295-0-0
    1. Antiques —Fiction. 2. Antique dealers—Fiction. 3. New York (N.Y.)—
Fiction. 4. Short stories.   I. Boniuk, Vivien. II. Title.
PS3603.O246 F35 2013
813—dc23   2013931639

Eyetooth Press LLC
NEW YORK
WWW.FAKED-OUT.COM

Dedicated to our forebears whose DNA endowed us with the collecting gene and to our families who have tolerated our obsessions—most of the time. Also, we are grateful to those in the trade: professionals, customers and friends. Their encouragement sparked our imagination and helped us create the stories in this book.

CONTENTS

INTRODUCTION

Twenty-four years ago we went on a cycling trip through the Cotswolds in England. In subsequent years we enjoyed many more biking holidays in the U.K., leisurely traveling through the lovely English countryside. Prior to or after the cycling, we would spend several days in London. Over the years we visited many of the antique shops and markets there, some of which are mentioned in our stories. On that first vacation, before leaving for our starting point in Oxford we shopped for reading material at one of London's numerous bookstalls. Among our purchases were, fortuitously, two short story collections: one was *Tales of the Unexpected* by Roald Dahl and the other, *Twelve Red Herrings* by Jeffrey Archer. Although we cannot expect to match the genius of these masters of fiction and the short story, we were inspired to begin writing short stories by two examples in particular: Dahl's *Parson's Pleasure* and Archer's *Cheap at Half the Price*. Each dealt with a facet of the antiques trade interspersed with a twist generated by the vagaries of human nature.

David Rago (publisher of *The Arts & Crafts Quarterly* and later *Style 1900*), recalling that Gustav Stickley had published fiction in his *Craftsman Magazine*, encouraged us to submit stories. Four were originally published in those magazines.

The paucity of fictional anthologies with antiques and art as common themes stands in sharp contrast to the current widespread interest in this area. This is exemplified by the enduring popularity of the British and American versions of the *Antiques Road Show* and its many offshoots, including *Pawn Stars* and *American Pickers*.

About 20 years ago, we met Irene Stella, founder of Stella Show

Management. Irene is a seminal figure in the growth of antique show management and continues to operate leading New York and national events. Irene not only gave us our first opportunity to participate in a major event, but she helped to fine-tune our buying and marketing skills. It was this exposure that enabled us to grow professionally and participate in shows in major venues throughout the country.

Our own experience in buying and selling antique jewelry, historic medals, New York memorabilia, books and art lends authenticity, we believe, to these diverse stories. However, the most important aspect of this experience is recognizing the relationships that develop between dealers and their customers. Woven into this world are the very human qualities that influence these events, including greed, jealousy, deception, irony and always the unpredictable element of chance. These and many more factors permeate the characters and plots in this anthology.

We had great fun inventing and writing these fables. We hope you share in our enthusiasm while reading them.

Arthur Cobin
Vivien Boniuk
New York, December 2012

ONE

Faked Out

On that Thursday afternoon in 2008 at Christies' New York auction room, Susan Hines sat on the edge of her seat as Lot #238 in Fine Arts and Sculptures came up. She wondered how the fabled Joseph Cornell box art sculpture titled *Pharmacy* would fare in the immediate post-crash art market. Ten minutes later she had her answer: Lot #238 quickly blew past its low estimate of $1.5 million. After competition from two phone bidders and a stone-faced buyer's representative in the audience, the final hammer price, including all commissions and fees, was $3,778,500. Susan Hines was a late-middle-aged woman, dressed unobtrusively in clothing from Target. She smiled broadly and strode confidently out of the gallery. Reaching 48th Street near Rockefeller Center, she continued at a brisk pace, heading back to her Upper East Side apartment a little over a mile away.

Joseph Cornell (1902–1973), innovative American artist, experimented with many 20th-century art forms. However, he is remembered mostly for his boxes. These creations featured unusual assemblages placed behind glass-fronted boxes of various sizes, from the dimensions of a shoe box to that of a medicine cabinet. Cornell created hundreds of boxes, initially selling them inexpensively. Fame intervened, increasing the prices to the low and middle five figures. After Cornell's death in 1973, better examples realized six figures. The Christies sale of *Pharmacy* in November 2008 established a record for Cornell's work.

Susan Hines, a retired nurse, had trained and spent her nursing career at the Cornell Medical Center, rising to the position of charge nurse on the orthopedic service. She loved the patients but not the paperwork. Her choice of career had been inspired by her late Aunt Catherine, a pioneer in the vitamin and health store field.

Catherine's father, Mel, owned and operated a drug store, aptly named Flushing Drugs, in Flushing, a working-class section of Queens. During the depression and war years, Catherine worked in the store. Although Mel encouraged Catherine to go to medical or nursing school, the young woman loved the drugstore atmosphere, and enjoyed advising the customers on purchases that would satisfy their various health concerns.

A frequent customer at the drugstore was the emerging artist, Joseph Cornell. He loved his visits to the little soda fountain, where he would sit on the revolving counter-stools as he discussed his artwork with the Hines family, both father and daughter. Many of Cornell's prescriptions were delivered personally by Catherine to his home on Utopia Parkway.

One day in 1946, Bill Gillis, a salesman for U.S. Vitamins, came into Flushing Drugs toting several suitcases filled with samples of a line of vitamins, minerals and nutrients in their own display cases. He suggested they be displayed at the front of the store, contrary to the then current practice of placing these items behind the prescription counter, with customers relying on the druggist for recommendations.

Within weeks, purchases of these "Health Pills" began to account for a significant percentage of their sales volume. Catherine convinced her father to devote window space to the "health stuff" to make passing customers more aware of their extensive over-the-counter vitamin and health products. Business boomed.

Fortuitously, a small retail space became available a few blocks away. With Catherine cheerleading, Mel took advantage of the opportunity to open another store with his partner/daughter, Catherine. This was the first health store in New York City, which had neither a soda fountain nor prescription services.

Ten years later, Mel retired. By that time, the partnership had opened eight "Certified Health Stores" in the New York Area. The fact that the initials on the logo—C.H.S.—could also stand for Catherine Hines Stores was not a coincidence.

During those busy and profitable years, their friend Joseph Cornell advanced from struggling artist to a big name on the art scene in post-war New York City. Despite his new-found fame, Cornell chose to live in his old neighborhood, where he and Catherine continued their close friendship. When Joseph Cornell died in 1973, Catherine owned over thirty Cornell boxes, all of which the artist had especially chosen for her. The business traded on the Amex under the symbol CHSP, with over a hundred stores located throughout the eastern seaboard of the United States.

Catherine's brother, Kevin, who was Susan's father, had fallen out with the family after the war. A returning veteran, he was troubled by alcohol addiction and suffered a downward spiral leading to suicide when Susan was seven years old. Catherine stepped up to the plate, supporting her sister-in-law Nancy and little Susan, through her school years and then nursing school. Fiercely independent, Susan accepted the financial help, insisting on working in the original Flushing store to repay her Aunt Catherine. While the three children

Catherine had with the erstwhile vitamin salesman Bill Gillis forged successful careers with CHS and made appropriate marriages, Susan focused totally on her nursing career.

In 1999, an elderly Aunt Catherine, approaching 80 and now living in a ten-room cooperative apartment on Park Avenue and 72nd Street, called her niece, Susan. They agreed to meet for lunch at *Nantes*, a cozy bistro in the East 80's. Other than at Christmas or other holiday gatherings, Susan rarely saw the family. Even casual observers at the restaurant would have noted a striking resemblance between the two women twenty-five years apart in age. They had the same sapphire eye color, aquiline noses, slim figures and short wiry hair, one head salt-and-pepper, the other completely salt.

It was not until dessert and coffee were served that Catherine broached the sensitive subject. "Susan, you have always been a completely unselfish person."

Her niece smiled, shook her head and replied, "No, Aunt Catherine, that's not entirely true. However, I won't bore you with a recitation of my many human faults."

"Susan, the reason for this luncheon is to discuss with you my association with the artist, Joseph Cornell. At one time, I had a very large collection of his signature boxes. Over the years, I disposed of some through sales to dealers and gifts to family members. Most recently, soon after Cornell's death in 1973, I donated ten of the best examples to the MCAM—Manhattan Contemporary Art Museum."

Catherine paused to sip her coffee. "Actually, I'm rather annoyed with them, because they took them out of the permanent collection on display and relegated them to the cellar! They are anticipating a retrospective on Cornell for the 50th anniversary of his death, but that won't be until 2023."

"I agree, Aunt Catherine—you have a right to be furious about that."

"Well, that is only part of the reason I invited you to lunch. For years, collectors and dealers have been badgering me to help locate Cornell's masterpiece, a box titled *Pharmacy*. The actual owner and location are unknown at this point. Meanwhile, twenty years ago, I was approached by a Toronto dealer with a supposedly similar piece that Cornell finished just before his death in 1973. Curiously, its title is *The Drugstore*. Considering the subject, I'm sure it would not surprise you that I purchased it for $120,000. I do not know its present market value."

Catherine stopped speaking as she looked at Susan to evaluate her reaction and to take one more bite of the usually forbidden chocolate mousse.

"I can certainly understand your attraction to the subject—it is, after all, the family's original business and the place where you met Mr. Cornell," Susan said.

"If I told the museum about it, they would be on my case to donate it, and even display it. After their behavior with my other donation, I would rather not do that, but would prefer that it go to you, Susan. Right now, I am keeping it in a large safe deposit box, into which it just snugly fits, at Citibank on 72nd and Madison."

Susan started to respond, but her aunt waved away her attempted reply. "If it is convenient, I would like to meet you this Friday at the bank. In contemplation of your agreement, I have rented a similar sized box in our joint names and have paid for ten years rental in advance. Now, only your signature as co-owner is required."

Catherine paused again and continued, looking directly at her niece. "At my death, which I hope will be toward the end rather than beginning of the rental, the box and its contents will be yours. It will be listed in my will and if you decide to sell it, my accountants advise me there will be no tax consequences for you."

"That's extremely generous of you, Aunt Catherine, but as you know, I never did anticipate benefitting from your estate and from your financial success. In any case, it is my sincere hope that there will be several extensions on the rental terms!"

"I know, dear. As the only real health professional in the family, I want you to have *The Drugstore* to keep or sell to make your future more comfortable financially."

Catherine refilled her coffee cup from the carafe on the table and wiped away a tear with her napkin. "One more thing—when the day arrives, let the museum know about your inheritance. First, it will spur their interest in purchasing *The Drugstore* should you elect to sell it. Equally important is the fact that it might elevate their interest in the Cornell boxes stored in the cellar enough to bring them up to the main floor. I was very fond of Joseph Cornell and his work deserves better exposure at the MCAM."

Ironically, Catherine Hines Gillis died, aged 87, just a week before the Christies Contemporary Art auction. Susan informed the attorney for the estate that the listed bequest was now in her possession.

Coming so soon after the record for the sale of *Pharmacy*, the contemporary art world was agog with the news of a heretofore unknown work by Cornell with the related title, *The Drugstore*. Nowhere was the buzz noisier than at the MCAM. After all, their great friend and benefactor, Catherine Hines Gillis, had donated previous important Cornell works. It was time for a working lunch of trustees and key museum personnel.

The cold and damp December weather reflected the mood at the MCAM Board of Directors meeting. The stock market was crashing, as were memberships and donations to the Museum. Towards the end of the meal, a short, bald man, wearing tiny octagonal steel-framed glasses, stood up and clinked his water glass to get the attention of the group. For the past fifteen years, Laurence Biscoy had been the director of the MCAM.

He began to speak in a firm voice. "First, I would like to remind you that both the Budget and Acquisitions committees have scheduled meetings in January. Today, I want to explore an issue with you that may relate to the charge of both committees."

The room had quieted and all eating had ceased. There was an expectant mood among the select group of directors, financial people, trustees and curators.

"I overheard a lot of small talk today about the record sale of Cornell's box titled *Pharmacy*. Also mentioned was the recent death of our benefactor, Catherine Hines Gillis, and the discovery of the previously unknown Cornell work, *The Drugstore*, in her estate."

There was a ripple of muted conversation around the large Directors' table as Biscoy continued. "Well, getting that box and our difficult budget situation may seem incompatible, but in fact they may be synergistic. It's simple. We need to find a rich benefactor who will buy that piece from the estate. The huge positive publicity generated will be important in the acquisition. Obviously it is a question of numbers. Our main source of operating income is entrance fees and memberships. *The Drugstore* will help our economic health—if you can stand that analogy."

After the laughter had stopped, Biscoy pointed at curator Mark Franklin, a nerdy, thirty-ish man sitting at the foot of the table. Slightly overweight, with long, un-groomed hair, wearing an open-collared shirt and ill-fitting hound's-tooth sports jacket, he had little to recommend him. What elevated his stature was the Princeton degree and some large family donations to the museum, which had helped grease his way into the curator's position.

"A few days ago, I explored the situation surrounding *The Drugstore* with Mark and I'm happy to report he has some ideas for us on that subject."

Franklin stood and began to speak with a pronounced Greenwich accent. "Well, the first thing I found out through my connections at Christies is that the German buyer of *Pharmacy* has absolutely no interest in selling and certainly less interest in donating it to us. Moreover, our recent, somewhat frosty relationship with the family of Catherine Hines Gillis is not likely to result in their donating *The Drugstore*."

A trustee sitting near Franklin suggested that the Cornell boxes they had, now in storage, would also have increased in value and could be sold to raise money for operations in the anticipated lean recession years ahead.

Biscoy waved his hand in dismissal. "No, this is not the course the Museum has followed since its founding, which was, I might remind you, in the depths of the depression of the thirties. We need to be proactive."

He paused and pointed directly at Mark Franklin. "You're a Princeton man and when we hired you, you bragged about your classmates and connections to billionaires in the hedge fund business. Well, pretend you're back at your eating club, Tiger Inn, and persuade one of them to buy *The Drugstore* for us."

"OK, I'll try."

"Let's see if you can make it happen. I'm willing, with the agreement of the Acquisition Committee, to make a deal, provided that it costs us only tradable assets; certainly not cash, which we don't have right now."

There were no interruptions as Biscoy continued. "Besides the usual BS—meaning a dinner and a plaque—I expect a request for a trusteeship to seal the deal. I'd sign off on that. After all, Catherine Hines Gillis knew the artist, and loved the subject. With the recent record sale for *Pharmacy*, that box is probably worth a few million dollars."

After the Christmas holiday, Franklin went to work on the project. His workshop was the Princeton Club, where the guests were always more impressed than the members. Timing was not great for hedge funds; most had been decimated by the financial downturn. However, by the fall of '09, the worst appeared to be over. Finally, Franklin's buddies began to show interest in the Joseph Cornell box story and the prospect of a trusteeship at the MCAM. In all of Franklin's conversations, the largest sum mentioned was $200,000.

By early 2010, Franklin had decided to contact Susan Hines directly to gauge her interest in selling the box. She agreed to meet him for a drink at the Princeton Club Bar. The two had little in common. For Mark, it was like fishing without bait, waiting for the fish to request what it would like to nibble on. Susan stated that she had no immediate plans to dispose of the box.

Now it was a year since that Directors' meeting and Biscoy began to push Franklin, intimating that his curator position might be at stake. Mark stumbled on a possible candidate at a friend's bachelor party: Jacob Stone had been Mark's classmate (Princeton '96).

With a Stanford MBA added to his Princeton credentials, Jacob was now a rising star at 'Literal Funds,' one of the few hedge funds that had squeaked through the recession unscathed. Jacob had bragged drunkenly about the firm's success. He was appropriately admiring of Mark's status as curator at the MCAM. Before the evening ended, they'd agreed to meet for dinner at 'The Palm' steakhouse to catch up on things. Mark texted Jacob the next day to remind him.

After the waiter at The Palm had presented generous sizzling portions of sirloin along with steaming creamed spinach and hash browns, Mark began to woo Jacob with Cornell box history. Franklin was initially surprised at Jacob's knowledge of contemporary art and his grasp of the New York art scene, finding him to be particularly knowledgeable about Joseph Cornell.

With his button-down Oxford shirt and stylish sport jacket, Jacob Stone looked the typical preppy Princetonian. A muscular, tall, former public high school fullback, he'd won an academic scholarship to Princeton, where he quickly shed his working class look and focused his sights on Wall Street.

"Does the Museum have any Cornell boxes in its collection?"

"Yes, Jacob, and I'm speculating, but the Hines-Gillis family has a personal connection to Cornell and donated the original ten, so I'm thinking that maybe we could do a swap. Considering that *Pharmacy* went for almost four million dollars at the time of the crash, any deal would still involve significant cash."

"How much?"

"I'd say, for starters, a million dollars plus the Museum's ten boxes."

As they left the restaurant and headed in opposite directions, Jacob shook Mark's hand and said, "I'll talk to our CEO, Jim McKay, and see whether the deal is do-able. The firm would really love the cachet of this association with the MCAM."

"Well, throw one other offer at him."

"What's that—a hot date?"

"Seriously—tell him we'll give a trusteeship to the firm with lots of positive publicity if that would seal the deal."

After Mark had presented a broad outline of the Museum's desire and plan to own *The Drugstore*, Susan Hines accepted a dinner invitation the following week. The Museum would honor Cornell's memory with a huge retrospective show and place the new acquisition prominently on display in the main atrium. Further, they had a potential donor who might suitably reward Susan for her generosity.

The Palm was within walking distance of Susan's apartment and they got down to business over his lamb chops and her lobster.

"Susan, I'll be frank. This is just conversation at this point. We're negotiating, but neither of us knows where we stand."

He paused and then added, "I certainly can't assume anything on your part."

Susan replaced her wine glass and said in a polite tone, "I understand that all is conjecture at this point. I won't agree to anything without advice from my attorney and accountant. You, of course, must defer to the decision of the Board of Trustees at the Museum."

"Here is our situation. We have a donor who would pay you a million dollars. For their part, the Museum would return five of the ten boxes your aunt donated over the years. You would have your choice."

Susan took another bite of lobster and a sip of her Batard Montrachat. "*The Drugstore* may be an American contemporary masterpiece. I would want all ten of the family boxes returned in any deal."

In a sarcastic tone, Susan added, "They have all been buried in the cellar for years. The ten boxes plus $1.5 million would represent fair value to me."

By the end of the meal, an outline for the deal was established. It was now up to the unmentioned donor, the Museum and Susan's counsel to agree on the details and draw up a contract.

Laurence Biscoy reluctantly approved the loss of all ten of the Cornell boxes, plus a trusteeship that, McKay demanded, would be occupied by a junior person—Jacob Stone—in the name of the firm. For Jacob, a partnership would be the unmentioned but expected dividend when the contract was signed.

Everything was in place for the lawyers' approval. The ever-careful CEO of Literal Funds demanded an independent appraisal of *The Drugstore* prior to writing a check for $1.5 million. A search by Jacob turned up George Kohl, a Philadelphia-based certified independent appraiser.

At the Citibank safety deposit site, Kohl inspected and carefully photographed the Cornell box with Susan present. He prepared his report and met with Jacob Stone at the firm's office a few days later to express his conviction as to the authenticity of the work. In doing so, he pointed out the basis for his reasoning on certain design details specific to Cornell's work. He then presented a bill for $60,000, which represented four percent of the $1.5 million appraised value, along with the document. He was paid on the spot.

About a month later, the Museum held a formal gala dinner for two hundred donors and staff in the atrium. A section of the Surrealist gallery was rearranged to temporarily showcase *The Drugstore*. A large sign had been prepared, describing Joseph Cornell's life and contributions to 20th-century art. A separate plaque commemorated the generosity of Literal Funds to MCAM and their appreciation of contemporary art.

When Jacob Stone arrived at work the next day he was directed away from his cubicle to a corner office facing the Woolworth Building, where he was greeted by a smiling crowd of his fellow workers and Jim McKay.

"Surprise—partner!"

The celebration continued with champagne and a posh catered brunch in the corporate boardroom.

When Jacob called Susan to report the news, he caught her on the way to the airport en route to London and Berlin to celebrate her good fortune.

The party at Literal Funds ended at two p.m., when the staff returned to their various desks to take care of the billion-dollar business. The euphoria at the Museum continued for a month. Their rude awakening occurred during the unrelated visit of Craig Withers, Sotheby's Worldwide Senior Appraiser of Contemporary Art. At Laurence Biscoy's insistence, he'd been asked to evaluate *The Drugstore*. Craig had examined the piece closely. He specified why this could not possibly be the work of Joseph Cornell: the materials used were not available when the work would have been constructed.

Finally, he stated, "This is a fake."

An angry conference call to Jacob Stone and Jim McKay ended after many expletives were exchanged.

The Museum had lost a donation valued at $1.5 million and probably twice that in the loss of the ten Cornell boxes.

When Jacob Stone went to work the next day he was stopped by the receptionist, who said, "The Boss wants to see you."

Jacob was not surprised so much by the summons as by the presence of *The Drugstore* sitting on McKay's desk.

McKay said, "You've cost the firm $1.5 million—but worse, the negative publicity is devastating. You're finished. Here's your severance—you can have this goddamned box which I want you to remove immediately, along with your personal effects!"

Although devastating, the job loss did not mean starvation for Jacob. His five years at the firm had left him with a portfolio worth several million dollars. There could be no legal recovery from the Philadelphia appraiser—an opinion was an opinion.

Unfortunately, the fallout from the awful affair was worse than Jacob could ever have envisioned. His name, his former position, and the fake multi-million-dollar box attracted the attention of the media—saturating the tabloids, TV broadcasts, and internet blogs—and within a few months, the sleek glossy antique and art magazines. Jacob even chose to avoid the Princeton Club bar, one of his favorite hangouts.

When the call came a few months later, Jacob hung up after he heard, "How about *The Drugstore* as a leading acquisition for the International Museum of Fakes and Forgeries?"

His cell phone rang again a few minutes later. "Don't hang up— this is Walter Meeks. I know you used to work for Jim McKay; maybe you recognize my name. My fund is Storm Securities."

"Oh, sorry, Mr. Meeks, of course I know your name. Your hedge fund is much bigger than McKay's. Is this really you or is this another cruel joke?"

"If you're willing to take a chance on the veracity of this call, be at the Oyster Bar at 1 p.m."

The Oyster Bar, although primarily a seafood restaurant located in the Grand Central terminal, is also a well-known meeting spot in midtown Manhattan.

Jacob arrived ten minutes early and found two empty stools at the bar. He ordered a double Wild Turkey. By 1:10 p.m., Jacob mused that the disappointment of an empty seat and fake invitation was preferable to another kind of unpleasant surprise.

Jacob was hunched over his drink when there was a tap on his shoulder. He turned and immediately recognized Walter Meeks. "You weren't joking."

Meeks laughed. "I guess not! What are you drinking?"

They moved to a table after Meeks ordered a refill for Jacob and a Manhattan for himself. Over the course of the next hour, Jacob related the entire episode to Meeks. Jacob was completely taken aback when Walter Meeks described the concept of his new museum, which was based in London and already under construction.

Without pausing, Meeks added, "All that terrible publicity that you have described and I have noted has made your fake *The Drugstore* infamous. I want to buy it from you for $250,000."

"That's a very generous price, Mr. Meeks, and of course I accept."

Jacob offered the famous hedge fund CEO his hand and continued humbly, "Look, I know you're busy and probably have to get back, so please don't feel you have to waste any more time with me."

"Actually, I do have one more important matter to discuss."

Then he stood, smiled and said, "I've looked carefully into your background and the job you did for your former firm and I'd like you to come work for me. There is a senior position available that I hope you'll accept and, as part of your duties, you will be the liaison with the Acquisitions Director of the International Museum of Fakes and Forgeries."

TWO

The Silver Cup
From Asprey

S imon Wells Ashton, seventy-seven years old, still enjoyed his visits to London's antique markets. English by birth, but a resident of the U.S. for over seventy-two years, his main reason for frequent flights across the Pond was to find stuff for his various collections. When asked, he would simply reply that collecting instinct was embedded in his British DNA. Tall, with a beaked nose and almost bald, he resembled a stork as he clawed through jewelry and Olympic and military memorabilia, which were his main collecting passions. A successful career in dentistry and prescient investments in gold and platinum now provided for a more than adequate retirement income to indulge his hobbies.

Simon was one of the members of a small group of children who had been fortunate enough to be sent to families in America during the London Blitz of World War II. Most children were sent for their safety to the English countryside for the duration of the war.

If it's Saturday morning in London and you are a bona fide collector, you are required to be at Portobello Road. At seven a.m. Simon was armed with takeaway coffee and was starting through the first stalls at the top of the road. Having arrived the previous day, he looked forward to scouring the markets at Camden Passage, Covent Garden and Alfie's through the next week. The rest of his time would be occupied with West End theater and the new trendy restaurants in London. In between he would peruse the fine shops at Gray's Passage that had survived the recession. Through all his searching he felt like a kid with a generous allowance looking for candy! But always at the back of his mind was his lifelong search for the silver baby cup from Asprey's that had been left behind by accident in the rush to pack him off to the safety of America seventy years earlier.

Just seven weeks after arriving safely in New York City to stay with his Aunt Ethel, his mother's older sister, the tragic news arrived that his mother had died during a bombing raid in London. Soon after, Aunt Ethel was notified that Simon's father, Malcolm Ashton was presumed dead. Flight Lieutenant Ashton, Oxford graduate and RAF pilot, went missing over the Channel south of Brighton after a dogfight between his Hurricane and a German ME109. All of Simon's vital documents had been destroyed in the fire and collapse of the building in which his mother had been staying in Chelsea. Simon was later issued a substitute document of his birth, and because of his orphan status, Aunt Ethel obtained American citizenship for him. All his succeeding U.S. passports recorded London, England, as his birthplace.

The passage of time and a good and happy marriage blessed by three fine children helped ease the pain of his childhood tragedies. The recent death of his wife, Ann, renewed the buried grief for his barely remembered parents.

After the war ended, the RAF sent Simon an official picture of his handsome dad, complete with flight hat, copies of Malcolm's RAF wings, and his numerous military awards and medals. This sparked Simon's lifelong interest in collecting British military memorabilia. The one object he longed to have more than anything was his silver Asprey baby cup that had been left behind in the rush to send him off to America. He could visualize the three raised rabbits on the outside of the cup, with his initials, S.W.A., engraved between the ears of the three bunnies. His mother, Laura, always called it his Asprey cup. When Simon had arrived in America and realized the cup had been left behind, he cried bitterly for days for his "bunny cup."

Ironically, a letter had arrived from his mother at the same time as the news of her death. She had written that she had the cup and would keep it safe for him until all three of them were together after the war. Simon had been searching without success for years for his cup or a similar one, at shops and shows in Europe, the U.S. and on the Internet. Yet he kept looking.

When he finally happened upon something, it was totally unexpected. On a cheap stall at the bottom of Portobello Road, he looked through an untidy pile of fairly recent, low-end Olympic pins. He found a participant's plastic ski badge with a damaged ribbon from the Salt Lake City Winter Olympics 2002. The elderly dealer quoted "five quid." Simon offered four, which the dealer accepted, and as Simon was handing him the four one-pound coins, an American quarter slipped through his fingers along with them.

The dealer inspected the common piece from the American State series, this one from Kentucky with a horse on one side. "Can you spare it, mate?" he said.

"Sure, take it!"

Quickly, the old man dropped the coin with a clink into a banged-up, blackened cup near his strongbox. The noise attracted Simon's attention to the cup and he noticed the initials S.W.A. between what appeared to be rabbits' ears.

Trying not to show his excitement, he commented, "That's a pleasant old cup—may I see it?"

"Yeah, but it's not for sale."

"Where did you find it?"

"Don't rightly remember and what's it to you anyway?"

As he spoke, the old man dumped the small collection of coins and bric-a-brac onto his table and handed Simon an almost black and heavily dented, small, cup-shaped container. At that moment, Simon thought that if the cup was from Asprey and fit his memory of his baby cup—he had to have it at any price. He even considered a grab-and-run if the dealer refused to sell it to him. But being a truthful and honorable man, he merely told an abbreviated but compelling version of his childhood circumstances, all the while examining the cup.

"That's a sad tale, which I can indeed relate to! My folks were in London during the Blitz and told me lots of unhappy stories about those times..." The old man paused for a moment while balancing the cup first in the palm of one hand and then the other. "I guess it weighs around four ounces, which would put the scrap value at about eighty quid—so go on, it's yours for ninety."

Rather than taking out his magnifier to check for the Asprey signature and possibly arousing the old man's suspicion, Ashton simply handed the dealer a 100-pound note and walked quickly away before the man could make change—of the hundred or of his mind!

All the way back up Portobello Road, Simon thought that it might be just another baby bunny cup in silver plate or even a cheap reproduction. Finally, he found benches near the Notting Hill Gate Tube stop where he could sit and in the bright midday light examine the cup more carefully with his loupe. After rubbing off some of the tarnish on the bottom with his handkerchief, he breathed a happy sigh when he identified the Asprey tower mark.

Sunday was spent at a West End matinee, which Simon scarcely remembered, so occupied was he with thoughts about the Asprey cup. Early Monday morning, Simon left his South Kensington Hotel for a quick run through the Covent Garden market, although his mind was not on the assorted "rubbish" at the various stands. Just before ten o'clock, he grabbed a taxi to Asprey's on New Bond Street and arrived just as the doors were opening. After a few inquiries, he was directed to the office of the young assistant store manager, Jack Quarles, who listened with sympathy and interest to the Ashton family saga.

"Specifically, how may I help you?" asked Quarles.

Simon replied, as he handed the cup to the young man, "I'd like to know when this model was made, because when you examine the cup you will see that the date hallmarks are worn away and are almost impossible to read. Perhaps you have records in your archives of the years this model was manufactured and how many were produced?"

As Simon spoke, Jack carefully examined the cup with a loupe. "Well, I can tell you, without even consulting our computer records, that this particular model cup was retailed only at our Edinburgh store."

"Are you certain?"

"Yes, definitely." He handed Simon back the cup and the loupe, indicating where one could see the auxiliary Edinburgh mark.

"Look, Mr. Ashton, if you have time, I can get some support from our IT specialist and get more information this morning. Let me get you a cup of coffee and the *Times* and I'll go right to work."

"That's most appreciated and exceedingly kind of you. I'll be grateful for any information you can give me!"

About forty minutes later, Quarles returned with a few pages of computer printout that he handed to Simon as he said, "This design,

Three Bunnies, was produced between the Wars in 1920–1939 and production ceased soon after World War II began. In those twenty years, it was by far our most popular baby cup design, with over 38,000 examples produced. We estimate that by 1948 all the cups remaining in stock had been sold. After that, it could be special ordered until 1968 or throughout another twenty years of production. We are estimating about 45,000 *Three Bunnies* cups in total were manufactured. In the year of your birth, 1935, our records indicate that 1,800 were made. Unfortunately, the year stamp of the hallmark on your cup is not readable and therefore the cup could be from any of the fifteen years earlier or later. I'm afraid we were unable to find in our archives any sales figures from the store in Scotland for that year.

"In my opinion, the chances of your cup being the very one that survived the Blitz, especially since it was retailed in Scotland, is questionable. On the other hand, if you do a calculation using these three letters of the alphabet, S.W.A., in that order, then the odds strongly favor you... so why don't you assume that you have found the original missing cup?"

Jack rose and shook Simon Wells Ashton's hand; a very disappointed Simon thanked him graciously. He left the office and Asprey's, which was now beginning to bustle with the day's retail trade.

On his way back to South Kensington, Simon stopped at a pub, purchased a Bass Ale on draft and brought the mug back to a booth in the rear where he could ponder his next move. Should he just take Jack's suggestion and cherish the cup without further research to prove it was his very own and a memento of his lost family? He was on his second pint when he made his decision. He would check sources and records of a possible stay by his parents in Edinburgh in the mid-1930's. By eight p.m. that evening he was sitting in a room in a central Edinburgh hotel, chosen for its proximity to City Hall and the Vital Records office. He had taken a British Midlands flight from Gatwick rather than the long overnight rail service. After a restless night, filled with self-doubt, he concluded that the most likely reason for his parents' possible visit to Scotland was for a holiday and it was highly unlikely that there would be any 75-year-old hotel registers available for his perusal. He certainly had no knowledge of any relatives on either parent's side that might live in the area. Out of curiosity, before leaving his room, he checked out the name Ashton, as well as his mother's maiden name of Wells, in the local phone directory and online. There was none listed.

A little Scottish morning mist and rain dampened his mood, but at the Vital Records Department at City Hall he encountered a cheerful, diminutive woman. She stared at him over her half-moon readers as he related his quest and announced that she would try to help him, undoubtedly influenced by his poignant story. He gave her the full names of both his mother and father.

It took just a few minutes for her to peruse the records and he actually crossed his fingers as she called him back to the desk. "I'm sorry, I checked everything for the city and surrounding area for all available records of home or land ownership, tax rolls, marriage certificates or birth certificates for Malcolm Ashton or Laura Graham Wells and there is none. Just glance over my shoulder and you can see the screen yourself." As he turned to leave, she exclaimed, "Wait! I do see a birth certificate for a Simon Ashton dated April 8th, 1935."

"That's me!" he cried.

"You were born in the hospital in Stirling, which is a city not far from here."

When Simon returned to London late on Tuesday, the idea of taking his usual run through Camden passage on Wednesday morning never occurred to him. Instead, promptly at nine a.m., he was at London's General Records Office anxious to find another piece of the puzzle: his parents' date of marriage. The clerk informed him that they could search almost all of Britain for that information, given a range of possible dates of the marriage. Simon asked if he could include a time period from 1934 to 1935. After listening to his tragic tale, which had never failed to arouse a storm of sympathy even in ordinarily uninterested bureaucrats, the clerk said he would personally look into the matter. After all he said, "Your mum was killed by the Jerries and your dad was a war hero!"

While he waited, Simon called Glasgow's General Register Office and after half-an-hour of waiting, he got a negative response from Scotland's second city.

The clerk in London finally returned. "I'm really sorry, mate, but there was no record of any marriage between those two parties for the entire decade of the 1930's in all of the UK."

Despairingly, Simon stumbled to the nearest waiting room bench. Even though he had his precious cup, he was apparently a bastard. His parents had not been in love enough to marry. He sat quietly for fifteen minutes, thinking of what his parents had gone through in the summer of 1940 at the height of the bombing in London. Between early August and late September, his mother had lost her life in the collapse and fire in her building in Chelsea, and only seven weeks later, his father was shot down near Brighton. He decided that he was being petty and insensitive to their memories by his upset over the lack of a formal marriage.

As he strode down the long gloomy hall toward the exit, the clerk who had so helpfully tried to find records for him came rushing after him; Simon was sure it was only to offer his heartfelt condolences.

"Excuse me, sir! We found the marriage certificate. It is dated July 8th, 1940. It's the original and somewhat damaged by smoke, probably from one of the many bomb strikes that did minor damage. Under these really extenuating circumstances, my supervisor has authorized me, although it is not our usual procedure, to make a copy for our records and we are giving you the original!"

THREE

The Talisman

"An object held to act as a charm to avert evil and bring good fortune."

P aul Corwin awoke to a familiar sight. As a physician practic-
ing internal medicine in West Palm Beach, he often attended
patients in the Emergency Room. However, he had never
seen those surroundings from a horizontal position, groggy and remote,
lying on a gurney.

A woman in green scrubs, with undyed, graying hair and a make-
up-free face, was adjusting an intravenous needle taped to his left
arm.

"You're a lucky man!" she said, seeing he was awake. "Guess your
number wasn't up today. That medal in your pocket saved your life—
because otherwise that 45-caliber bullet would have gone straight
into your heart!"

As she spoke, Corwin carefully reached with his right hand to
touch his heavily bandaged chest.

"Be careful! There are some pretty nasty bone bruises there."

On that fateful November Saturday in West Palm Beach in 1965,

Paul Corwin, M.D., was a vigorous, athletic man in his late thirties. The last thing he remembered—before he'd woken up on the stretcher and then drifted off into a morphine-assisted narcotic trance—was the forceful thump and ringing sound of something very powerful hitting his chest.

Paul was one of the early-bird buyers at a house sale. The mansion on the shore of Lake Worth belonged to a recently deceased prominent attorney. Corwin lined up at seven in the morning with the other eager buyers and dealers anxious to get a low number so they could be among the first to rush into the house looking for treasures. He loved these house sales. Paul now looked for smaller items to satisfy his collecting passion, since his own home was already crammed with furniture and decorative items. His wife, Hilary, had laid down the law: nothing bigger than a bread box would be allowed into the house.

Paul's late father, also a physician, was a decorated World War I veteran; hence, among the things that fascinated and attracted Paul was historic war memorabilia. This particular house sale was disappointing; nothing piqued his interest at all. As he was about to leave, he spotted a small den to the left of the entry way. Inside were a large oak desk and a glassed-in bookcase, from where he caught the glint of a bronze medal propped up on a small plastic stand. He opened the unlocked bookcase and carefully removed the medal, noting that it had an image of a "doughboy going over," the classic image of an American soldier from the First World War. What really excited him was recognizing the medal as the famous Williams College Commemorative World War medal that had been given to all the Williams College Alumni who had participated in the war. His father, Edward, owned this medal, being a proud alumnus of Williams College. Edward had graduated in 1917 prior to his war service. After the Armistice, he'd completed his undergraduate studies and attended Medical School at the University of Pennsylvania.

At the open garage door, the lady in charge of checkout and payments gave the medal a quick look and said, "That will be three dollars."

Corwin strode happily back to his three-speed bicycle propped up on its kick stand. He zipped the medal into the breast pocket of his light, tight-fitting windbreaker and mounted his bicycle. His mouth watered in anticipation of the coffee and Danish he would enjoy in a few minutes at the Dixie Deli. As he made the turn onto Dixie highway he noted the flashing lights of a police cruiser speeding towards the Florida State Bank on the corner opposite the Deli. Then came the hard thump on his chest and oblivion.

After another hour, the morphine had worn off, the X-rays of his chest and EKG were read as normal and the ER physician was ready to discharge him. "Dr. Corwin, I'm Dr. Greg Sandler. That high-velocity 45-caliber bullet hit the medal in your pocket almost straight on, badly bruising your chest and rib cage and leaving a nearly clear impression of the medal on your skin!"

As he spoke, he handed the badly dented medal back to Paul, laughed wryly and said, "You're going to have an interesting scar there to remind you of this lucky day!"

Paul answered with considerable aplomb, considering his recent experience. "Things that end well are fun to re-tell." And re-tell he did on many occasions and for many years afterwards.

Dr. Corwin credited the good things that happened to him and his family over the years to the magical powers of the Williams medal that had saved his life. He carried the dented medal with him wherever he went. At the top of the blessed events list for Paul and Hilary, three years later, was the unexpected later-life pregnancy for Hilary and the birth of their only child, Jan.

Paul's internal medicine practice prospered and he took in two young partners to share his crowded space in the early postwar building conveniently located near the West Palm Beach General Hospital. Corwin was pleased when the adjacent space, formerly occupied by a pediatric practice, became vacant. The landlord offered the Corwin group a package that included reconstruction of the expanded space and a fifteen-year lease with an option for five more years. The final proposals were presented at a meeting of all parties and their attorneys.

Dr. Corwin would later recall that as he turned the Williams medal over and over in his hand he was overcome by feelings of indecision and uncertainty about the long-term rental commitment. "I'll be very frank – I have serious doubts about going ahead with this plan," he told the landlord. "I wish to discuss it privately with my attorney and I'll get back to you very shortly."

Paul's concern centered on committing to paying a high rent—for fifteen years with no escape—for offices in an older building. Furthermore, West Palm was booming and his friend Dr. Henry Lombard, an ophthalmologist, had suggested that a select group of ethical and competent physicians get together to build their own facility: West Palm Beach Medical Arts Building. Corwin did not agree to the lease arrangement and one year later moved into a brand new suite in his own building. The Medical Arts Building was enlarged twice over the next twenty years and became the largest medical building in the area. In 1984, all of the practices became affiliated with the University of Miami Medical School.

As luck would have it, the other rental property was destroyed in what was later determined to be an arson-precipitated fire.

In 1987, Jan Corwin was accepted into the pre-med program at Williams College. On that happy occasion Paul thought about giving her the Williams medal, but decided to wait for her graduation. This was another great day for the Corwin family and with Jan's acceptance to Yale Medical School and her graduation diploma she received the "lucky Williams medal" from her father.

"Jan, Mom and I are so proud of you!" Paul told her. "We know Grandfather Edward would be bursting his buttons to think this is the third generation of Williams College graduates in our family from 1917 to today in 1991. Always treasure this medal and carry it everywhere with you. It will bring you good luck as it has for me!"

After graduating from Yale medical school and completing an internship at Columbia in New York, Jan started her residency in ophthalmology at the University of Miami's Bascom Palmer Institute. Her decision to study ophthalmology was the result of her relationship with Dr. Henry Lombard, the ophthalmologist who was her father's main partner in the West Palm Beach Medical Arts Building. Dr. Henry's suite was next door to her father's office. When she was a little girl, Jan's father had brought her to the office on weekends. She would run next door to see Dr. Henry—he had so many fun things! He would let her look at all the optical equipment and devices. When Jan was in junior high she trailed Dr. Henry, in his office and in the surgical suite, watching the microscopic surgeries that ended with patients delighted with their new clearer vision.

Paul Corwin constantly reminded Jan that it had been while playing with the Williams medal thirty years previously he had decided not to continue with the rental, but to proceed with the plan for the Medical Arts Building with Dr. Lombard. Jan continued the tradition when she leased her own office space in the building after completing her fellowship in Medical Retina. Her best referrers were Dr. Lombard and his associates in the practice.

One day, in the garage of that same building, Jan met Walter Mason. She was particularly attracted by his clean-cut, athletic look in his tight-fitting bike pants and colorful shirt. The clincher was when he took his helmet off and she saw his crew-cut blond hair. He rode his racing bike daily to his successful orthodontic practice in the West Palm Beach Medical Arts Building. Their conversation started over a mutual interest in cycling and a whirlwind romance led to their marriage within the year.

Well, of course, Paul and Hilary were beyond excited about the birth of their beautiful twin grandsons, Jackson and Randolph. Jan had an easy pregnancy and delivery. With the help of her excellent nanny Martina and her mom's supervision of the childcare, Jan was back at work in two weeks!

The Gonin Retina Society was to hold their annual meeting in Auckland, New Zealand. Jan believed it would create a great opportunity for her and Walter to take that trip and then extend their vacation to visit Australia. The twins were still too young for such a long trip, but Paul and Hilary happily agreed to stay with the children and Martina.

Although the daily Air Pacific flight out of Miami International required a longer drive than the more convenient West Palm Airport, it required no lay-over, no change of planes and only a brief refueling stop in Honolulu. Unfortunately, on the day of their flight the limo service was forty-five minutes late due to a pile-up on the Sawgrass Expressway. More troubles came with weekend rush-hour traffic on I-95. They had planned to arrive at Miami International at five p.m. for a 7:30 departure. It was actually seven p.m. when the frustrated couple reached the security check-point.

They grappled with the frantic filling and shoving of bins and carry-on luggage by impatient and often rude travelers as they inched towards the screening machines. A fleshy, middle-aged woman immediately behind them, dressed all in red, was in such a hurry that she shoved her open tote bag into Jan's already crammed bin just before it entered the scanner. At the reclaim area, the woman in red grabbed for her bag, which had become up-ended in its passage through the tunnel. Its contents now mingled with items from Jan's own tote bag.

She exclaimed, "I'm sorry, but I'm very late for my flight," while quickly gathering several items from Jan's bin and shoving them into her bag.

Before Jan could reply, the woman in red (as she would be forever after) hopped from one foot to the other, putting on her shoes before running down the ramp towards the gates.

A few minutes later, Jan and Walter were making their own race to their gate, which—of course—was the last one on the concourse.

"Walter, stop!"

"What's wrong?"

Jan frantically searched through her pockets and purse. "I think I left the Williams medal at security—I'm going back!"

"If you do, we'll definitely miss the flight!"

"You run ahead to the gate—pull my carry-on. Hold the flight. I've got my running shoes on so it shouldn't take long."

Unfortunately, a quick but determined search of all the bins did not locate the medal.

Jan scribbled her cell phone number on her card and handed it to the supervisor. "I'm leaving the country, but this phone has the international chip so please call me if you find the medal. Leave a message. This medal has no value to anyone but me—but I'm desperate to have it back."

Jan, out of breath, reached the departure gate a few minutes later;

a quick glance at Walter's face told the story.

The agent said apologetically, "I'm really sorry, but the flight closed ten minutes ago."

"Jan, we would have made it if you hadn't gone back for the medal."

"Walter, that doesn't make me feel better and Dad will be so disappointed that I lost it."

Even the courtesy of the Air Pacific agent, who upgraded them to first class for their rescheduled itinerary, didn't lift their dark mood. They would be routed through Los Angeles, change planes there, and fly on to Auckland.

The woman in red, Claire Beck, barely made the Air Pacific flight to Auckland via Honolulu. She was anxiously looking forward to meeting her first granddaughter, Michelle. Claire had planned to pick up a few presents at the Miami International Duty Free store, but her delayed trip from Orlando had killed that plan. A few hours into the flight, it occurred to her that she might find something interesting to buy during the one-hour lay-over in Honolulu.

Claire hurried off the plane and located several shops. Her first purchase was a bottle of Moet Champagne for the new parents—and her. In a jewelry shop she found an adorable sterling baby set, consisting of a miniature fork and spoon with hula girls enameled at the tops and beautifully displayed in a colorful box. They would be perfect for baby Michelle when she was able to feed herself in a few years.

With only a few minutes to spare until the flight took off, Claire thought it would be prudent and more comfortable to visit the ladies' room in the terminal rather than wait to go on the plane. In the stall, she placed her purchases and her tote bag over the hook behind the door. A moment later a hand reached over and grabbed the tote bag.

Claire screamed as she hastily pulled herself together and ran yelling out of the ladies' room. "Stop that woman, she stole my bag!"

A nearby security guard, alerted by her cries, stopped Claire to question her. The woman, in the distance, disappeared into the late-night crowd of travelers in transit.

The thief, Linda Mauro, at 220 pounds and with a two-pack-a-day smoking habit, was not used to racing down terminal concourses. A native Hawaiian, with a sometime job as a drug mule, she had been roaming the terminal awaiting her nine a.m. flight departure for Bangkok to take a rare vacation. She was looking for a crime of opportunity where she could snag an unattended purse from an unwary traveler. The lady in red with the eye-patterned tote bag looked like an easy mark—and in worse physical shape than Linda herself. She had not expected her to come out of the toilet stall so quickly in hot pursuit! Glancing at the unusual embroidered eye on the red tote bag, Linda realized that the bag would be very easy to spot. She reached inside and grabbed a wad of U.S. currency—fifty-dollar bills! There was probably $500 there—enough to really enjoy her vacation in Bangkok, including some of their readily available coke.

Alarms sounded! She tossed the bag into an open trash can just by the food court and slipped into the nearby ladies room where she stuffed the wad of cash into the back pocket of her blue jeans. She changed from a glittery, black top to a plain white T-shirt and put on a baseball cap. Then she casually walked out and headed to a bar at the other end of the terminal.

Claire, meanwhile, was frantic. Gone were her credit cards, driver's license and cash. The security guard had taken her to an office to make a full report and fill out the details of the crime for their computer files.

"Oh my God, the flight has left—with my carry-on baggage and all my checked luggage!" Claire cried desperately.

A pleasant older man, clearly the supervisor in charge, reassured her, "We have notified Air Pacific about your situation and everything will be waiting for you in Auckland."

"How am I going to get there anytime soon, with all my personal stuff missing?" Claire sobbed.

"Our security people are all on the case. They're scouring the garbage bags, which are transparent. Your red bag with the distinctive eye should be easy to spot! Most thieves throw stolen purses in the garbage. We have also alerted the rental cars and outside bus and taxi services to be on the lookout for the bag."

Claire mumbled a thank you and put her head down on her arms on the desk.

"Can I get you some coffee?" the man asked.

"Thanks, no—just please keep on searching!"

Claire couldn't believe her eyes when, half an hour later, a beaming policewoman walked through the door of the security office and handed her the slightly rumpled but intact red tote bag with the distinctive eye pattern.

After a quick examination of the contents, Claire cried, "I'm so excited and lucky—all my cash is missing, but everything else is here!"

She caught her breath and added, "There's something heavy at the bottom of the bag." She pulled out a three-inch diameter, round bronze medal with a deep indentation in the middle. "That's not mine—I wonder where it came from?"

The supervisor volunteered, "Someone probably dumped it in the garbage and its weight dragged it into the bottom of your bag."

Claire jubilantly replied, "Whatever! I'll consider it my good luck charm from now on!"

Later that afternoon, Air Pacific found space for Claire on a flight to Auckland that was scheduled to arrive very late in the day.

Claire called her daughter Jill and recounted the story and its happy ending. She suggested to Jill that, as it would be very late when she arrived, she would prefer to stay overnight at a hotel in Auckland to refresh herself after her trying ordeal. The next morning she would be ready to meet her new granddaughter, Michelle.

The breakfast room at the Oceanic Hotel was pleasant and welcoming and Claire felt rested and happy as she clutched her red tote bag tightly and looked about for a vacant table.

Jan and Walter had just finished breakfast. Their re-routed journey had been completed only very early that morning. Jan was scheduled to attend a seminar that morning on new treatments for macular edema and, after asking Walter how he would be spending the day, she exclaimed, "Walter, look at that great tote bag with the eye on it that lady is carrying! She's looking for a table for breakfast. Wave her over so I can find out where she got it."

Claire saw the nice-looking couple gesture towards the vacant chair with an unused place setting and walked over to them. "Thanks, I'd love to join you. I'm Claire Beck from Winter Park, Florida."

Walter said in surprise, "What a coincidence—we're from West Palm."

"I love your bag!" Jan said. "Since I'm an ophthalmologist, I'm very partial to eyes—where did you get it?"

"Oh, this is a limited edition bag by Lulu Guinness. I bought it last year in the West Village, New York, at her shop there."

Soon the three were chatting animatedly, enjoying their common origins and backgrounds in Florida. Jan told her story of missing the flight and the loss of her lucky charm at the security checkpoint in Miami.

Claire said, "I have a missed flight story too. Someone grabbed this bag from the hook in the toilet stall in Honolulu. They took the cash, but I was lucky enough to get everything else back. The distinctive eye bag was easy to spot in the garbage bin. But I have a lucky charm too! When I examined the contents of the bag, there was something extra in there—a banged-up medal that I had never seen before. So it's my lucky charm now, since it helped me get all my personal effects back!"

As she spoke, she pulled the Williams medal out of her bag.

Jan screamed, "I can't believe it! That's my lucky medal that I lost at the security checkpoint in Miami."

Claire happily returned the medal as Jan wept with joy.

Claire was so delighted with the encounter that she invited her new friends Jan and Walter to meet her daughter Jill and baby Michelle, who were coming to pick her up. As they walked out of the breakfast room, they analyzed the events at Miami security and agreed that the mix-up must have occurred when the bags were upended while passing through the scanner.

They were so involved in their happy, animated conversation that they did not notice the headlines, repeated in various iterations and languages on the newspapers at the lobby stand, "*Honolulu to Bangkok Air Pacific Flight #542 Overdue and Presumed Lost at Sea with 248 aboard!*"

FOUR

Audubon's
Brown Pelican

Everyone on the antique tour hated the hotel in London. The location was advertised to be a few stops on the Tube from the Portobello Road antique markets, but instead the nearest Tube station, Earl's Court, was a six-block walk through a questionable neighborhood. The hotel—pretentiously named The Royal Windsor Arms—was combined from several adjacent Victorian-era homes and still managed to project the atmosphere of a rather seedy rooming house. Though the meanly proportioned rooms all had individual baths, they were badly in need of modern upgrades. The London Olympics and resultant shortage of hotel rooms had prompted the change from the usual more luxurious digs. The tour participants were informed that they were lucky to have any respectable (a matter of opinion) place to stay in the summer of 2012.

Jane Forsten had picked up a brochure promoting the antique-buying trip to England during one of her monthly runs through the antique shops in South Tampa. A senior rep for the blue-chip pharmaceutical firm, *Aliza*, based on the Florida Gulf Coast, Jane's passionate hobby was collecting 18th- and 19th-century medical memorabilia. After fifteen years of collecting, her "stuff" filled every nook and cranny of her two-bedroom condo in Clearwater Beach, a town just north of St. Petersburg, Tampa's sister city.

Jane had been hired by Aliza after graduating with an M.S. in pharmacology from the University of Florida, up I-75 in Gainesville. She'd married her classmate, Joe Cruise, and they had moved to the condo in Clearwater Beach.

After three uncomfortable months of living together, Joe had "come out" and left her for the waiter at the local coffee shop. Life went on. Except for a brief stint in Atlanta, her pharmaceutical career was happily arranged around the Gulf Coast, rewarding her with a low six-figure income with full benefits. Since her experience with dating sites was uninspired and uninteresting, she busied herself with her work, her friends, her swimming, kayaking and other water activities, as well as her collecting passion.

Jane was now in her mid-forties, very attractive, with a long torso, long arms and a long face crowned by black, curly, unmanageable hair, usually tied up in a high ponytail.

"Hey, Jane," Gail, the proprietor of the multi-dealer antique mall, *Look Back Again*, in South Tampa had said. "If I had the free time, I'd go on this ten-day antique tour they're offering in this brochure and escape the humidity for a few weeks."

Jane had read from the brochure, "Only eighteen lucky antique lovers can be on the magical tour this July!" She'd grumbled, "It's probably going to be all old farts from up north, over sixty, collecting fans and canes to lean on and getting ready for the nursing home."

"Well, well, well, aren't we snobby!" Gail replied. "You could see a few plays, hit a few English pubs, drink warm beer and whatever...

it's sure to be cooler than here and more interesting this time of year. If I didn't have to manage this shop and three annoying teenagers, I'd be first in line to go on that trip."

Jane had replied, "I'm a little depressed and the thought of sharing a room with some stranger with poor hygiene or paying the single supplement isn't really appealing."

"I think you've exhausted the sources of medical collectibles in the Tampa Bay area," Gail had countered. "England is a terrific repository for your kind of stuff. Think of all the 19th-century apothecary shops, old hospitals and medical offices from a hundred years ago and more! You'll find loads of stuff at great prices and the exchange rate is pretty good now."

So, in early May with the temperature and humidity in the Tampa area already in the nineties, Jane had filled out the online details for Olde But Goode Tours and, after only a moment's hesitation, pressed the "complete purchase" button...

All sixteen people who had signed on for the London Antique Scene tour gathered in the sparsely furnished lobby of the Royal Windsor Arms. They paraded en masse to the King's Black Cat pub, a few blocks down Templeton Place, for the first night's get-together. Those unfamiliar with pub etiquette were instructed to order and pay for drinks at the bar, and then carry their own drinks into a small seating area toward the rear that had been reserved for the group.

Katie and Doug, the husband-and-wife team who were the group leaders, stood with pints in hand on a small raised platform. Their Midlands accents enhanced their warm and enthusiastic welcome speech. They suggested that everyone in the group introduce themselves (even though they all had been given name tags) and include their city of origin and special area of collecting interest.

Fourteen of those on the tour were identified as partners; the only two singles were Jane and a guy. Contrary to Jane's expectation, the group did not originate from the Northeastern U.S., but rather from Houston, St. Louis, Colorado Springs, Buffalo, Seattle and Toronto, Canada. Collecting interests included silver, majolica, Victorian jewelry, porcelain figures, British Arts and Crafts and pottery. When it was Jane's turn, she said she was from Tampa—since most people had never heard of Clearwater—and mentioned her interest in medical collectibles. The last person to speak was the other single, a fiftyish, tall man, bald but making up for his lack on top, as so many of the hair-challenged did, by sporting a thick salt-and-pepper beard.

"Hi, I'm Elliot Gaines from Sarasota, Florida," he said and then, winking at Jane, "at least I have the company of another Floridian just up the road from me. My interest is vintage books and prints of flora and fauna."

After the buzz from the introductions had died down, Elliot approached Jane. "Let's toast Floridian collectors and our own London Road Show."

Jane liked him immediately—*finally, a guy with personality—and not bad-looking, either.* They sat next to each other at the pre-ordered dinner paid for by the tour and managed to choke down the pub fare, greatly assisted by refills of draft Bass Ale. Their shared geography was a great conversational starting point. They compared experiences with antique shops in the Tampa Bay and Sarasota area, as well as the regularly scheduled seasonal antique shows in Southwest Florida, sharing stories with many laughs.

As far as discussing their collecting interests, Jane admitted that her beachfront condo in Clearwater Beach was bursting at the seams with her collections of art work, devices, glassware, china, advertising figures and old signs and explained how it tied in with her career in the pharmaceutical industry.

She looked at Elliot. "Your turn."

"Well, I started with stamps, which my father collected, and then books while I was growing up in Philadelphia. I studied business at Penn and about fifteen years ago moved to Florida after I got a job with the Ritz Carlton group in Naples. Just before the crash, I was transferred to the Sarasota operation—and fortunately, I am still working there."

He stopped for a moment. "I'm really partial to English trifle—would you like to share one for dessert?"

"Why not? We're on vacation and an extra couple of pounds are to be anticipated." She added, chuckling, "I guess in this country that would be considered a pun."

Smiling at her, Eliot said, "You look great to me, so a few more pounds of you would only be better." He added, "Getting back to my shopping interests in London, I've become very interested in old, illustrated books on flora and fauna including botanicals, areas in which we both could be interested. Although you can buy these things online, I prefer to handle and examine a book before I buy it."

Listening attentively, Jane was taken with his flattery and hoped that the dim pub light had masked her uncontrollable blushes.

Elliot continued, "I'm really looking forward to visiting a lot of antiquarian bookstores in London and maybe picking up a few bargains at the street markets. I know it's nine p.m. here, but to us Floridians it's only four p.m.—how about a long walk over to South Kensington before we turn in?"

"Sure, I'm up for that. Let's go back to the hotel first—I want to put on comfortable walking shoes."

An hour later, they were sitting outside at a cafe watching the late London crowd take advantage of a pleasant summer evening. Sipping her decaf cappuccino, Jane asked Elliot a question that had been on her mind all evening. "How did you manage to remain single all these years?"

"Fair question and I accept your asking me as flattering."

"Well, you've made me feel comfortable talking to you, but I suppose that was presumptuous of me. I've already told you about my marriage experience."

Elliot smiled, signaled the waiter for refills and then responded, "Of course, there were relationships along the way. I was very close to marrying a woman with two teenage sons. I loved her and was willing to accept the challenge of raising step-kids, but she went back to her husband and I never found out if they had better luck the second time around."

Over the course of the next week, with the group, they experienced both the Covent Garden and Camden Passage street-markets. In between, they stopped at retail antique shops and bookstores in various sections of the city, travelling by tube with their weekly passes. On the Kings Road, Elliot found a beautiful boxed set of an Edwardian era, illustrated series on English songbirds. Later the same day, on Kensington High Street, Jane bought a circa 1880 "Ray" machine in excellent condition; included was the original case, all of the attachments and an instruction booklet. Elliot joked that they could try it out that night on their aching feet, as the plug was already appropriate for the British electrical system.

Jane was very pleased with the trip. London was certainly fun. Their itinerary included two West End shows, one certainly bound for Broadway. Everything was made more enjoyable by Elliot's company. The pre-arranged meals were unexciting, but Elliot and lots of good draft beer made even these meals seem special.

Elliot and Jane were now inseparable.

The last Friday night was "dinner on your own." Armed with a recommendation from an antiques dealer at Gray's Passage and a plug for the boeuf bourguignon, they traveled by Tube to a small French restaurant in Knightsbridge. The Belgian waiter suggested a St. Estephe claret to follow their Kir aperitifs. Even though they changed their selection to the Dover sole, it didn't seem to matter that they were drinking a red wine with fish. The couple had pre-ordered chocolate soufflé for dessert and the rest of the wine and espresso were perfect endings to the meal.

They took a cab back to the Royal Windsor Arms and Elliot suggested a nightcap in his room with the XO Martell Cognac he had purchased duty-free in the Tampa airport on the way over. Jane accepted with alacrity, completely comfortable with Elliot and their relationship, which was happily consummated that night.

Saturday morning in London for antiques people means Portobello Road. Elliot and Jane were both in a tired but happy mood.

"I think they could sell me anything," quipped Jane.

"Well, I'm sold on you," was Elliot's sly answer.

Surprisingly, among all the wares available, they were only able to find a few trinkets intended as gifts for friends and family.

After a stop for fish-and-chips at the bottom of Portobello Road, they retraced their steps to the Notting Hill Gate Tube stop. From there, they went to Edgware Road on the Circle Line, destination Alfies, a short walk from the station. Alfies is a group of quality dealers in an interesting rabbit warren of a building that is manned on Saturday afternoons by dealers anticipating trade from the Portobello crowd.

Jane found some miniature, early Victorian apothecary jars in amazing original condition, which the dealer carefully bubble-wrapped to avoid breakage. She was delighted also to find an early traveling dentist's kit. At the stall of a dealer who sold primarily Victorian jewelry, Elliot spotted a beautifully bound volume of hand-illustrated botanicals from the late Victorian period. They were both drawn to the book, but Jane insisted Elliot have it for his collection.

As they turned a corner on the top floor, they said in unison, "Look at that print!"

What had attracted their attention was an extremely large print of Audubon's Brown Pelican, the brown pelican being a ubiquitous, much-loved Florida bird. Audubon had painted two versions: one with the pelican roosting in a tree and this one of a pelican standing on a beautiful, empty Florida beach.

Jane exclaimed, "That would look really great in my living room overlooking Clearwater Beach!"

Elliot countered, "I really must have that for my collection. I know that Audubon worked in England after 1826 and here produced his famous and now very valuable double-elephant folio, 'The Birds of America.'"

The dealer removed the poorly framed example from the wall so they could examine it and, noting their obvious American accents, added, "Shipping is no problem, since I can remove it from the cheap frame and put it in a hard tube I have that you could carry home."

Again, almost in unison, they said, "How much?"

The dealer replied, "You know this is a later reproduction and rather common; however, the paper is good and the colors are bright. I was asking eighty pounds, but for cash I'll take seventy and don't worry about the VAT."

Although it was not clear which of the two was the purchaser, finally they settled on sixty pounds, each handing him thirty pounds, and left happily with their prize.

Back in Florida over the next six months, their relationship continued and became more committed. Elliot enjoyed weekends with Jane in her condo in Clearwater Beach. Many of the mid-week nights were spent at Elliot's luxurious, but small apartment at the Sarasota Ritz Carlton. Sarasota happened to be at the mid-point of Jane's territory for Aliza Drugs. In addition to each other's company, they enjoyed the restaurants and cultural activities available in one of the best small cities in the U.S.

Although the M-word—marriage—was never mentioned, they did discuss buying a house together in the Sarasota area, so they could live comfortably in a larger space than either of them had separately. They looked at Longboat Key, a barrier beach island that began about four miles from downtown Sarasota, which besides being convenient to both of them also fulfilled Jane's strong preference for waterfront property.

As is often the case, their reach for a house appeared to exceed their financial grasp. Their broker showed them many available properties, which even in Florida's severe real estate slump did not begin to suit their budget of $600,000.

They both fell in love with a white Modernist house, of 2,900 square feet, on the edge of Sarasota Bay. Built and originally intended for a couple from Boston and completed just before the crash of 2008, it had never been lived in and was still owned by the builder.

Originally listed at $1.45 million, the agent claimed the builder's rock-bottom price was $875,000, most of which he needed to pay off his construction loan. As they walked through the house, with its red Spanish tile floors, floor-to-ceiling windows with views of the water from almost every room, both Jane and Elliot could picture happily living there. A top-of-the-line kitchen and two generous bedrooms and a den completed the picture. The only mild drawback was the smallish lot, but it was well screened from its neighbors by dense tropical foliage. A small swimming pool fit snugly between the house and the Bay.

The broker, sensing their serious interest, explored their finances. He estimated that the Clearwater condo could fetch $125,000 in this depressed market. Jane owned it free-and-clear and could add fifty thousand in cash towards the purchase. Assuming a similar contribution of $175,000 from Elliot, which he said he could manage, that would still require a $500,000 mortgage to purchase the Longboat Key property. Under the present economic climate, banks were not happy to lend that amount.

As the broker said, "The banks are figuring you could lose your jobs tomorrow and the last thing they need is to own another property."

The broker spent several more weeks showing them properties in the $600,000 range. None of them appealed; most needed repair work and/or had un-enticing views of only the street.

Elliot said, "Well, I figure in two years, if we save and the stock market recovers, we'll have enough to buy that house."

"Yes," Jane countered, "and then the real estate market will have recovered and the homes we like will be in the million-dollar range!"

Over dinner one night, Elliot brought up their meeting and their happy stay in London, with their near-fight over the Brown Pelican print. "I've got an idea—how about getting the print framed? We can share it now and it will bring good luck for the day when we can buy the house we really want."

The framer, Bill Marks, was an old friend of Elliot's and had a shop in downtown Sarasota, a short walk from the Ritz Carlton. He had framed most of Elliot's collection and was considered an expert in print evaluations.

"Very nice, good quality," were his first comments as he unrolled the print carefully from the hard tube, placed weights on the corners and began to bring out frame and mat samples for them to evaluate.

They had pretty much made their choices when he said, "Let's see if we need to add some extra backing for protection."

Bill then removed the weights he had placed on the corners of the giant print and, as he held it up, the light revealed some markings near the edge of the print. "My God, this is an original Havel print!" he exclaimed.

With his hand-held magnifier, he showed them the lack of the tell-tale dots that would be present in a reproduction and further pointed out the "J.Whatman" watermark and plate number in roman numerals.

"Where did you buy this?" he said excitedly.

"In London," was their response. Elliot added, "Why do you ask?"

"Well, that explains everything! This is an extremely rare original print from the first Havel edition. It's in near-perfect condition. This version of the Brown Pelican of Audubon is one of the most sought-after of the over four hundred birds that Audubon produced in England around 1830—give or take a few years—as part of the famous *Birds of America Folio*."

Jane tried to sound casual and laid-back. "I guess it's worth more than the sixty pounds we paid for it."

Marks answered, "A LOT more—as I recall, one like this sold at Christies New York about two years ago for $237,000. High quality stuff like this is recession-proof."

"Are you serious?" cried Elliot.

"I am and if you are interested in selling it, I know the Christies representative for South Florida and I will contact her for you. Besides, tell you what, guys, I have a nice inexpensive, recent laser-produced Brown Pelican print that, to the untrained eye, looks exactly the same. With the frame and mat choices you picked, I can do the package for $350."

That night, Elliot proposed marriage and Jane accepted.

After dinner, they took a drive out to Longboat Key to their dream house and Jane remarked that the real estate company sign was still displayed on the lawn. "Look! The house is still for sale."

Elliot happily replied, "Not for long!"

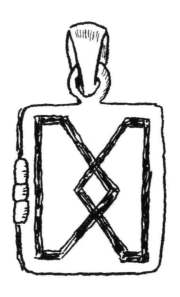

FIVE

Remembering
A Winner

B ella Bash, diminutive and plump, completed her perusal of
the Elephant's Trunk Flea Market in less than two hours.
She was bright and observant and very venal. Spotting un-
dervalued items at flea markets and reselling them at a profit on eBay
allowed her to supplement her retirement income.

Fiftyish and recently divorced from her second husband, an assistant school principal, Bella was happy to be out of the New York
City education system. As a kindergarten teacher, she relished the
short hours and lack of homework, but did not enjoy the hassles of
dealing with the parents or administration. In the divorce settlement,
she had kept the rent-stabilized Bronx apartment, now jammed full
of her inventory. Although mostly successful with her "finds," Bella
lamented not making the big score—an unrecognized treasure,
which she would buy for peanuts and that would fetch thousands or
even tens of thousands at a top auction.

The drive from the Bronx to the New Milford, Connecticut,

market, had taken only seventy minutes in the light early Sunday morning traffic. A glance at her watch confirmed that it was not yet ten a.m. Bella Bash found an unoccupied bench and in the bright sunlight examined the three pieces of pottery she had bought. They were undamaged, confirming her earlier inspection. They should earn a tidy profit on eBay, with good photos and an informative write-up. The pottery, a small abstract oil painting and a few pieces of signed vintage designer jewelry made up her take for the day. Not bad.

Just as she was opening the sippy-spout of her coffee, about to take a bite of a large cinnamon bun, a gray-haired woman thrust copies of *Antique Trails Northeast* onto the table next to her. Bella glanced at the lead story, "Resurgence of the Doll Market," thinking sarcastically to herself, "Well, that headline makes my day!"

Finishing her coffee and bun, she leafed through the paper and noted in the advertising section a promo for the antiques area in Stamford, Connecticut. She had never shopped there. Most of the listed malls opened at eleven a.m., which would be perfect timing for her. It was about a 40-minute drive and not out of the way on the return trip home.

While driving south on Route 7 and then southwest on I-95, she carefully planned her approach. Bella's technique of shopping was very important, because her buying and reselling method was not ethical and was quite possibly illegal. The antique malls represented sellers who rented cases or cubicles to display their wares, which would be shown and sold by the staff of the mall. Unlike most buyers who purchased for themselves or in the case of dealers for resale at shops, shows or on eBay, Bella had added a questionable twist that allowed her to generate a more predictable profit. She would photograph the item in the display cabinet and then list it for sale on eBay as if she already owned it. When Bella accepted an Internet bidder's offer at well over the listed price, she would return to the mall and buy the item. She then shipped it after the buyer's check cleared. This was her no-risk, no-investment, unethical and probably illegal methodology. On the rare occasion that she returned to the store and the item was sold, Bella would notify the disappointed eBay buyer that the piece had been damaged in packing or some other deceit. The sale was cancelled and the check returned to the buyer.

All of this required a compliant retail staff member who permitted her detailed close-ups of the object. Most did, since their goal was to sell the merchandise for the renters of the display cases. Bella rationalized that it was a win-win for everyone: the mall owners, the renters, the eBay buyers and especially for her. She had grossed over $100,000 in extra income the previous year to supplement her teacher's pension!

The GPS sounded woodenly, "Your destination is on your left," as she pulled up to a modern six-story building with offices on the top floors. "Fairfield Antiques" was spelled out in large forties-style letters over the entrance.

Bash was greeted by a man and woman as she trilled, "Good morning, guys, can I get you some coffee at the Starbucks next door? I'm going to grab some before I start shopping." She knew that they would have their own coffee available in a large Keurig coffeemaker. They would politely decline, but it would set the right tone for her later photography requests.

Right on cue the sales representative, wearing a badge that stated, "My name is Jack Gates, how may I help you?" replied, "Thanks, you don't have to leave—we have our Keurig machine down the aisle and some cookies as well—help yourself!"

Bella prepared her coffee and began a quick circuit of the fifty or so glass cases to check the general quality of the merchandise. While doing that she would note the lighting and see if there were some things to photograph with her Smartphone without their noticing to avoid having to ask permission.

Her best profits and easiest sales had been with items of fine jewelry. It was much easier to pack than lighting and pottery, and since the buyer paid all shipping and insurance, that was okay by her.

"Beautiful store you have!"

"Thanks! If you need to see something just speak up. We've got the keys."

Bella determined that the store had great possibilities. There was lots of attractive silver jewelry in the $200–500 range. Within fifteen minutes she asked them to open three cases. She noticed a large rectangular silver locket on a medium-weight silver chain and asked to see it. Jack Gates carefully lifted it out and handed it to Bella, commenting, "This could be worn by a man as well as a woman."

"I like it—may I open it?"

"Of course, however, it has a difficult catch—let me help you."

After two attempts to open it with his thumb nail, Gates succeeded and handed the open locket containing a small photo to Bella.

Bella laughed. "The picture looks like a black Scottie—maybe Roosevelt's dog, Fala—very thirties."

She saw potential immediately as Gates checked the tag and commented that it seemed reasonable at $210 considering the age and the amount of silver contained in the 2x2½-inch Deco-style locket and chain.

"From the style, it's undoubtedly thirties," Bella commented as she examined it with her loupe. "Most likely German since it's stamped '800'."

Without being asked, Gates volunteered, "I know this dealer gives fifteen percent off, but that's it. She doesn't like to be called for a lower price. You're looking at about $180 net and I assume you are a dealer with your state tax resale number and don't pay sales tax."

After pausing, he continued, "This dealer, Jane Downs, is a well-known locket expert. She has a personal collection of several hundred unusual ones, so she either has a duplicate of this or decided it was one of her less interesting examples."

Bella sensed that this was the moment for her ruse. "Actually, I'm buying this for a very fussy customer. Would you mind if I remove it from the case and take some photos with my Smartphone?"

"No problem!"

"If I could place it on this table, I have a little velvet backdrop I carry with me so the photographs show the object better."

"Go right ahead!" Jack said, and then jokingly added, "Good thing the film for Smartphones is cheap!"

Bella explained that her customer was out of the country for a few weeks and out of touch. She would have to wait a few weeks to complete the purchase.

"Well, of course, it is subject to prior sale, but come back again in any case."

Bella commented as she left the store, "If he says yes, I will call you immediately. Would you hold it for me for just a day? I will come back and complete the sale."

In the trendy Nomad Restaurant in the Flatiron District of Manhattan, Linda Quail remarked, "Kevin, you worry about your mom too much!" Linda was referring to Kevin's recently widowed mother, Jane Downs, who lived in Greenwich, Connecticut.

Although Kevin's father (a retired OB-GYN specialist) had left his wife Jane financially well off, with a beautiful house and the estate to support her needs comfortably, Kevin did worry about his mother.

"All she does is play with antiques that she tries to sell at that antique center in Stamford. The rest of the time she runs around buying lockets for her collection. She must have over two hundred by now! I think it is an unhealthy obsession with the past!"

Linda and Kevin had picked Nomad for lunch because of its proximity to the pricey loft they shared. Linda was employed at a PR firm in the nearby Empire State building. Kevin, a Penn graduate and free-lance journalist, worked at home. His fluency in both German and French, which he'd learned at an early age from his Swiss grandmother, gave him versatility and access to several print and on-line European journals. "Stringer" would have been his title in the past, but his many American contacts, creative approach and fluency in German had landed him regular employment with *Der Spiegel*. Downs was knowledgeable about the US political scene as it related to European concerns; however, his special area of interest and expertise was the history of international sporting events since 1900, particularly the Olympic Games.

"It's Mom's 65th birthday next month and I'm looking for a really unusual locket to give her. It has to be really special, considering she has so many."

Over dessert, they discussed how to go about finding such a unique item. "I looked at Tiffany, Cartier and more than a dozen antique shops in town and so far I've seen nothing that appeals to me."

Linda took a final mouthful of strawberry-rhubarb pie and another sip of coffee. After a thoughtful pause, she looked at Kevin and offered, "EBay is tedious and chancy, but you can still find great stuff."

"I'll look tonight, but I prefer to examine jewelry before I buy it. For example, with a locket, part of the attraction is how it opens and closes. Even if it is pictured in both positions, it's not the same as handling it yourself."

That evening, Kevin started his eBay search. In retrospect, he recalled his attraction to that particular locket was because of its Deco styling, which the seller described as probably German, from the thirties. Most of his mom's lockets were feminine and traditional and he doubted that she had one like this. It would be a great addition to her collection. The photo of the locket in the open position showed a black-and-white image of a Scottie. So far there were five bids— the highest at $225—but the reserve was not yet met. There were three days to go, so he put it in "watched items" for re-assessment.

Over the next few days, there were more bids. The price was up to $430 by an hour before the end of the auction. He decided that his maximum bid would be $503, which he left as a last-minute bid. A few minutes later, the auction was over and he was the winner of the locket at $485. Kevin completed the transaction using his PayPal account and noticed that the locket would be mailed from somewhere in New York State.

The birthday party at his mother's home in Greenwich was a few weeks later. Linda was traveling in Europe on business and could not be there. When the present was opened, Jane Downs stared at it with an astounded look on her face. When she opened the locket, her jaw dropped even further. "Where the devil did you buy this?"

"Actually, on eBay. Do you love it for your collection?" Kevin said, misinterpreting the look on her face.

"Son, you just bought and gave me my own locket!"

"How is that possible?"

Jane indicated he should join her in the study. She carefully reviewed her sales list from the Fairfield Antique Center. She asked Kevin what he had paid for the locket and more importantly, the exact date that the eBay auction closed. After further analysis, it was clear that the sale at Stamford occurred a day after the eBay auction closed.

Jane explained, "This eBay seller must have photographed it earlier, put it up on eBay and returned to buy it only after the auction closed."

"Well, she was lucky it hadn't sold in the meantime! Incidentally, is this legal?"

"I have no idea, but we have been had! She bought that piece from me for $180 and made a profit of over $300 without even having to lay out any money! A no-risk deal for her—and if it had been sold earlier, she would claim it was damaged and withdraw it. That behavior is really scurrilous!"

Kevin stared at the photo of the dog. "Well, I guess it was a dog of a present for your birthday!" As he was speaking, he pried away the photo with his finger, thinking he might give it to Linda and put a photo of himself as a baby inside instead of the dog. There was tarnished silver visible underneath.

"Incidentally, Mom, where did you buy this?

"When your Dad and I went to Berlin about ten years ago I bought it at the flea market there."

"Mom, after all that, I'm going to take it home with me. Maybe Linda would like it. I'll put one of my baby pictures inside. I think another present would be in order for you. Maybe someday we'll all laugh about this!"

"Don't worry about the present and when you locate the humor in this, please let me know!"

Back in the loft, Kevin polished the locket and presented it to Linda on her return after telling her the sad story.

"I like it!" was her first response.

She opened the locket, laughed at Kevin's baby picture and using her long sharp nails played with the locket's mechanism. She asked Kevin for a magnifying glass and, after examining the locket carefully, activated another concealed catch to allow a tiny miniature silver plaque to slide out of the rear of the locket, behind the original space that had held the photograph.

"Kevin, check this out—I think there's an engraving in German."

Picking up the magnifying glass, Kevin read the small, old-fashioned German script. It was engraved under five interlocking rings, which he recognized as the symbol of the Olympic Games. It was engraved "Berlin 1936" and Kevin translated into English, "For Jesse Owens, a true hero" and the letters "KSVD." He Googled those letters in the German language and found that they stood for the Christian Social People's Service, described on Wikipedia as a German anti-Nazi organization banned by Hitler in 1933. The engraving on the locket verified its continued existence three years later as an underground organization. Further research confirmed all this history.

Even though it was after 11 p.m., Kevin called his mother, excitedly describing what they had found. He promised he would bring her a very extra special 65th birthday present!

The next morning, Kevin took lots of pictures of the locket and its inscription and spent several hours on the German Internet doing extensive research. That evening, he wrote a lengthy article to be submitted to *Der Spiegel*. He was confident that in the current Olympic year, 2012, there would be interest in this unique item involving the 1936 Olympics. It was extra special because the locket exemplified the political uproar of the time. Most unusual were the connections of the iconic American athlete Jesse Owens with the anti-Nazi Christian group.

Three months later, Bella Bash was sitting at her usual bench, post-shopping, at Elephant's Trunk. It was the last week for the flea market before winter. Today had been a great success for her. Piled on the table were more than a dozen "steals," including three oil paintings, two great signed bronzes and assorted jewelry. The coffee and the cinnamon roll tasted even better than usual. She was not even annoyed when the same gray-haired woman thrust the Antique papers on top of her items. Midway through a large bite of the sweet roll, she was startled by the large picture almost filling the front page. She spat out the roll before she choked on it, as she absorbed the details of the story accompanying the picture.

"Rare and Highly Important Historical 1936 Berlin Olympics Find!" was the headline over a picture of "her" locket that she had sold on eBay. As she read further, her face got redder and her expression more aghast. The part about its being purchased on eBay was particularly galling. In a final act of rage, she swept her purchases off the table as she read that the world sports community and historical scholars as well were in an uproar over this find: "While the owner has no current plans to sell this treasure, experts from the leading auction houses, after reading the *Der Spiegel* article and examining the photos, estimate the auction value to be in excess of 80,000 Euros."

SIX

The House in the Hamptons

Considering his seventy-two years of active physical life, Sean "Cable" Carson was nimble and athletic. But even at six-foot-two, he still needed a stepladder to pull the oversized canvases off the walls of his sprawling 10,000-square-foot Park Avenue apartment. Earlier that wintery December Saturday morning, Sean had selected the eight most valuable artworks of the dozen 20th-century European oil paintings he owned. He included two Picassos and two Braques from the teens, two large fauvist period Derains, a Modigliani and a large Klimt. He carefully wrapped each in protective blankets over cardboard protectors, estimating their total worth at nearly 200 million dollars. He would have taken more, but even his spacious Cadillac Escalade would not accommodate additional artworks and rental of a truck would have attracted unwanted attention.

It took several trips on the service elevator and most of the day to load them carefully into the large SUV parked in the subterranean garage. Fortunately, he encountered nobody on the elevator or in the garage and his servants, husband-and-wife team James and Bertha McEwen, had been given the weekend off. Sean planned to return later that night with similar large, framed-but-worthless substitutes to fill the wall spaces he had just left.

At four p.m., he pulled the Escalade out of the garage onto 82nd Street and turned right on Lexington. He headed to the Midtown Tunnel and the Long Island Expressway which, after two-and-a-half hours should bring him to the house in East Hampton.

The weather was worsening on that mid-December day, with snow starting to accumulate on the grassy edges of the highway, but Sean did not have the luxury of waiting another week. The forecast called for heavy accumulation of snow by dawn on Sunday, but he would be back well before midnight. Traffic was light and Sean made excellent time, arriving at the turn-off for Route NY 27 just after five p.m. as darkness fell, hastened by the cloud cover, and snow was falling.

Sean felt safe and secure in his Escalade cocoon as he listened to old Artie Shaw CDs. His mind drifted back to his first trip to this site almost thirty years before and under very different circumstances.

Sean offered Victor Slayton a neat three fingers of 18-year-old Macallan single malt from the bar of the chauffeured Lincoln limousine. They both had attended graduate school at Harvard fifteen years earlier, Victor for his Masters in Architecture and Sean in the M.B.A. program. Their paths had never crossed at that time.

Sean commented, "It was easy for me. I was able to keep the same apartment I had when I was an undergrad at MIT."

"Not the same for me! It would be a really long commute from Providence, Rhode Island, where I went to Brown. In architecture, you need easy access to a really good library and the drafting studio," was Slayton's reply.

After another sip of the Macallan, glancing across at Sean, Victor continued, "I'm really excited about the building site being right on Georgica Pond. It's almost seven acres and very near the ocean on the southern border. My plans will put the public areas and the decks on the upper levels for maximum views. The seven bedroom suites, projection room and service areas will be at ground level. The landscaping, including keeping the natural vegetation, will support maximum privacy."

As Sean nodded his approval, Victor continued, "I hear you're a golfer and there is room for a putting green, along with a par three 130-yard hole."

"Well, that sounds like fun!" said Sean enthusiastically.

At two previous meetings, Victor had developed specific ideas about what Sean wanted. He had been given carte blanche in the design. At the last meeting, at Slayton's Madison Avenue studio, Victor showed Carson aerial photos of the undeveloped land. Using slides with progressive on-lays of drawings, he was able to project the finished house.

"If you approve, Sean, I will build scale models that will portray the finished project."

"I'm really not sure what type of home I prefer, although that Hampton-style house you just projected looks pretty good!"

After the lights came on, Sean continued, "I have a Park Avenue apartment with high ceilings and period moldings. It's decorated with museum-quality American 18th- and early 19th-century furniture from Boston, Philadelphia and New York.

"My Palm Beach home, circa early 20th Century, is a Mediterranean-style mansion facing the Atlantic Ocean across Ocean Boulevard. The furniture is French Art Deco by Ruhlmann and other designers who decorated the Normandie. I want this house to have a different look!"

"My plan is for something very livable and different from your other homes. The primary materials will be steel and stone, with lots of glass. With that modernistic look, it should be furnished sparely, but I assure you it will be very comfortable."

In the early 1970's, at thirty-two, Sean Carson had foreseen the demand for cable television to satisfy the entertainment desires of those in metropolitan areas. At that time, there was access to only a small number of channels and the sale of TV antennas was still booming.

Sean's senior thesis at MIT had proposed a new concept: bundling TV signals in a cable to increase capability and number of programs available. Initially his work was supported by the Department of Defense, as they could foresee many important national defense uses for such a system. The classes and degrees were much less important than the significant contacts Sean made, both at MIT and Harvard.

By 1972, Sean had built his first trial cable system in Salt Lake City, Utah. It stretched south from Logan, through the city proper to Provo. Although the project didn't make headlines at the time, it did catch the attention of groups with venture capital. By the end of the seventies, Sean "Cable" Carson as he was now known was the senior partner in over twenty cable systems around the U.S.A. Further acquisitions and consolidations made him the second-largest cable operator in the country, second only to VCC (Vision Cable Communications).

The Lincoln limousine left the expressway and was at the western fringes of the first Hampton villages. The towns were deserted and the trees stood bare in the early December cold. Just after Wainscot they turned right, heading toward the ocean. When Georgica Pond came into view, Sean signaled the driver to stop by a stand of leafless maple trees.

As they exited, Victor pointed. "If you agree, that will be your property running straight down to the pond, with over 800 feet of direct pond frontage. On your right it stretches to just short of the Atlantic."

"Where do I sign?" was the enthusiastic response.

"Glad you like it! When we get back, I'll put your attorney in touch with the owner and you can sort out the details."

Victor was shivering as they had left their coats in the limo, but Sean didn't seem to mind the 30-degree weather.

"What are your specific ideas about the interior of the house?" Victor inquired.

Sean replied, "I don't feel like focusing on a particular genre of decorating. Just get some comfortable new stuff, built-ins, all compatible with your 'spare' look, augmented with odds-and-ends from local antique shops. Wall treatment could include landscapes and the like from good local artists."

Slayton grabbed his coat from the car as Carson continued to gaze proprietorially at "his land."

"Actually, I know Kate Morris, who is a decorator based out here. I've worked successfully with her on a few of my other commissions in the area. She's a no-bullshit type who gets the job done. Another plus is that she's great looking and if I were single I'd be very tempted…"

"Okay, get me her number. I'll set up a meeting with her in the City after we've sealed the deal. Let's get back now."

After a stop in Southampton at Julian's for a celebratory lunch with more cocktails, the ride back was uneventful.

Within six weeks, all the legal documents for the purchase were completed and signed. The deal was easy since no financing was required. Victor Slayton completed his plans within the next month, with a few changes suggested by Sean. The town of Easthampton gave fast approval for the project and the necessary building permits were issued. The projected date for completion of the house was Easter of the following year.

Soon after, Kate Harris and Sean Carson met for lunch at the Harvard Club. Many heads turned at the sight of the attractive woman with her wavy, shoulder-length auburn hair and Kelly green tailored form-fitting suit as she entered the mostly male occupied dining room. Kate Harris strode in confidently, burgundy leather briefcase in hand. For a moment Sean wondered, "Who is the lucky man meeting this actress for lunch?"

Then Kate approached his table. "Hi, I'm Kate and you're Sean, I presume?" She extended her hand, which he grasped happily.

"A drink before lunch?"

"Fine!"

He ordered a Wild Turkey Manhattan with extra cherries; Kate said she would have the same and commented, "I confess it's my first time here. This is the closest I've been to an Ivy League education, although another client did take me to the Yale Club."

Carson laughed. "All the Ivy Clubs are the same—they're filled with self-important people!"

"From the way you said that, I guess you don't consider yourself important."

"Well, we're all important to somebody. I guess I can say immodestly that I'm important in the Cable industry."

Carson proceeded to give her his standard three-minute spiel on his professional background.

Kate smiled often until he finished. "Yes, you are important!"

The waiter interrupted with their drinks and menus for the lunch with a recitation of the specials of the day.

"Anyway, let me fill you in about my decorative objectives for the Hampton House. I expect that Victor has already given you some background on my other homes on Park Avenue and in Palm Beach."

Kate reached into her leather briefcase and extracted a large ring-binder notebook. "I made some notes and have some preliminary ideas and suggestions."

Sean nodded for her to continue.

"At your convenience, we could stop by the Design Center on 57th Street. They have some excellent contemporary furniture by Knoll, Milo Baughman and others that I think would work well. Bear in mind that, while it is still early in the year, the best designer furniture can take up to a year for delivery."

"Sounds like a good idea."

"In addition, I have excellent sources out on the East End for decorative objects and even hand-crafted furniture and artwork. It can be hit-or-miss, but if we find things out there storage will not be a problem."

"Go on—I like your ideas!"

"I've seen the plans. The project is spectacular even by Hampton standards! The design magazines are going to line up to feature your estate."

After a good luck clink of their highball glasses and a first sip, Sean said, "Kate, please prepare the appropriate documents that will give you financial authority for designs and .purchases."

The waiter took their order: Dover sole meuniere for both.

"I want you to see this commission through to completion," Sean continued.

"Thank you—that was quick, but we haven't even discussed my notes!"

"Use your professional judgment. Get stuff that's available—I don't like back orders! I want to be able to use the house as soon as possible. I'd like the kitchen in working order the same day the builder installs the lock on the front door. And I don't need foreign-sounding appliances."

Kate was still smiling as he continued his rant.

"I've got museum-quality furnishings in my other homes. In East Hampton, I don't want crap, just excellent contemporary furnishings and decorative items. You can feel free to fill in with interesting things you pick up from local shops. In addition to your contractual fees, I'm prepared to pay you a considerable bonus for getting this done well and on time."

He stopped speaking and glanced at her for any reaction. Kate continued to smile and nodded her acceptance.

"Now, let's enjoy lunch. I've had the sole before—you're really going to like it! Now it's time to tell me about you."

By dessert, Carson had learned that Kate was ten years younger and like him had never married. Her first words after sampling the Dover sole were, "I'm a townie—born in Sag Harbor into an old fishing family. I did get a degree from Parson's School of Design in New York, but I'm really a country girl at heart. Before the real estate market boomed in the Hamptons, I was able to buy a small historic house in Bridgehampton."

"Do you spend much time in New York?"

"I have a girlfriend in the travel business, who is frequently out of town, and I use her apartment."

"How about dinner next week?"

"That would be nice."

"Great! If you like, I'll pick up some theater tickets. Any preference?"

"Not really, although I do enjoy musicals a lot."

Their relationship started warmly, but was not consummated until several dates later.

In spite of Sean's initial insistence on no interim involvement in the project, Kate suggested he drive out to see the partially cleared property. The site was even more spectacular than he remembered.

He could envision, in the late spring light, the amazing views the finished house would provide.

"In a few weeks excavation will begin and, just so you know, some of the furnishings are selected! How about drinks and lobsters at Gozman's out at Montauk?" She was referring to the easternmost village at the tip of Long Island, noted for its views, fishing, surfing, State parks and beaches, and increasingly for its new homes and estates and an atmosphere far more casual than the Hamptons.

Kate beamed at him over dinner and suggested he cancel his limousine back to the city and stay with her. He didn't need much convincing.

The affair went well and lasted throughout the fourteen months of construction of the Hampton house. The sunny fall day of the walkthrough was memorable for two reasons: first, Carson's unexpected reaction to his new estate.

"My God, Kate! I gave you carte blanche, but this place looks like the furniture department at Sears during a clearance sale."

Then he pointed at some of the artwork and continued, "I've seen better art stuck up with magnets on the refrigerator!"

"Of course, you're joking."

"No, I'm dead serious and very angry!"

Kate looked at him with tears welling in her eyes. "Well, I've got other news I hope you take better!" Seeing no reaction, she blurted, "I'm four months pregnant!"

Then came the second memorable moment.

"Kate, this is my response. This was your choice. I have no heirs and don't want any."

She stared at him, speechless.

"Of course, I'll take care of the cost of the abortion and I'll send a check."

"That sounds like the instructions you gave me for decorating the house: 'Just give me an address and the amount and I'll send a check.' Well, we're hardly talking about taking delivery of a table here!"

They never saw or spoke to each other again. A few weeks later, Sean hired a local real estate firm to manage the property. Over the next three decades, he returned a handful of times. The annual rent of $750,000 attracted few takers. Carson didn't care and the neighbors were happy with their view of the quiet and empty property.

In early 2001, Sean Carson was featured in a *Wall Street Journal* article on American billionaires. In the interview, he touted the foresight he and others in the cable industry had shown in predicting technological advancements. In the nineties, his firm had pioneered developments of internet and satellite data transmission that helped gain virtual monopolies. The home computer was entrenched as the new king of the household and hand-held devices were in the development stages. The dotcom revolution arrived and Sean was happy he was late to the party since the bust-up was spectacular.

Sean Carson steered the bulk of his business-related hedge fund's venture capital into a project in China. With the cooperation of the Chinese government, they installed TV and computer networks in the newly built cities in that country to access the internet via cable. The agreement was a fifty-fifty partnership with the goal of networking all technology in China through this cable system. Contrary to the financial downturn in the U.S. in 2007–8, the cable network system in China was hugely successful.

Unfortunately, other investments in Carson's fund were not as successful and the fund was forced into bankruptcy. The US investors were wiped out and sued Carson. After spending $100 million in legal fees and more failed appeals, Sean saw his wealth dribbling away. The Chinese partners were uninterested in the results of U.S. legal proceedings and refused to release his share of the profits of the successful Chinese operation. The next recourse was the World

Court. Their judgment could be imposed on China, but that was years away.

Things did not go well for Kate either. Several real estate busts and financial downturns, as well as competition from New York City decorators, had decimated her business. She struggled to raise her illegitimate son, Glen. Now twenty-eight, a graduate of East Hampton High School, he had signed on with the local police department. The local crowd felt sorry for him because his mother, Kate, was wheelchair-bound from the ravages of multiple sclerosis. She was now in a nursing home, paid for by Medicaid, for which her pauperized state qualified her.

Sean's senior attorney, Harry Block, called him at home late one night. "Here's the story. A college friend works for the Department of Justice—and this is off the record."

"Okay, Harry, my bills with you are up-to-date, so maybe you owe me something."

"Someone in the Marshal's office listed the properties they intend to seize to satisfy the judgments against you. They didn't list the house in the Hamptons—I guess because you have hardly ever been seen there and it is held in a different corporate name."

"Well, what of it?"

"My advice—which I will deny giving you—is to take your best, most valuable paintings off the walls in your Park Avenue apartment and move them to Long Island. Bring back some cheap stuff to fill the spaces on the walls. At worst, it will buy you some time and hide a lot of assets. They will soon also grab everything in Palm Beach."

"How much time do I have?"

"My final piece of advice is-do it tomorrow!"

Artie Shaw was hitting the high C on *Begin the Beguine*—the last track on the CD—as Sean entered Bridgehampton. The road was becoming narrower, snow-covered and treacherous. He found the turn-off for Georgica Pond and his house with difficulty. Sean sighed with relief as he entered the long circular drive leading to his dark estate. He had brought the front door keys, which moved smoothly in the lock. Carson flipped the entry hall light switch just as the beeps of a tripped alarm began. This meant that he had only minutes.

"Shit, I don't know the code!"

He made a quick decision to unload the car quickly. The alarm would not be heard by his neighbors and it would take at least twenty minutes for a response from the police station. He had unloaded all of the paintings into the hall when the phone began to ring. If he didn't answer, there would be no record of his having been there to alert the Marshal to his valuable property or his criminal attempt to hide it. He would skip exchanging the paintings, as he could easily find some other cheap replacements pre-framed in a poster shop in the City. When the alarm company called him the next day, he would say the matter was taken care of.

Patrolman Glen Morris was talking New York Islander hockey with his buddy, Bill, at the counter of a diner in East Hampton when his hand-held radio crackled. "Possible break-in and burglary reported by Alarm Company at 88 Georgica Drive…"

Glen thought, *Another false alarm. No self-respecting burglar would go out on a night like this. It's probably just a cold weather malfunction.* "Hey Bill, I'll be back in twenty minutes."

"We'll keep the coffee warm for you!"

As Glen entered the long circular drive, he noticed a large SUV exiting from the other side at a dangerous speed considering the poor road conditions. He immediately put on his flashers and siren and followed the SUV as it turned west on Highway 27 in the direction of New York City. Glen kept a safe distance behind as he called for back-up from the Southampton department (whose jurisdiction they were entering). Glen's training reminded him to remain cautious and avoid an accident. The policeman feared that, at its current rate of speed, the large SUV would soon leave the Hamptons and be on the four-lane highway to NYC. He alerted the NY State police who assured him that a trooper in the area would follow up immediately.

Suddenly, about 500 feet ahead the SUV made an abrupt right turn onto a secondary road. When Glen reached the turn, he saw only an empty road ahead. He proceeded cautiously and soon noticed skid marks. The SUV had spun out of control on the slippery road and apparently hit a large tree before careening down into a small ravine.

Sean called for help and then scrambled down the embankment. The SUV's headlights were shattered and the horn was blowing from the pressure of the body compressing it. The doors were crumpled and would not open.

An ambulance and other police cruisers arrived in less than ten minutes. When the driver was finally freed, it was obvious that he had died instantly from multiple severe injuries, the most serious of which was a broken neck.

When Kate Morris told Glen that the famous victim of the crash was his biologic father, he was shocked. The press was, of course, obsessed with Carson, the details of his life and the circumstances of his death. Glen's paternity and the coincidence of his involvement in his father's death only served to increase the frenzy. When it became known that Sean 'Cable' Carson had died penniless, the story became less interesting.

Eighteen months later, the World Court made its ruling in favor of the Carson Hedge Fund. The Chinese partners would be forced to pay all the creditors, of which Sean Carson's estate was the largest. The payout would come from the earnings of the last seven years of the highly profitable Chinese business—with interest. Those who had raided Carson's personal assets were forced to return them. When all was said and done, Sean Carson's estate was valued for tax purposes at $8.5 billion.

Several months later, DNA tests done on tissue saved from the mandatory autopsy was compared with that of Glen Morris. The conclusive results put to rest the claims of some remote relatives against the Carson estate.

Glen and his mom had a big celebration at a local restaurant after the decision was handed down.

They had another, even more splendid celebration right after Kate Morris moved into the house at 88 Georgica Lane with her retinue of servants and nurses. On the night of the party, the line of cars belonging to invited guests reached back to Route 27.

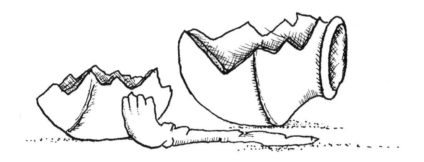

SEVEN

The Reservation

"Little Vic" Rizzo, aged 84, kept his hard hat on. It was cold and drafty in the construction shack. He had just come down the temporary elevator after seeing the topping-off of the 48-story tower building.

"I only wish my dad were here," he thought, "to see the American flag flying from the tower of this development with a clear view of the Empire State Building forty-eight miles away."

Over sixty years earlier, he had stood on this very spot on Long Island near Hauppauge, New York, a year after Technical Sergeant Vic Rizzo had been discharged from the army following an eventful tour on the European front in World War II. He'd joined the family construction business, started in the late 19th century by his immigrant grandfather from Sicily.

Vic was raised in a comfortable brick house in Bay Ridge, Brooklyn, which his father had built before the war. "Little Vic" was a handsome feisty Italian lad, barely five-feet-four in his shoes, even-featured with penetrating blue eyes and dark, thick, straight hair. He would perform his Sinatra imitation at the slightest urging. His mother wanted him to take advantage of the GI bill and go to college so there would be a professional man in the family.

"Momma, the war was my college. I was an army engineer and learned lots of practical things, as well as a lot of other good and bad stuff. I only want to work in the family business and make some real money!" he told her.

So Vic joined the business and learned from his father, Rocco, that the only way to make money was to do good work using other people's money, concentrating on something you know is in demand. What people needed and wanted in the post-war years was housing for returning servicemen and their expanding families. From the perspective of the Rizzo Construction Company, this would be rental homes, since many of the veterans could not even afford the down payment on the $6,000 Levittown tract houses. They wanted to raise their children in the suburbs, not the gritty old apartment blocks in the outer boroughs of New York City.

Rocco put it this way: "The vets want to live in the country." To him, the country meant housing within commuting distance of the City, where most of the family breadwinners had jobs. The problem was that in the still-green suburbs, rent was too high for blue-collar families with children.

At that time, the extended Rizzo family together had accumulated $300,000—definitely not enough for the project they envisioned. Through involvement in the parish, they met the priest's brother-in-law, Sal Capelli, president of the small but rapidly growing Brooklyn-based People's Trust Bank.

Discovery of The Reservation building site was fortuitous. Ken Gold, their broker, was given the task of locating a hundred contiguous acres on Long Island, within forty miles of Manhattan and convenient to the Long Island Railroad. The plan was to build 600–800 rental garden apartments with a large, centrally located community center. The search had been fruitless until one Friday afternoon in August, when Gold's Chevy blew a tire on his way out to Montauk for a weekend holiday. While Gold waited for the local garage man to arrive to change his tire, conversation with a few of the locals led to a revelation. There were rumors of an ancient Indian burial ground in that area—possibly haunted. Therefore, the locals referred to the tract of land as The Reservation. Although 175 acres was much larger than the family had requested or probably could finance and it was almost 48 miles from Manhattan, Gold met with the owners and put together a proposal. A year later, after overcoming legal and tribal objections, People's Trust Bank provided financing. In early 1952, the completed units were finally available for rental.

The response was overwhelming and within sixteen months every unit had been leased, leaving a waiting list of over 200 buyers. With regular rental income, the loan was soon paid down and the line of credit increased for future investments. Over the ensuing years, Vic Rizzo bought out the rest of the family.

By the early 1960's the real estate boom had fizzled, lessening the demand for rentals. The ever-prescient Little Vic Rizzo realized that he would soon be stuck with aging rental buildings. The garden apartment, low-ceiling look did not readily lend itself to condo conversion. The more affluent buyers of the day wanted larger homes closer to the City in Nassau County. Even a complete rebuild of The Reservation would probably not be successful.

In 1968 after a golf game with Craig Kenyon, the Rizzo Construction accountant, Vic got the idea during post-game drinks at Craig's exclusive Sound Gates Club on the North Shore that a country club on the property could be successful.

"Craig, how much does it cost to join this club?" he asked.

Kenyon was momentarily at a loss for words. "Vic, you're a friend, so here's the no BS story. We have no Jewish or Italian members, although we can bring them as guests. They mostly have their own clubs anyway. An applicant is recommended by two members and if approved by the board pays the non-refundable $10,000 initiation fee. Then, the annual dues are $1,200 with a minimum for spending in the bar and dining rooms. The typical member spends north of $7,000 per year—not counting the private parties and affairs."

"How many members do you have?"

"Probably around eight hundred." Kenyon paused. "Why are you interested in our financials?"

"Oh, nothing personal, but I'm thinking of building a new country club and the information you just gave is very instructive! A quick analysis of your figures tells me that you have a base budget of six million dollars and that does not include extras like weddings, golf tournaments and corporate rental of the facilities."

That evening, Vic made the decision to pursue building his country club on the Reservation property. He surmised that the burgeoning population on Long Island would welcome an open membership country club. There were three big obstacles: finding a partner for financing; clearing the legal hurdles for town permission; and getting rid of the last few recalcitrant tenants. In the final analysis, all these problems would be solved by money.

Vic's new partner, Island Equity Associates, agreed to demolish the units and supply the capital for designing and building the new facility. The deluxe club would have thirty-six holes of golf, a sprawling clubhouse, six tennis courts and two swimming pools, along with a spa facility. Since Vic had supplied the now valuable acreage, the partnership split was fifty-fifty.

The Reservation Country Club was completed in 1971 and became a financial success, with debts repaid and positive cash flow by

1976. Although management was independent, the performance contract carried a strict nondiscrimination policy for membership.

As befit their improved financial status, the Rizzo family left Bay Ridge behind and lived in a small mansion on the "Gold Coast" overlooking Long Island Sound. Rizzo's business interests included office buildings and corporate parks; he had also accumulated a large stock market portfolio. In 2001, Little Vic was 75 years old and life was good! His children were educated professionals, Johnnie a lawyer and CEO of RRE (Rizzo Real Estate) and Melissa a pediatrician on staff at North Shore Hospital. Vic's mother would have been proud of her professional grandchildren!

Along came the dotcom bust and the events of 9/11, which combined to cause a real estate and business disaster on Long Island. Many of the Company's office parks were half-empty and the Reservation Country Club was operating in the red. The firm's accountants suggested they might have to close it down. After much research and study, in 2006 Johnnie decided to reconvert The Reservation back to residential usage, which was still in demand. This time, the plan was to build a high-rise cluster of buildings containing 800–1,000 luxury condos positioned around the existing renovated clubhouse, with its pools and tennis courts. In the initial offering plan, the putting green would remain and the 36 holes of golf would be converted to a par 3, nine-hole layout. The difficulty of dealing with the remaining club members and the town was again solved by good lawyers, money and time. By March 2008, the excavation for the first tower was underway.

About four weeks later, a construction worker digging the foundation discovered various human skeletal parts at a depth of twenty-five feet. The County ordered all work stopped and the discovery was prominently mentioned in the national media all that spring. The Native American community and its leaders immediately assumed that analysis of the remains would confirm the 90-year-old rumor that the site was, in fact, an ancient Indian burial ground. Some scientists claimed it was essential to carbon date the skeletal remains. The results were reported that September: the human bones were at least 700 years old. Therefore, they must be Native American: The Reservation was a sacred burial site that should receive protected status. A few weeks later, the stock market crashed and the banks canceled their commitment for the new luxury development, already on hold because of the discovery of the bones. For the first time in 60 years, the Rizzo family business, RRE, was in big trouble.

Billy "Red" Highcloud, the titular chief of the thirteen histori-cally recognized, Long Island Indian tribes, contacted the Rizzo Company. Though CEO, Johnnie directed the call to his dad. The phone conversation was cordial and a meeting was arranged on what turned out to be a cold Sunday morning in early December. The two men, one short and wizened, the other tall and broad-shouldered, climbed down into the cordoned-off excavation and inspected the area carefully. Since the temperature was near freezing, they agreed to continue the conversation at a nearby diner in Commack.

"Mr. Rizzo…" Billy began once they were seated in the warm restaurant.

"Please, call me Vic."

"Okay, Vic—I'm Billy."

"Perhaps we can still salvage something from this difficult situation."

"I'm listening."

They both ordered burgers and hot coffee and between chews the conversation proceeded.

"Vic, this economic situation is going to get worse quickly and in my opinion will not improve for years. However, I think there is one recession-proof use for this property."

"I know you're thinking the C-word—casino," Vic said and then laughed out loud. "As you know, there is a vociferous anti-gambling crowd out here, but I'm thinking of an interesting twist that might improve our chances for success."

"What's that?"

"In these bad economic times, politicians are scrambling for ways to raise money to make up for falling tax revenues. They would probably approve the casino, contemplating the tax revenue increase, if there was a way to make the idea more palatable to the public."

"I'm listening—what do you have in mind?" Billy said thoughtfully.

"I've done some research and lots of relics and artifacts such as arrows, old hard-shell clams that were used for wampum, cooking utensils, clay dishes, sharpening rock implements, etcetera, were found in Middle Island—that's just seventeen miles east of here."

"Yes, I know about that, but so far no things like that have been discovered here."

Vic looked around to make sure their conversation was not being overheard. "What I have in mind is a mini-museum over the area we just inspected. During the winter, some of your Indians—sorry, I mean Native Americans—"

Billy laughed. "You can call us Indians—I'm not P.C.!"

Vic continued, "Your people could throw artifacts from Middle Island and other areas on Long Island into the excavation area and then cover everything with dirt. No one will notice anything during the winter and by the spring, when the snow melts, trusted members of the tribes will come here to inspect and then uncover the relics. We'll suggest to the politicians that they build a museum/casino directly over the site—with emphasis on the museum, which will be a remembrance/memorial to the souls who were buried there."

"That's a great idea, but after the material is discovered and analyzed some snot-nosed professor is going to claim it's from a different site."

Vic laughed. "By then their research will be drowned out by the noise of a thousand slot machines ka-chinking."

"You're a funny man!"

Vic continued, "Look at it from the standpoint of what is important to your members: a dissertation by some Master's candidate from Podunk U on relics and artifacts discovered at The Reservation; or the billions in funds from a casino that will benefit the entire tribe? Case closed!"

"Yes, you're right."

"Billy, you and I can fight over this land. Your lawyer will say that the remains prove it belongs to the Tribes. My guys will say that my company owns it—and point to my longstanding legal title. Ten years from now, I'll be dead and my son will still be fighting with you."

"I hope not, on both counts!"

"Billy, here is my general plan. I contribute the land; then, using my influence over the local politicians who owe me, I'll concentrate on the huge potential for the County and local towns. I'll also stress the construction employment, tax income and jobs the Casino will bring. Finally, I'll use the museum as the cover to convince the anti-gambling do-gooders that the whole plan is kosher. Incidentally, we can probably keep at least one 18-hole golf course to increase the appeal of the new resort."

"You make sense. Every year delayed costs $1.5–2 billion in gross casino revenue. I'm sure we can work out the details and get the casino deal done. Let our lawyers make their money figuring out the fine print and percentages. Otherwise, we're losing money!"

Both men stood and shook hands…

The chief engineer, James Kelly, got up from his seat in the cold construction shack, smiled at Vic and offered the shivering old man his jacket. "Mr. Rizzo, you were looking out at New York City from the top of $1 billion—The Reservation-Museum-Casino-Golf Club! You won't believe this coincidence, but almost sixty years ago, my grandfather started his family on this spot in a cheap rental garden apartment with a view of a brick wall!"

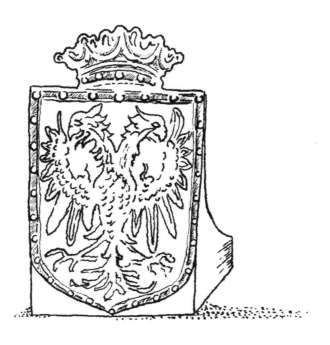

EIGHT

Weighted Bookends

In today's culture of Kindles, Nooks, and Pads, the concept of rows of shelves containing neatly arranged rows of books is passé. Past generations appreciated the esthetic of the book shelf, the rows of books secured by artfully placed weighted bookends. Publication and collection of books is diminishing, but the bookends and their collection are dying a slower death because bookends are interesting figural objects and collectibles unto themselves. They come in all styles, sizes, materials and ages. Typically they are in pairs, mostly mirror images. As decorative objects, they can stand on their own. In the following tale, we follow a pair of very special and unusual bookends, created under fire and stress, separated by circumstances and possibly reunited in the end...

Fritz Karl hurried from the side exit of his Babelsberg film studio in Potsdam, just fifteen miles southwest of Berlin, the destination his nearby apartment. It was the fall of 1930 in Weimar Germany; the crowded tram was filled with many other anxious commuters glancing at evening papers, which described the ever-worsening economic news. Front-page photos recorded the strife on Berlin streets between Nazi gangs and Communist Labor Union members. Nevertheless, for the moment, Karl's position as a rising film director at Universal Films A.G. (commonly known as UFA) was apparently secure. In the past year, the studio had successfully completed the conversion to all-sound, full-length features. Karl's marriage to the talented and beautiful young British actress, Sarah Holmes, was going well and most of the time he was shielded from the increasing disruptions that weighed on Berliners.

"Dear, how did it go today?" was Sarah's greeting as Fritz entered the modern flat.

The building and furniture—all straight lines and angles—were designed by an architect who had studied under Walter Gropius at the Bauhaus. Blond furniture, Expressionist art and Art Deco-style lighting blended for a striking modern look. Straight out of central casting, Fritz Karl's angular youthful appearance and shaggy mop of blond hair was a stereotype for "young, blond, Aryan man" and blended perfectly with his surroundings.

"Let me sit down and have my martini and I'll fill you in on the latest." (A brief visit to Hollywood had introduced them to the cocktail habit, one they had continued for several years living in London and now in Berlin.) A casual observer would not have pegged Sarah Karl as a film actress. Unassuming in manner, with very blond, Nordic, regular features, blue eyes and medium-length, white-blond hair, she spoke English with a pronounced Midlands accent. "Small-town English girl" was her stereotype and she would have seemed perfectly at home working as a clerk in a Birmingham chemist's shop. Sarah had, in fact, graduated from film school in Berlin. Fluent in German, learned as a child from her native-born German mother, her bilingual skills had advanced her career.

The Karl family, including Fritz's father and uncles, had been bankers for several generations until a mutant creative gene propelled Fritz from the financial side of the film industry into directing. During introspective moments mandated by the overwhelming and frightening social and political crises, Fritz reflected fearfully on the increasing anti-Semitism. He was concerned that a revelation about his maternal half-Jewish grandfather might impact his and Sarah's safety. Grandfather Louis, a colonel in the German army and a decorated hero, had lost his life in the service of his beloved country in Flanders in 1915.

Most of the time Fritz was calm, knowing that many Jewish directors, such as Fritz Lang and Billy Wilder, as well as Peter Lorre and other Jewish members of the film industry, were doing quite well and not suffering from obvious discrimination.

"Well, the news is that I have been selected to direct a film in Paris," Fritz told Sarah. "It's probably just a lightweight Boulevard comedy, but what the hell—it's a month in Paris for us! What's your news?"

"Let's skip the martinis tonight—I have something else in mind!" From under the table, Sarah pulled out an ice bucket that contained a chilled bottle of Moet champagne, along with two crystal glasses arranged on a silver-and-black Art Deco tray.

As he deftly pulled the champagne cork, Fritz said, "Okay, I'm ready for your news—what's your next starring role?"

"How about—mother?"

Fritz embraced Sarah excitedly. "Of course you mean in real life?" Her radiant smile was his answer.

The next several months were eventful in many ways. The deepening depression in the USA exacerbated the already dire economic and political situation in Germany. Karl's banker relatives predicted that even if Hitler were defeated in the next election the outlook for the film industry was extremely bleak. On the other hand, if Hitler were to be victorious, the nationalization of UFA Studios in order to produce propaganda films was a foregone conclusion.

Over the previous five years, anticipating the coming economic chaos, Fritz Karl had presciently been buying gold bars and storing them in a wall safe in his flat. When unable to secure additional bullion through his banking contacts, he bought high-karat gold jewelry—which at the time seemed expensive but was now a bargain, based on the outlandish inflation. Another source for his gold purchases was his nephew, Dr. Mark Strauss, a dentist with a fashionable office suite on Unter den Linden in Berlin. In addition to highly sought-after dental skills, Dr. Strauss was a skilled amateur sculptor.

By the beginning of 1931, Fritz Karl owned a combined weight of just under 380 ounces or about twenty-four pounds of almost pure gold and high-karat jewelry. Dr. Strauss was able to refine the jewelry into near 24-karat gold. The original plan for buying and hoarding the gold was as a hedge against the spiraling inflation. In the current situation, having gold easily exchangeable into any currency (then $12,000 in U.S. dollars) seemed the best guarantee for a safe and prosperous life in Germany or elsewhere.

Baby Marlene arrived in the spring of 1931, along with Herr Hitler's increasingly improving prospects. President Hindenburg did not seem at all perturbed by the coming election. Those in the film community with any Jewish background were fleeing to Hollywood if they could, not even pausing to consider whether their talents would be welcome there. Somewhat surprisingly, Alexander Korda, the Hungarian-born director and Karl's mentor, also chose Hollywood over England, in spite of Korda's many British connections.

Named for the famous German actress Marlene Dietrich, baby

Marlene was a happy distraction as the Karls planned their exit. They were now resigned to selling their special flat and its contents at way under its expected value. Using his banking family connections, Fritz transferred his funds to London banks. Sarah, meantime, hoped to get work in the West End theaters in London, if not in the struggling British film industry. All the while they were extremely grateful that Sarah's British passport would get their small family safely out of Germany.

Transferring the melted-down gold threatened to be a much more difficult problem. Dr. Strauss devised an elegant and creative solution: he proposed that he make a plaster cast of two bookends. The design would be a shield-shaped design mounted on a square base and bearing the heraldic symbols of the Karl family's Bavarian crest. This design had presided over the entrances of all the Karl-owned banks for centuries. Molds would then be prepared, the gold poured to fill the molds and the "sculpture" would be finished with six coats of polished black enamel. Each bookend would weigh well over eleven pounds.

The year 1933 found Hitler firmly and triumphantly ensconced in Berlin and the Karls somewhat less securely in London. Walking, talking and busy baby Marlene was a constant joy. On several occasions that year Fritz had been tempted to melt one of the bookends. Since the price of gold was somewhat deflated he delayed, and they were saved financially by Sarah's modestly successful stage career.

The thirties marched on inexorably and Marlene grew into a beautiful and extremely bright student. She was enrolled and soon at the top of her class in one of London's excellent preparatory schools, conveniently located near the Kings Road not far from their Brompton Road flat.

Alexander Korda, meanwhile, had departed Hollywood and returned to England to form London Pictures. He invited Fritz to join the new studio. In 1933, London Pictures received a Best Picture nomination for an Academy Award for *The Private Life of Henry VIII*. By the end of the 1930's, J. Arthur Rank and his famous gong had absorbed Korda's company. Fritz Karl was now an important film director. World War II provided huge opportunities for motion pictures, both with the government and in the private sector. Unfortunately, shortly after the war, the new medium of television substantially weakened the British film industry.

By the early 1950's the Karls, then in their sixties, chose to retire and enjoy life in their beautiful Knightsbridge home. Marlene was a pre-med student at Cambridge and within ten years she would become a qualified specialist in obstetrics and gynecology. She had added a credential by undertaking postgraduate training in the new discipline of infertility studies at Johns Hopkins University in Baltimore. This led to a successful Harley Street consultancy practice in infertility.

To complete their lives, Sarah and Fritz Karl wished only for a son-in-law and grandchildren. Their wishes came true only partly— no son-in-law—but a pair of fraternal grandchildren, one of each gender, born to their daughter Marlene through the new science of artificial insemination, which had been introduced by her specialty. Their disappointment at this unconventional arrangement was superseded by their great joy in the grandchildren.

When the twins, Janet and Dean, were eight years old and the grandparents were in their late seventies, Sarah and Fritz drafted new wills leaving their entire and now impressive estate to Marlene. Even at such an early age, the twins demonstrated radically different interests and personalities. Sarah and Fritz were confident that Marlene would fairly distribute what was appropriate to each twin. As a special family memento, each twin, under the terms of the will, was to be given one of the special bookends with instructions that they were never to be sold, as they carried the spirit and soul of the family's good fortune. They were meant to be handed down to future generations. Marlene was never told of their history and special composition.

Janet, the granddaughter, qualified as a teacher in early childhood education and worked in Bury St. Edmonds, a town northeast of Cambridge, where she had trained. Although serious about her work, Janet thoroughly enjoyed kicking up her heels on weekends at the local pub, The Raven's Nest. In the mid-nineties, she met an American Air Force officer stationed at nearby RAF/USAF Mildenhall airbase. A quick courtship resulted in an even shorter marriage. The good news was that her ex-husband soon flew away for good across the Atlantic and out of her life forever. Shortly after the ill-fated marriage, Marlene bought Janet a little cottage in Bury St. Edmonds. In retrospect, Janet's happiest childhood memories were of summers spent with her twin brother Dean and their mother in a charming rented cottage facing the North Sea just north of Southold on the Suffolk coast in East Anglia.

Janet's brother Dean, by contrast, was more a city boy He inherited his grandfather's love of film, unfortunately without the requisite creative and financial skills. Gambling seemed a quicker path to success and—as usually happens—just the opposite occurred. Since Marlene controlled Dean's trust fund, she kept him in a small flat so he could live a reasonably—if unearned—comfortable life. After buying Janet the cottage, Marlene felt she should do something for Dean. In an attempt to change his focus, she bought and furnished for him a condo in a new development near the area where the family had summered so happily years ago.

Dean took a train to the coast with his mother and had to utilize his best theatrical skills to gush over the view and the "charming little village." On the trip home he vowed never to return and schemed how he could unload the cottage without arousing his mother's ire, thus allowing him to put the money to better use.

Time passed and true to human nature all three continued on their respective paths—Janet was teaching, her mother was bringing unexpected joy to infertile couples and Dean was muddling along, occasionally involving himself with some modest film project but never achieving much success.

One day, as Janet dusted the shelves in her cottage, the heavy bookend tipped over and fell on the stone cottage floor. A careful examination revealed a break where the scroll met the family crest. Her attempt to secure the cracked piece with crazy glue left an ugly, irregular line. A call to her mother and subsequent enquiries at the University produced the name of a competent repair shop in nearby Cambridge. The owner dealt with commissions from the sculpture department.

The repairman, Simon Quarles, was a fiftyish, compact, bearded man with round wire-rim glasses, his eyes magnified by the thick spectacle lenses. Quarles commented on the heaviness of the book-end and the crest, and was given an abbreviated family history by Janet. He easily pried the pieces apart, but although his eyes widened at the sight of the very yellow inside core he did not make any comment to Janet, merely asking her to call in a week for an estimate.

The moment that the shop door closed, Simon took out his set of bottles of acids and touchstone; his heart raced each time the core material resisted the increasingly concentrated acids. Nine, fourteen, eighteen, twenty-two karats—the strongest acid could not dissolve the core material inside the bookend, indicating that it was made of almost pure gold! In case the acids had deteriorated, he rechecked their potency against gold pieces of which he knew the karat content; the acids were accurate. He carefully scraped the paint from several other areas of the bookend and repeated the same test with the same results. He then weighed the bookend at eleven pounds, nine ounces, Googled the latest spot gold price and checked his math twice before concluding that the bookend was worth well over 200,000 pounds!

The customer had seemed pleasant and intelligent, but was obviously unaware of the gold composition of the bookend. In recounting the family history, she had said her grandfather had brought it from Germany in the thirties. He was probably some grasping, corrupt, rich Jew. Serves her right to lose this treasure! Simon's plan was simple: make the repair sound more complicated to give him time to fashion a copy. However, it should not be so expensive that she would reject it, return in a hurry to reclaim her property and look elsewhere for a cheaper price. In the end it was easy. When he told Janet it would take several weeks and cost 90 pounds, she said she was not in a hurry. He reassured her that the result would be pleasing, adding, to himself, "especially to me". He would call her when it was ready.

Simon Quarles put aside the boring little lamp and sculpted figural repairs that ordinarily barely paid the rent. He went right to work. First, he cemented the broken pieces with epoxy and took two impressions, one using flexible dental impression materials and several plaster impressions, which he cut in two pieces that he would later re-join. After several attempts, the reinforced mold could be filled with lead. After days of buffing the lead and adding many coats of black lacquer paint, he carefully polished and prepared the surface to match the original patina. Five weeks later, he was satisfied; the customer would be easily fooled by his craftsmanship. He practiced his speech saying he had to re-finish the entire piece to cover the break, but when the time came he did not need to use it. Janet admired the wonderful result, paid him and carried the replica bookend wrapped in tissue paper and bubble-wrap to her car.

Ironically, the mate bookend was already used to rough treatment from Dean. He kept it on the floor near his radiator. Dean would periodically kick it around and curse his grandfather Fritz, the cheap bastard, who'd left all the money to his mother and left his grandson only a crappy old bookend. One day he kicked it into the radiator, forgetting he had taken his shoes off. As he was muttering expletives and holding his damaged toe, he put the bookend on the table.

Dean noticed a penny-sized, irregular, yellow-colored spot where the black had been scraped off. "Hmmm! Funny color for plaster—which must be covering the lead interior..."

A more careful examination revealed a few other smaller areas of yellow under the black paint. Further scraping uncovered more yellow, which he thought might be a brass alloy over the lead. This might merit a special expedition to his gambling buddy Irv Staub, a back-street antiques dealer: Irv was always happy to fence stolen jewelry and other valuable objects. Irv was only sixty years old but looked ninety, with his pasty, pudding complexion and grizzled gray beard. Many times and many years in and out of prisons will do that.

After Dean pointed out the yellow areas, Staub, without comment, scratched on a piece of slate with the exposed parts of the bookend and applied acids to the scratches.

"I don't believe this," he said incredulously, "but this tests like bloody gold! I have to drill down to see how far the plating goes." Using a fine, long dental drill mounted on a small hand-held motor, he drilled about three inches into the bookend from various sites.

The drill went through easily; Irv carefully gathered the dust and tested it with his acids. "Bloody solid gold! Where did a rummy like you get this?"

"Never mind that! What is it worth?"

"My scale only goes to eight ounces. Go next door to the fruit market and we can get the weight and estimate its value based on the spot gold price per ounce."

The shop's scale finally stopped at eleven pounds and nine ounces. Dean did not return to see Irv but kept right on going to his flat, where he hid the bookend in a ledge in the flue of his rarely used fireplace. He could easily calculate that the bookend was worth over 200,000 pounds.

Over a Bass Ale at his neighborhood pub, Dean calculated that Grandpa Fritz, that wily old bastard, had smuggled his fortune out of Germany under the noses of the Nazis. Then it hit him! Janet had the other bookend and shouldn't bookends be together? They started as pairs and should stay that way! He cooked up his scheme: he would generously offer her the detested condo on the Southold coast, which she loved, in exchange for her bookend. The real estate market was soft and the condo wasn't worth more than 40,000 pounds now. Besides, he would no longer have to pay the insurance, condo fees and taxes out of the measly stipend from his mother. If he had both bookends, he could melt his, settle all his debts and invest in some property in currently hot East London real estate. He could enjoy trips abroad, sample the pleasures of Monaco and live worry-free from now on—and of course, he would have Janet's bookend in reserve.

He presented his sales pitch to his mother, claiming that he was so involved in his projects he would be happy to turn over the Southold condo to Janet. Marlene thought this was very generous of him…

"Janet, I'm going to pick you up on Friday evening and we'll drive together to the shore; we'll stay overnight in my condo. And bring your bookend—I have a surprise for you."

On the drive to the Suffolk coast through beautiful East Anglia, Janet kept asking about the surprise. "Dean, please give me a hint!"

"You'll see when we get there."

Once they arrived, Dean asked Janet to bring her bookend to a table on the terrace overlooking the sea. He had placed his bookend next to two freshly prepared martinis. "Janet, I'd like to give you this condo. I know you have always loved weekends out here since we were kids and I'm more at home in London. I'm signing the property over to you and in return I'd like to own both bookends and keep them together in London."

"That's more than generous. I will accept, but only on the condition that you feel free to come here as often as you like!"

They happily clinked glasses and Janet invited Dean to dinner, but he declined, saying he had an important appointment back in town. Janet said she would get a cab to the train station after the weekend; her load would be lighter without the bookend. Dean left hastily, gloatingly carrying both bookends.

After Dean left, Janet made herself a second martini and dozed off on the patio in the warm salty summer air, watching the sailboats wend their way along the horizon back to Southold.

Around 8:30 p.m. Janet was awakened by the sound of fire engines racing along the coast road. Flames and black smoke were erupting out of a second-floor flat in the next building. Within a few hours the fire had been extinguished, saving all the other flats except the one that was the source of the fire.

The morning edition of the East Anglia Herald carried the tragic details. Janet was shocked to see the picture of the victim and the report on the front page.

"Simon Quarles, an artisan from Cambridge, was tragically burned to death in his recently purchased seaside condo last night. Police speculate that he was working on a project when his acetylene torch accidentally caused a gas canister to explode. Sadly, he did not die immediately, but must have suffered a great deal while trying to crawl to safety. A lump of smoke-blackened material from the project he was working on was found fused to his charred hands…"

Her call to Dean telling him about the fire went to voicemail on his cell phone. Dean was lying in a drunken stupor in his disheveled apartment. He had not noticed that it was in even more disarray than when he had left for the gambling club: his belongings had been thrown about. Even the artificial logs from the gas fire in the vintage fireplace, where he had placed both bookends the night before on his return from Southold, were shattered.

Dean had seen Irv Staub at the Bank of the Thames Members Only Gambling Club the previous night. Dean had avoided direct interaction with him, recalling sheepishly how he had failed to return as promised after weighing the bookend in the fruit market. As soon as Irv spotted Dean entering the Club, the old man cashed in his baccarat chips and left the premises, Dean's empty flat and his bookends the destination.

Janet stared quietly out to sea pondering the events. "Well, at least after all, Grandpa Fritz and Grandma Sarah are resting in peace and would be happy that the bookends are united…"

NINE

Great Uncle Jack

T he large banner over the entrance of the new WestSide Museum advertised the *Jack Quinn Collection of New York Society Memorabilia: Objects from the first half of the Twenti-eth Century*. Susan Quinn Clark, curator of the collection, barely glanced at the banner. She quickly climbed the one flight of stairs to the already crowded rooms that housed the exhibit of her great-uncle's collection. The Museum was located on West Seventeenth Street in the newly fashionable Meat Packing district, just a block from the High-Line Park. This was a stunningly successful urban park fashioned from an abandoned elevated rail line that snaked a couple of miles through the area near the Hudson River. Smart shops, restaurants and galleries had soon followed, with the final show piece currently under construction: the relocated Whitney Museum of American Art.

Jack Quinn (1907–1999) was definitely not from New York High Society. Quite the opposite: his father, Edmond, had been a late 19th century Irish immigrant—one of those pejoratively called "shanty Irish." Edmond had obtained work on construction of the New York subway system at the turn of the century in order to support his wife and only child, Jack. Edmond was more accomplished than a mere laborer and was quickly recognized by his peers and superiors for his abilities as an artisan in the mechanical, electrical and tile trades. These were key skills over the decades of subway construction in NYC. Young Jack was enthralled by his father's work and became a favorite among his father's co-workers. He was allowed on the building sites as their little mascot, where he precociously learned the mechanics of the trades.

The Quinn family lived in the upper east Eighties of Manhattan, then a neighborhood of primarily Irish and German immigrants. Edmond's only sibling, an older brother named Kevin, found work as a doorman/handyman at a white-glove building on Park Avenue. Kevin married and had a son, Edmond, who was named after his talented uncle. Tragically, the elder Edmond died in 1918 in a not-rare subway construction accident. Following the death of his brother Edmond, Kevin generously took in Jack and his mother, Morag, to share quarters in the Park Avenue building on the servants' floor, where he lived with his wife, Sheila, and the young Edmond. Young Edmond and Jack Quinn were brought up as *de facto* brothers.

In 1919, when Jack was only twelve years old, an interesting incident occurred one Saturday morning. A man with a large, flat, wrapped object came to the entrance of the Park Avenue building where Kevin was on duty as doorman. Kevin agreed to hold what was declared to be a painting for delivery to a resident who was expected back later the same day. Young Jack, who was keeping his uncle company, politely asked the person what was the subject of the artwork. The man, who was in his thirties, carefully uncovered the painting, which depicted an old house overlooking the ocean.

Young Jack asked, "Did you paint this?"

"Yes, I did this in Maine and my name is Edward Hopper." Hopper leaned over and brought the painting down to the level of young Jack's eyes so he could better view the scene and the signature.

After a short pause, Jack responded simply, "I like the colors—do you have any more paintings like this? It's beautiful!"

"Yes, I have a studio downtown and some day, if you like, maybe your parents will allow you to come down and see my work and how I paint."

"I'd love that! I'll ask my mom," Jack replied enthusiastically.

Over subsequent years, the two became friends and many years later Hopper gave Jack a signed sketch.

Young Jack was not a good student. The lessons he had learned at his father's side and his inherited artistic sensibility made him an excellent artisan and mechanic. By the late 1920's, he was a freelance handyman, much in demand by the Park/Fifth Avenue Upper East Side crowd. Recommendations through Uncle Kevin and the doorman fraternity kept him busy with all sorts of fix-up jobs and eventually complete apartment renovations. Then came October, 1929, and many of New York's high society—both old money and new—were hard hit. Some residents moved away; others hung on after the crash and managed to keep their properties, surviving financially by cutting way back on their life-style. During this period, Jack's cousin Edmond (whom he thought of as his brother) was able to graduate from City College with a teaching degree and later married another teacher, bringing up their family (a boy and a girl) in Queens throughout the war and early post-war era.

However, this story is primarily about Jack Quinn. A good eye and a sense of style, along with dexterity and personality, turned out to be a winning combination for the times. As the Depression deepened, Jack actually got busier. Barter became the favored method of payment by his customers. As payment for simple plumbing and toilet repairs, he might be given souvenirs from the famous NYC night clubs, such as the Stork Club, 21 Club or El Morocco. That was tableware, silver, photos and autographs of celebrities, movie and stage stars and politicians.

More importantly, the newly idle would educate him about their artwork, sculpture, lighting and furniture. This enlightenment came in handy when floods, fires and other accidents caused more extensive damage. These losses were often not covered by insurance. Then, Jack's work became more elaborate and expensive. Armed with his growing decorative knowledge, he knew which painting or artifact to point to in order to satisfy the repair bill. Some of the former *grandesdames* of the time were not beyond giving up a piece of their now devalued jewelry to make sure that their bathrooms continued to look and function as they should.

By the early 1940's Jack had accumulated a large selection of art and furnishings, as well as cash from sales of some of the items. He filled his new home in Queens with many treasures. Jack never married and remained very close to Edmond's extended family, becoming the beloved Uncle Jack to the generations that followed. By 1972, his baby cousin, Suzy, was born to Edmond's son, Bill. Jack was ecstatic and the two became inseparable. Suzy's first complete sentence was, "Where my gweat-uncle Jack?"

Whereas Suzy's parents and sister loved seeing Uncle Jack, Suzy became positively devoted to him; she loved visiting his house and going to museums and restaurants with him. When the opportunity arose to buy a place directly on Long Island Sound in nearby Stamford, Connecticut, Jack purchased it, planning that the family would come for weekends. Later on, Suzy would fondly remember being served dinner with Stork Club plates and silverware. Sometimes Jack would insert the menu for dinner inside an old night-club folder. Ashtrays, vases and photos added to the authentic effect.

The other rooms in the house were decorated with paintings of old NYC restaurants, Central Park scenes and shops on Madison Avenue. It was like living in the New York of the thirties and forties. Everything seemed so special to young Suzy. During this time Jack continued to acquire and sell artwork at auctions and private sales. As a result of prudent selections, Jack's collection of American art of the period was significant and contained some excellent examples of the Ashcan school, whose style he greatly admired. Included were works by Luks, Lawson, Bellows and Sloan. As a result of the exposure to Great-uncle Jack and his collection, Suzy decided to major in art history. She earned her Ph.D. from the highly regarded NYU Fine Arts department.

When Jack died in 1999, Suzy found many treasures in the Queens house and in the Stamford house, both of which she inherited along with the contents. Jack had bequeathed cash to Suzy's sister, Mary, who was more than happy with that arrangement.

The Jack Quinn Collection (or Great-uncle Jack Collection as it was popularly called) was hard to categorize. The installation in the WestSide Museum recreated the furnishings and life of well-heeled Society of early- to mid-century New York City. There was particular emphasis on the period between the Wars. A typical Park Avenue apartment was set up and there were examples of shops, clubs and restaurants that they frequented. In the case of the clubs, rare lighting, signage, table settings and furnishings were all authentic and original. Walking through the large installation one felt as if one were back in 1935. Overseas tourists were particularly awed by "Olde New York." The Museum became a destination, not just a stop on a "High-Line Tour."

The blueprint for all this had occurred about three years earlier when a group of art patrons, hearing rumors that the Whitney Museum was moving downtown, established the WestSide Museum dedicated to New York art of the Twentieth Century. This move coincided with the boom in the Meat Packing District and seemed a natural choice. Unfortunately, the Museum was underfinanced and poorly publicized. The first eighteen months were a disaster and the Museum was in danger of closing.

After Uncle Jack died, his legend surfaced and was documented in the New York and national media, including the *New York Times, New York Magazine* and the *New Yorker.* A video of Uncle Jack with his collection, taken just before he died, became a YouTube sensation. The Directors of the WestSide Museum contacted Susan Quinn Clarke. They offered her an opportunity to showcase the Jack Quinn Collection as a way to promote the Museum. Suzy agreed to put the exhibition together from material taken from both homes and from items that were in storage. The outcome of this endeavor exceeded all expectations! The Museum became profitable. Enthusiastic visitors waited in line for tickets. The institution made huge profits from sales of gift shop replicas of New York City High Society mementos.

The recession of 2007 caused severe financial losses for Suzy. She lost her untenured position at City College. Her marriage had broken up a year earlier. Suzy wondered whether she could afford to keep the Connecticut house, which had lost much of its pre-recession value. A day never went by when she did not bless Uncle Jack, who was indirectly responsible for her $150,000 per annum curator position at the WestSide Museum. The terms of her contract were simple—either side was free at any time to cancel the contract. It all seemed too good to last…

Suzy took a call one Monday morning from the Museum Director, Clair Davis, and her world crashed.

"Good morning, Ms. Clarke. Something extraordinary and much unexpected has occurred. We have received a bequest of a very large and important collection of New York school, post-war abstract art worth well over $100 million. I don't have time to give you the details, but the terms of the gift specify that we take possession and display the art without delay. Therefore, in keeping with our agreement, we will need you to disassemble and remove the Jack Quinn Collection immediately so we can begin reconstruction of the galleries next week. That gives you four days to remove your material. Of course, your curator position will be terminated."

Suzy was shocked—primarily at the woman's cavalier attitude—and replied, "Of course, you will make decisions that are in the best interests of your institution. Given the fact that Uncle Jack's collection has contributed to the successful establishment of an institution that had such a shaky start, I would assume that you would show a little patience. Please allow me the time to find another entity that might accept this collection."

Ms. Davis interrupted. "I'm sorry, that could take weeks and maybe months. You have the rest of this week—that's four days—to contact another institution and then the next week to remove everything from the space." She added sarcastically, "I don't expect a line forming to fight over your stuff. Please give our movers an address where we can ship everything."

Angrily, Suzy gave the Stamford address and made a mental note to have a friend in Connecticut be available to receive the huge shipment.

After she'd hung up, Suzy sat motionless staring at the phone. She briefly entertained the idea of calling the Whitney and finally, in desperation, picked up the instrument. A curator there whom she knew was polite and sympathetic. After listening to her plea, he made it clear that the Whitney was actually paring down its own holdings because of space limitations in the new building which, in any case, was still years away from completion.

Suzy could not bear the thought of being at the Stamford house when the truck unloaded Uncle Jack's collection. Her friend Jamie, handy and reliable, agreed to be present and oversee the operation in order that, somehow, everything could be squeezed into the Stamford house safely.

A couple of weeks later Suzy returned to Stamford, realizing that she would have to decide which items to sell and what would have to go into storage in order to clean up the house for sale, which was now a financial necessity.

Suzy would always recall that fateful Saturday morning. She was walking through the house, clipboard in hand, starting at the attic. Suzy worked her way back to the ground floor, making notations and comments on the inventory list. Yes, there were some valuable items she could transfer to her already crowded home in Queens, but there were other things that she loved but would need to sell just so she could retain that residence. It was a heart-breaking experience. She was exhausted mentally and physically and wished Great-uncle Jack were there to put his arms around her and soothe her as he did when she was a child. However, there was still the cellar to deal with. Suzy switched on the basement lights at the top of the stairs and proceeded down, using a flashlight to augment the dim basement lighting. Boxes of stuff had been crammed into the already crowded space and she noted with annoyance that her bicycle had been toppled by the movers pushing the cartons around. Apparently, that accident had also loosened a piece of the decorative paneling long ago placed by Uncle Jack over the old cellar walls.

Suzy worked her way through the piles of stacked cartons and was relieved to find that, evidently, the handlebar of her bicycle had only been loosened by the fall against the wall, which in turn had caused the damage to the paneling. She picked up the bike, straightened the handlebars and made a mental note to tighten them before she rode the bike again. As Suzy started to push the thin panel back in place, she noticed a framed painting resting on the floor, hidden behind the loose panel. Apparently, although the nail was still present in the old cellar cement wall, after all these years the picture wire must have corroded from the weight of the painting, causing it to fall undamaged to the floor. She carefully freed the artwork and noted how its entombment had left it almost dust free and with its colors still bright. Even by flashlight she observed that it was a well-done shore scene.

Suzy brought the painting upstairs to the dining room and held it up to the hazy but special light that reflected from Long Island Sound. It reinforced her admiration for Uncle Jack's choice of this location. What really shocked her was the signature. The scene, approximately two feet-by-three feet, not including the frame, was of this very property with the Sound in the background. The signature in the lower right corner was clearly that of Edward Hopper.

Suzy's reaction was immediate—she called Jamie, who was fortunately at home nearby in Greenwich and available. He was there in less than twenty minutes.

The rest of the day was consumed with removing most of the material from the basement. Fortunately the weather had cleared, so they were able to stack cartons in the yard. Then Jamie began to remove the rest of the paneling from the basement walls where they hoped to find a few more treasures. They almost gave up when under the next large segment of paneling they found the mummified remains of a rat. Much joy followed as the day progressed. Yes, there were more paintings! Eighteen signed Hoppers in all, the largest being five feet long. The subjects, all of Long Island Sound, ranged from Greenwich, north and east to Rhode Island. Curiously, while examining the stretcher on the last uncovered painting, Suzy found a yellowed envelope still attached to the back of the frame. She carefully extracted the contents. On a small piece of the artist's stationery was the following hand-written note:

"To my dear friend Jack Quinn, whom I have known for almost forty years, thank you for giving me the opportunity and encouragement to paint the shore again. Very different than the Maine coast and certainly a big change from city scenes, and it's only fifty minutes from Grand Central Station!"

TEN

The Tony Award

Every Monday morning, Peter Sturdivan, a Yale drama graduate student, attended a seminar on the history of the American theater. Professor Lynn Carlton's seminars were fascinating theater in themselves. But after Peter's party-intense weekend, even the scandalous careers of the Barrymore family were not holding his attention. He snapped out of his reverie when the next PowerPoint slide of a gold compact, cigarette lighter and money clip filled the screen.

"Anyone like to guess what I'm showing here?"

One smart-ass student remarked, "This is the stuff you couldn't sell on eBay."

Carlton laughed. "Well, here's another clue." The next picture was of the more familiar Antoinette Perry Award commonly called the Tony Award. It was a nickel-coated, silver-colored medallion with Antoinette Perry's profile on one side and the masks of comedy and tragedy on the reverse. An attached swivel secured the medallion to a black base. The professor continued, "I'm sure all of you recognize the famous Tony and I hope some of you will be nominated for this award during your future careers!"

More laughter followed. She returned to the earlier slide showing the various golden objects. "These were the awards in 1947 and 1948 and the more familiar medallion was introduced in 1949."

Peter Sturdivan would later recall that the last thing he remembered before dozing off was the gold cigarette lighter…

The Sturdivan family had emigrated from Holland in the late 19th century. Peter's great grandfather and great-granduncle brought their farming skills to the town of East Windsor in the fertile Connecticut River valley. Their expertise in shade tobacco farming would maintain the lucrative family business until just after World War II. The Sturdivan offspring were prolific and dominated by the Y chromosome. At one point, Peter counted forty-eight cousins with the Sturdivan surname. Peter's father, Martin, was born in 1950 in East Windsor, but had no interest in shade farming. Instead, he attended New York University in downtown Manhattan and his choice of a career in banking turned out to be both mentally stimulating and financially rewarding.

The seventies were an exciting time in Greenwich Village. Martin was active in amateur theater productions that flourished in the Village. It was at an off-off-Broadway production of Shakespeare's *As You Like It* that he met his theatrically more gifted mate and Peter's future mother, Lauren Gage.

Later, Martin would privately tell Peter that Uncle Hale Sturdivan (Martin's uncle and Peter's great-uncle) was an inspiration for his love of the theater. When Hale was a teenager, a bitter divorce tore the family apart. Hale had moved to Providence, Rhode Island, with his mother. The older brother, Sam, who was involved in the shade tobacco farm, stayed behind in New Windsor. Hale graduated from the Rhode Island School of Design (RISD) with a major in theatrical costume design. The divorce and the move had estranged Hale from the rest of the Sturdivan family, including his brother Sam. Hale's later success was well known and often mentioned as part of Sturdivan family lore.

Hale earned two Tony awards. The first came in 1948, the second year of the Award, for costume designs for the play, *I'll Be With You.* The play itself ran for only eighty-two performances. At the time the buzz was that without the wonderful and authentic 17th-century costumes it wouldn't have lasted a week. About fifteen years later, Hale won his second and final Tony for another unsuccessful play, a revival of an Aeschylus Greek tragedy. The modern costumes were considered inspired and cutting-edge and Hale Sturdivan was selected over the other nominees.

Peter's excellent high school record and a perfect 1600 SAT score earned him acceptance at Williams College in Massachusetts. He was fascinated by the theater. His senior thesis in his major—economics—dealt with the impact of Broadway and the theater on the economy of New York City from 1900 to the present time. During his research he came across Hale's name several times. Peter made efforts to trace Hale's current whereabouts and discovered that Hale was involved with several projects as costume designer for London's West End theaters. Peter wrote a companion thesis, comparing the impact of the theater on the economies of New York City and London, which gave him the opportunity to spend several weeks in the U.K. capital.

He found the record of Hale Sturdivan having last been in London in 1989. There was some report of Hale's involvement in regional theater in Brighton in 1990. A discussion with a local pub owner produced a report of an older Yank who drank bourbon and talked about the theater. After that, the trail went cold.

Back home in New Haven to pursue a Master's in Economics of the Theater, Peter was aware of the great changes that were occurring in his chosen field. The Internet, corporate and Hollywood involvement and the current recession were causing dramatic changes in the way plays were financed, staged, promoted and publicized. Peter's career path was influenced by the family fascination with Uncle Hale. At Yale, Peter continued the search, utilizing the resources of the research library. He found nothing to indicate whether Hale was still alive at eighty-seven...

Peter's neighbor prodded him and he opened his eyes and noted the lecture was over. He slipped sheepishly out of the room and headed to the closest Starbucks, where a caffeinated latte stimulated his consciousness. He focused on the image of the cigarette lighter that was the first Tony award. Peter decided that if he couldn't find Great-uncle Hale, perhaps he could locate at least one of his Tony awards.

Over the next several months, Peter searched the Internet, eBay, Google, First Dibs and many other antique and collectible sites, but without success. He seemed to be searching for an ethereal needle in a virtual haystack. There were a few positive hits, for example, a listing on eBay for a Tony award for Best Actress in a Musical from 1972, awarded to Alexis Smith for the Sondheim musical, *Follies*. Hale's awards would have been one or two of a total of 700 Tony's awarded to date. The likelihood that they were available was slim.

A more proactive approach was in order. Peter placed a medium-sized ad in the leading antique newspaper in the northeast, based in Connecticut and affectionately called *The Newtown Bee*. The ad proclaimed that "top dollar will be paid for any information leading to the location of the two Tony awards for Costume Design awarded to the late Hale Sturdivan." Six months of weekly insertions yielded only calls and emails from various dealers wanting to sell him other theater memorabilia. Most annoying were offers to sell him cheap playbills. As completion of his degree approached, Peter would have to concentrate on a more pressing need—a real job in the theater.

Three months after Peter's last ad insertion in *The Bee*, a call came from a dealer in Hudson, N.Y. He reported that he had spotted the ad by accident while using an old copy of *The Bee* to wrap some glassware. Peter held his breath.

"Yes, I have the two Tony awards for Hale Sturdivan, although for some reason one is a cigarette lighter. But the other is a traditional award."

Peter interrupted him with a string of excited questions. "Where did you get them? Are they in good condition? How much are you asking? Where are you located? Can I come up tomorrow to see them?" and finally, "He was my great-uncle!"

The dealer, who had introduced himself as Lou Sommer, responded calmly, "Since he was your uncle, I'd love you to have them. Why not drive up tomorrow and I'm sure we can make a deal?"

"Give me your exact address. I'm coming from New Haven. I have a GPS. Is one p.m. okay?"

Lou gave him the street address in Hudson. "See you then."

Peter made it from New Haven to Hudson in two-and-a-half hours. The shop, Lou's Oldies, was one of many along Hudson's long Main Street. Some of the stores were permanently closed, obviously victims of the poor economy. Lou's place was an attractive store-front near the northern end of town. A glance through the window revealed a nice blend of country-style furniture interspersed with pleasant vintage lighting. Opening the door jangled an attached bell and announced Peter's arrival.

Lou seemed older than his telephone voice indicated, but his demeanor was warm and welcoming. After a few words of introduction and some brief niceties, Lou reached under the counter and produced an old wooden box. He raised the top and handed the box to Peter who stared, amazed, at the contents: a gold cigarette lighter and the traditional Tony lying sideways so it could be accommodated in the box.

Lou commented, "This is obviously not an original box for either piece."

Peter examined each item carefully, Lou handing him a magnifier so he could read the inscriptions. The lighter was engraved in neat script near the base on both sides: one bore Hale's full name and the award category, Costume Design; the other was engraved with the name of the play and the date of presentation, April 8th, 1948. The more traditional award was dated May 15th, 1964, with all the other pertinent information engraved on one side of the medallion.

"I love them! I hope you can make the price reasonable," Peter exclaimed and added plaintively, "He was my great-uncle and a huge inspiration in my life."

"Well, the lighter is 14-karat gold, so I paid a lot more for that one. On the other hand, the costume design category has less cachet than the acting and directing awards." He paused before asking, "Would you be interested in both?"

"Absolutely!"

"Okay, I need $1,500 for the lighter, which represents just a small premium over the gold weight. The other award would be worth more if it were for a star in an important play—it could have fetched up to $5,000—but I will do both for $2,600."

Peter breathed what he hoped was an inaudible sigh of relief and dismissed any thought of bargaining for a better price. "It's a deal!"

As Lou returned the awards to the wooden box, he pointed to a piece of folded paper at the bottom. "I didn't notice this when I bought the lot a few months ago from another dealer who was retiring—let's have a look."

Peter carefully unfolded the paper and saw a handwritten address in Hillsdale, New York, about twenty miles away near the Massachusetts border, just south of Albany. "Would that be the other dealer's shop?"

"No, his store was further east in the Berkshires, in Great Barrington, Massachusetts."

After many a thank you and a hug, the very happy young man headed east toward the Taconic State Parkway to go south and later east again toward New Haven. Lost in reverie, he missed his turn and accidentally got on the northbound ramp of the Taconic heading toward Albany. It occurred to him that he was heading towards Hillsdale. He spoke the address on the paper into his Smartphone and found that he was less than twenty minutes away. "What the hell—let's go for it!" he muttered.

His last GPS direction outside the town of Hillsdale led him onto a very long secondary road with no visible outlet. On one side lay recently harvested cornfields; on the other grew fruit trees, probably an old apple orchard, looking somewhat bedraggled and neglected. Toward the east, the foothills of the tree-covered Berkshires were just beginning to show autumn colors.

The GPS announced that his destination was on the right. Parked in front of a detached garage was a 20-year-old Subaru. The nearby house was an early 20th-century Arts and Crafts bungalow, with all its original features and still in decent shape. The crunch of Peter's Jeep on the gravel driveway had alerted the owner that he had a visitor.

Peter approached the small, elderly man sitting in an Adirondack chair on the porch who had abundant, longish white hair, even, real-looking teeth and bright blue eyes that apparently did not require glasses. "What brings you here, young man?"

Peter stared at the man, who appeared to be in his seventies and unperturbed by the sudden intrusion. "Well, I just bought some collectibles from a dealer in Hudson and this address was on a piece of paper in the box. I made a wrong turn going home to New Haven, so I decided to see if I could get more information from the person at this address about the original owner of the items."

Peter paused for a moment. "Well, now that I'm here, I was wondering if you could tell me anything more about the man whose name is engraved on these awards."

"Why are you interested, young man?"

"I'm sure I'm boring you with this, but the man who won these awards was my great-uncle, who probably died years ago. He would be almost ninety now. He was and still is a great inspiration to me."

"What is your name, young man?"

"I'm Peter Sturdivan."

"What was his name?"

"Hale Sturdivan, a highly talented artist and costume designer."

"Well, I may have good news for you, dear nephew—I AM Hale Sturdivan and as you can see I am very much alive!"

At that, the two embraced for a long moment and a tear rolled, hidden, down Peter's cheek.

Later, over cups of tea served in Minton China on an old tavern table, they continued recounting their histories.

"But, Uncle Hale, why did you stay out of touch with the family and why did you sell your precious Tony awards?"

"Many years ago I felt that, as the family had abandoned me, I did not want to be in contact with them. As time passed and my life went on, it was too complicated to reconnect and I was not sure how I would be received. As far as the Tony awards are concerned, I thought that at least someone interested in the theater might buy and enjoy them."

Peter hugged Great-uncle Hale again, this time looking directly into his sparkling blue eyes. "Your family is not estranged anymore. I'm glad you sold your Tony awards—otherwise I never would have found you!"

ELEVEN

The Gift

A t 4:30 a.m. on a December Sunday, the alarm reverberated harshly in a modest house on a tree-lined street in the Riverdale section of the Bronx. Bill Watson urged his late-middle-aged body out of bed. Coffee brewed as he listened to the radio weather report. It called for temperatures in the thirties all day. Bill picked out an extra-warm hooded sweatshirt and a pair of thick wooly socks; it always felt much colder in the flea market lot on 26th Street.

Seated at a 1920's gate-leg table (which he detested), he quickly drank his coffee and ate his cornflakes with milk and a banana.

For what seemed the millionth time, he mused about his life. Watson was always introspective, but had become even more so since his wife Cheryl had died three years previously, after losing a hard-fought battle to breast cancer. Bill was childless and lonely, having retired from teaching high school English. After Cheryl's death, his collecting bug had turned into a business. The nature of his business required that he sacrifice Saturday night social activities to be able to get up early for the Sunday flea market. It was no great loss for him, since he rarely had any kind of engagement to make him regret those early-to-bed Saturday evenings.

Bill recognized that the antiques business got him out of the house, gave him a purpose, provided a sort of social life and perhaps $30,000 net yearly to supplement his $48,000 pension. That sum, along with some modest investments and a tenant who occupied the top two floors of his house, allowed him to enjoy a comfortable life-style. During the week he spent time at estate and garage sales and combed the antique shops within a 50-mile radius to replenish his stock.

As Bill sipped his coffee, he surveyed the rectangular living space where he had arranged a nice collection of Arts and Crafts furnishings. The dream was to have his residence mirror a Stickley Craftsman home of the early 20th century. Unfortunately, compulsive collecting resulted in the antithesis of the spare look. Every corner was filled with "stuff" that he couldn't resist buying or trading for, although most had been bought very reasonably through his market connections. The latest purchase was an original Onondaga Morris chair complete with a rarely found label. On the flared-leg, L & JG drink-stand next to it was an exceptionally nice, scenic, reverse-painted Handel lamp. Above, he had hung a Curtis orotone photographic print on glass in its original frame.

The rest of the furniture, including a small settle, a bookcase, library table, server and liquor cabinet, were good, middle-of-the-road Gustav or L & JG pieces with original finish. They were complemented by tasteful examples of Rookwood and Marblehead pottery, mostly in soft green shades and earth tones. Muted track-lighting with the occasional generic Mission lamp, with a slag glass or mica shade, gave his copper collection and woodblock prints a rich golden glow. The total effect brought a wonderful feeling of comfort to his life. As he took a final sip of coffee, he was reminded of that one glaring weak spot in his living space: that common and poorly dimensioned dining table.

The van had been loaded the night before. As he backed out of the garage, he caught a look at his face in the rear-view mirror. Allowing for some of the lines from fatigue, Bill still had a reasonably wrinkle-free face for his 57 years and plenty of wavy, gray-sprinkled brown hair. Moving furniture on a daily basis kept his six-foot frame trim and firm.

After he turned onto the Henry Hudson Parkway on his way to the market on 25th Street and Sixth Avenue in Manhattan, he was on automatic pilot. Watson's thoughts turned to Mary Jane Johnson or MJ as she liked to be called. Although Bill had dated several women since Cheryl's death three years earlier, none had really struck any emotional response from him. He assumed they had felt the same toward him. Even though he was an educated and somewhat experienced traveler, his only passion was for antiques. Although sufficiently assertive in business, he was very shy with women. MJ was an exception. He felt very attracted to her. Although he was comfortable discussing business and making the usual next-door-vendor small-talk, he felt inhibited about furthering their relationship.

Bill had met MJ at the market the past summer when she started selling. Her space was just across the aisle from his, against the back wall at the north end of the lot. MJ was a tall, attractive, dark-haired woman, divorced and—he assumed—in her late forties. She was frequently assisted at the market by her married daughter, Linda. Bill and MJ were friendly neighbors, buying coffee and watching each other's merchandise during breaks.

They often talked about their respective lives, past and present, at down times, meeting in the middle of their common aisle. Through these bits of conversation, Bill came to respect MJ as a genuine person with very good values. As a result of these qualities and her attractiveness, for the first time since Cheryl's passing, Bill felt a strong sense of desire.

MJ was a registered nurse, currently doing *per diem* work. She was relatively new to the antiques and flea market business so she often sought his advice on purchases and prices. The interactions were comfortable and non-threatening for they handled similar merchandise: middle-level forties and fifties furniture and objects, with the occasional Deco and Arts and Crafts piece. MJ specialized in the accessories while Bill predominantly sold furniture. Even after months of market friendship, Bill could not overcome his reluctance to extend their relationship a critical step further and ask MJ for a date.

A slow-down for a two-dollar-fifty toll brought him back to the present. Underway again, he slipped back into his reverie. He was extremely annoyed at his lack of success at an auction just a few nights earlier in Queens. Bill had gone to the sale planning to pick up some good buys. There were none. Unexpectedly, there was an unadvertised addition to the sale: an L & JG pedestal table, #716 in the original catalogue, with four vertical supports that gave it a lighter, almost prairie-style look. Its 45-inch diameter was perfect for his smallish living space and carried the added bonus of original finish and two apparently never-used leaves, still in the original box. It would be the perfect replacement for his wretched gate-leg table. What's more, since he did not intend to resell it he could afford to pay a reasonable retail price. Cringing inwardly, he remembered almost word for word what had transpired.

"Lot #92: an L & JG dining table #716," boomed the auctioneer. "Can we begin the bidding at a thousand dollars?" When there was no response he had lowered the bid, first to eight hundred, then to five hundred and finally the action began. Several dealers were raising the bid, driving the price quickly to $1,900. After the auctioneer asked for $2,000, Bill decided it was time for him to raise his paddle. There was no counter-bid from the floor and for a moment he thought it was over.

But it wasn't. The auctioneer looked to his left and acknowledged a phone bid. "I have $2,100" he said and looked in Bill's direction for a counter. Bill thought for a second; believing the table was worth at least $2,500 and maybe several hundred dollars more he raised his paddle again. It was now a battle between Bill and a single anonymous phone bidder. He hung in until it was his turn to bid $3,000. Just before the hammer was to go down at $2,900, he raised his paddle reluctantly for what he decided was the last time. Unfortunately, a nod from the woman handling the telephone told him that $3,100 had been offered and when the auctioneer stared at him and implored him for $3,200, he shook his head.

Bill got up and strode angrily out of the hall. What bad luck! Without the phone bidder he would have had his table for two thousand plus the 15 percent buyer's premium.

The turn-off from the West Side Highway at 23rd Street brought him back to reality. He still felt angry, even two days later! In a few blocks he was at the New York version of the London Portobello Road market. He backed his van into his aisle in the rapidly filling market and one of the helpers who worked the lots helped him unload his merchandise.

It took about thirty minutes to unload and park his van and another thirty minutes to set up his booth. By 6:45 a.m. the job was done and the early buyers were already asking about his merchandise.

With the first early rush over, Bill slumped into a very lived-in Eames chair and for the first time noticed that MJ's booth was empty, even though it was approaching 7:15 a.m. Bill hoped there was nothing wrong; she was not usually late. He had been looking forward to sharing with her his disappointment at losing the dining table to the mysterious phone bidder at the auction. A moment later, he smiled as he recognized her van backing down the aisle. He hurried over to the driver's side and said, "Hi! I was worried that something was wrong, you're very late."

MJ, climbing out of the van, said, "I had to stop and pick up a table I bought during the week. Please help me get it off. I'm not selling it; I'm going to use it myself at home, so I'll put it back on the truck after I get my regular merchandise off."

As he swung open the door of the van, a shocked look came over his face. There was no doubt that the L & JG pedestal table was the very one that he had been outbid on at the auction in Queens. "Where did you get that table?"

"At an auction, a couple of nights ago. Actually, I wasn't even there, I was on the phone. Why do you ask?"

"I was bidding against you! Why didn't you go to the auction? And since when do you collect Arts and Crafts furniture?"

"I wanted to attend, but my daughter, Linda, was ill and her husband couldn't be with her, so I had to bid by phone."

"You didn't answer my question. Why did you want this table?"

"Bill, don't get crazy! I had no idea you wanted this table. After all, you got me interested in Arts and Crafts furniture. You're so enthusiastic about it. I loved the form."

Bill was almost livid. "I've wanted that table for years! It was the missing piece in my collection and would have fit right into my house!"

"Look, Bill. I've never been to your house and we've never talked about this before. If you really want it, take it now—it's yours!"

He made no response, just turned around and headed back to his booth.

In the next hour the market came to life and Bill mechanically went through the motions of dealing with his customers. His annoyance must have been apparent, because he made no sales during what should have been a peak time. About eleven, a customer inquired eagerly about posters.

"The lady across the way says you have some American Airlines posters from the fifties by McKnight Kauffer."

"Yes, I do," he replied, "They're $400 each. Do you want to see them?"

As Bill unrolled them, the customer said, "Are you aware he did much better work in the thirties for British Rail?"

"Yes, I know, and since you're such an expert, you should realize they go for a grand each at auction when you can find them."

In spite of Bill's unpleasant demeanor, the man eventually bought both posters for $675, presumably realizing that only the posters would go home with him, not Bill and his lousy attitude. Besides, they were a great buy.

It was approaching noon and, for the first time since the early morning, Bill allowed himself a glance across the aisle at MJ's booth. She was doing well, judging by the number of people picking through her stuff. Bill walked over and sheepishly thanked her for referring the poster buyer.

"You're very welcome. I hope you're not still mad at me over the table."

"No, of course not. In fact, I'm really embarrassed about being so insensitive and selfish. How could you have known I was bidding? As a matter of fact, I'm really pleased that you're getting into collecting Arts and Crafts. It's something else we'll have in common."

Though enjoying brisk sales, Bill still had nagging feelings of guilt about his behavior toward MJ. She had been more forgiving and gracious than his hostile attitude deserved and had steered the poster customer to him. The ball was clearly in his court. Either the relationship would go forward today or they would be nodding across the aisle at each other forever.

Bill crossed the aisle to her booth. It was past five o'clock and most of the dealers were packing up. He waited nervously while her last-minute sale was completed.

He spoke quietly. "I've got a great idea. After we've packed up, I'll take you to a new restaurant I know in Flatiron. We've talked a lot about wine and this is a newish place called Sonoma on West Nineteenth Street. They serve bistro-style food, with a wine bar that has about 50 different selections by the glass."

"Sounds like fun, let's go! What about the vans?"

"There's an indoor parking lot next door. That will give us plenty of time to pack up without rushing."

Sonoma was a typical loft-style restaurant in the trendy Flatiron district. It featured high tin ceilings painted creamy white, with classic columns recently uncovered and restored.

"It's really crazy that an argument over a table has led to our first dinner date," quipped Bill.

"Maybe we should go to more auctions—who knows what a settle might lead to?" MJ said with a slightly tipsy giggle. "Listen, Bill, I really want you to have that table. I offered it to you sober and I'm even more adamant now that I'm feeling so mellow and happy. You were right when you said it belonged in your collection. There will be lots of tables for me to choose from in the future."

Bill reached over and squeezed MJ's hand. "That's very generous of you, but I feel just as strongly that you should begin your collection with that table, especially after the way it has brought us together! Look, it's after ten. I've got to get to the Bronx and you have almost as far to go to Brooklyn. No fights tonight. I'll call you tomorrow."

The parking attendant brought up both vans. They embraced tightly for a long time and then kissed goodnight. Bill climbed into his van and headed back to the Bronx up the West Side Highway, in quite a different frame of mind than when he'd started much earlier that day.

There was very little traffic and as Bill rounded the last turn into his street he pressed the remote garage door-opener and drove into his attached garage. He spotted something at the last moment and stepped hard on the brakes just in time to avoid crushing it. It was the table!

Jumping out of the van, he was momentarily blinded by headlights behind him. "Who's there?"

"It's me!" MJ exclaimed as she hopped agilely out of her van.

"I don't understand! What's going on?"

"Linda drove it up here today and persuaded your tenant to let her put it in the garage."

"You're crazy!"

"Yes, I am—crazy about you. Do you think if you pulled your van way to the right mine could slip in beside it? If we take the table inside now we should have lots of room."

Bill performed the task with alacrity, silently saying a prayer of thanks to the original owner of the house who had had the foresight to construct such a spacious garage.

Next morning, the happily lounging couple sipped their seconds of coffee beside the newly installed table. The wretched gate-leg table had been banished to the basement.

"Let's see how the table looks with the leaves in; I'd like to see how many people we could seat for our first dinner party together," Bill said, joyfully contemplating the days—and nights—of happy companionship ahead of him with MJ at his side.

As he unpacked the leaves from the original box, a yellowed, crumbling envelope slipped out. It contained a bill of sale, handwritten in a spidery style and dated September 12th, 1905, at Fayetteville,

New York, for thirty-five dollars. In the envelope, along with the bill of sale, was a note.

> *"My darling Margaret,*
> *The past twelve months with you have been the very happiest of*
> *my life. This table is most sturdily built, but it will not outlast our*
> *love for each other.*
> *Yours forever, Edward"*

Bill handed the note to MJ. She read it quickly, smiled and whispered, "Know something? I think Margaret and Edward would be very happy if they knew their table had survived and found a home—with us."

TWELVE

The Kid

Warren Wexler (Double W, as he was known to his admirers and patrons)—a fortyish, short, swarthy man with curly hair—popped out of a cab. His destination was the Leo Castelli Gallery at Number Four, East 77th Street. Dressed New York urban chic style—jeans, open oxford blue shirt and short, tight, brown leather jacket—he strode confidently into the still empty gallery. The large print, plain black-and-white sign at the entrance proclaimed: "WW—A DIFFERENT VIEW!" The scheduled opening was an hour away. Wexler headed towards the gallery office at the rear, barely glancing at the forty strikingly bright canvases artfully displayed on the stark white walls of the gallery. He rapped gently on the office door and without waiting for permission entered the office. Carol Lawrence, the middle-aged gallery manager, rose from behind the mid-century modern desk, hand extended, to greet him. "Hi, Warren; thoughtful of you to come early! We're expecting a big crowd—we sent out over 500 invitations."

"Let's hope they bring their checkbooks!" He paused as he dropped into the comfortable leather-covered Eames chair next to the desk. "Actually I could use a real drink—vodka on the rocks from your personal bar, not the standard wine or beer. I really despise these openings!"

Carol, at fifty-two, was just beginning to show the inevitable effects of gravity on her classic featured, still attractive face. Her bright red dress, matching red Christian Louboutin pumps and red coral earrings and necklace, accentuated and enhanced her excellent posture and five-foot-ten height. With her jet black, shingle-cut hair and round tortoise shell glasses, she epitomized the 'academic art historian meets gallery manager' look.

As Carol fixed his drink, she commented, "The caterers will be arriving soon. We picked Empire City Edibles to cater. They're great—you'll enjoy the nibbles!"

"Well, I rarely drink, so if I drop off, please wake me when the crowd arrives." WW's last thought before closing his eyes was of his first visit forty years previously as a seven-year-old to the original Castelli Gallery then located a few doors away…

It was just before five p.m. when Lillian Wexler pulled her new Chevy Malibu up to the entrance of PS 87 in upscale Forest Hills, Queens. She was just in time to see Warren exiting the school, loaded down with art paraphernalia from his three-day-a-week, after-school art program for talented students.

Lillian beeped and Warren scampered into the front seat after dropping his stuff into the back. "Did you have fun today?" she asked.

"Yes!"

"Will you show me later what you did?"

"Yes."

Warren's parents lived in a comfortable, three-bedroom, rent-stabilized apartment near Queens Boulevard. Lillian was then in her late thirties, her husband Jeff three years older. Both worked in middle management for New York City agencies. Jeff was an accountant at the Department of Health and Lillian was an administrator at the Housing Authority. Warren's older twin sisters, Hope and Merle, had occupied all of Lillian and Jeff's time since their birth thirteen years previously. Warren's unexpected arrival six years after his fraternal twin sisters was a joyous addition to the family. The girls were Daddy's; Warren was Mommy's golden son.

Both parents shared a passion for art. Warren, early on, exhibited artistic talent, perhaps inherited through Great Aunt Gail (Lillian's mother's maiden sister). She was the art director of a Madison Avenue advertising agency, Blue International.

As Lillian pulled up to a just available spot (alternate side parking eight a.m. to six p.m. Monday and Wednesday), she asked Warren, "Can you guess where we're going after dinner?"

"I hope, I hope to an art gallery opening!" said Warren.

"Yes—and it's in Manhattan!"

"Goodie, goodie, goodie!"

In those years, children's spare hours were spent in front of the TV, watching kids' programs and cartoons. They played baseball and stickball on the streets and playgrounds with their friends. Not the Wexlers! Dinner conversations centered on Picasso, Braque and the motivation behind Cubism. Some nights, they might discuss Monet and the Impressionists. More recently, they had focused on Abstract Expressionism. Their home was filled with art, sculpture and books about it. They had been buying good quality prints, pastels and original oils from little-known contemporary artists at local galleries and street fairs. Warren would recall later the excitement in the Wexler house when, after much discussion and deliberation, they had purchased a signed Picasso print for $750. It was hung in a place of honor in the entrance foyer, a specially purchased spotlight focused on it.

Names like Motherwell, Jackson Pollock, Cy Twombly and Willem de Kooning were mentioned in the hushed tones reserved in most families for God.

"Warren, Merle and Hope are going downstairs to play with the Jackson girls after dinner, so it will be just you, me and Daddy going to the opening."

"Can we leave soon?"

"Yes, right after dinner. Remember to brush your teeth. We'll get on the subway and be there by eight. Do you think you can stay awake?"

"Yes, I can."

Warren ate quickly, excused himself and ran into his room. Bright, very verbal and alert, with his curly hair and large head he was quite striking, even though he was unusually small for his age. Most adults on first meeting him thought he was a five-year-old kindergarten student. His talent and love for art were apparent even in pre-K: the art teacher had told Warren's parents that he had a natural sense of proportion, dimensional scale and sense of color that was way beyond even the oldest students she taught.

"Warren, we're ready to leave."

"I'll be right there, Mom," he said as he grabbed his small sketch pad, a grease pencil and a few crayons.

It was 1970. The Leo Castelli Gallery was at Number 18, East 77th Street, between Madison and Fifth Avenues. Unlike most of the other invitees at the opening, who grabbed the wine and finger food first, the Wexlers slowly perused the paintings. Artists represented included Frank Stella, Robert Rauschenberg and Ad Reinhardt in one room and pop art by Roy Lichtenstein and Andy Warhol in the other large room.

"Hey, Warren, what do you think of all this—pretty amazing, eh?"

"I like it," was his simple reply.

"How about some of those little cakes for dessert?"

"No thanks—you and Dad go—I want to walk around more."

The Wexlers encouraged their children's independence. In those days, with the artsy crowd and the small but open space, they felt comfortable allowing Warren to roam on his own.

Just as Lillian and Jeff were enjoying a few brownies and fresh cut-up melon from their shared plate, they literally bumped into Leo Castelli's personal secretary, Jane Fesco.

"Jane thanks so much for the invitation—this is really exciting."

"You're welcome! Keep your eyes peeled for some big names lurking about!" Jane paused to be sure she had Lillian's attention. "Mrs. Wexler, I'm really grateful for your intervention with the Housing Agency. I'm next on the list to get a big one-bedroom at 'The Veranda.' It's affordable and only a few blocks from Central Park."

"You're welcome. I was glad to move you to the head of the list and now you have the fun part coming—decorating it!"

Warren had his little secret. His parents thought he brought his artist supplies and pad to the exhibitions to make quick sketches to bring to school to show his teachers; however, for the last year, the tiny boy had been circulating among conversing adult groups and, when he heard the name of an artist that his parents had mentioned, he would get their attention by calling out their name or even tugging at their clothing. Whatever the conversation, it would always stop at the sight of the cute little boy. He was certainly adorable, dressed in his preppy outfit of blazer, chinos and miniature tie, sketch pad in hand, looking up at them from barely thigh height.

"Are you an artist, Mister?" he said to a man in a grey suit.

"No, but the man next to me is Jasper Johns."

Warren turned to him. "I've seen your paintings in my parents' books."

Johns looked down and said in a higher-pitched tone than usual, "Are you also an artist? I see you have a sketch pad and crayons."

"Yes, I am," Warren said and with dramatic flair raised the sketch pad and continued in his childish voice, "Would you please make a little picture for me?"

This was Warren's ninth gallery opening. Although he didn't know about keeping score, he had successfully got an artist to sketch something on his pad and sign it at least once at each show. Jasper Johns reached down and picked the kid up. Warren was so light and small he was able to cradle the boy in the crook of his left arm while he held the pad. He took first a red and then a yellow crayon from the little boy's closed fist and quickly filled the page of the sketch pad with intersecting strokes. Then he scribbled his signature with a black crayon.

"Gee thanks, Mr. Johns, that's beautiful!" Once he was back on the floor, Warren carefully placed the pad and crayons in his mini-blazer pocket, which was barely large enough to contain even the small sketch pad. Later in the evening, after Warren's parents had put him to bed, he got up, turned on the light, retrieved the sketch book and carefully printing the letters he added the date and "party at Leo's" on the back of the drawing.

Over the next few years, Warren grew older and bigger—which made getting his "free" pictures from artists more difficult. Leo Castelli had moved his gallery to Soho, but the invitations from Jane Fesco for the gallery openings continued to arrive. Her ongoing gratitude for her rent-stabilized apartment generated other invitations as well. The Wexlers were on the regular invitation list for openings at the Sidney Janis Gallery on 57th Street, as well as the numerous galleries then popping up in Soho and the West Village. Different artists were featured, including Jim Dine, Josef Albers, Mark Rothko, Claes Oldenburg and many others.

Although they kept no specific records, the Wexlers must have attended well over a hundred events over the next five years. Many of the sketches Warren gathered were by "flavor-of-the-month" artists, who paid for their own openings, had a little flurry of interest in their work and were never heard from again. By the time Warren was twelve, his top twenty-five signed sketches were done by the likes of Poons, Kline, Twombly, Serra, Motherwell, Dine, Rothko, Albers and of course, Jasper Johns, and even a mini "dripper" from Jackson Pollock. De Kooning was one of several artists who declined little Warren's request for a sketch.

The year Warren turned thirteen, his older twin sisters Merle and Hope were well into their pre-law studies at Brown University. Their good grades made their dream of Yale Law School (or some other Ivy League law school) a real possibility. Meanwhile, Warren Wexler was winning local, regional and even national competitions. The awards were based on his imaginative style, neither impressionistic nor abstract, but which could be described as 'radiant' and seemed to have universal appeal. Warren attended a special city high school that focused on art while also providing strong emphasis on academics. He took private studio lessons from a noted artist, too. In his junior year, three events occurred within the span of a week that would have a substantial effect on his future.

First, his father was suddenly dismissed from his job under circumstances that remained secret and were apparently scandalous. Two days later, the twins were both accepted to Yale Law School. The Wexlers assured the girls that enough money had been saved to pay their tuition for the next three years if they could supplement it with income from summer jobs.

The third event was Warren's mother tearfully telling him that his private art lessons could not continue beyond the end of that month. Warren was more concerned for his parents' distress. Frankly, he was getting tired of his teacher and felt he had learned everything he could from him. His focus as a high school senior would be applying to and getting accepted at the prestigious Art Institute of Chicago.

"Mom, please don't cry! Senior year is tough and I'll need extra time to get the good grades I need in my regular academic subjects."

In January of his senior year, Warren was notified of his acceptance to the Art Institute. Sadly, Jeffrey Wexler had still not gotten a job, so Warren was not surprised when his parents told him, across the kitchen table, that they could not afford to send him to the Art Institute of Chicago. He could see that they felt worse than he did.

"Warren," his dad said, "There are excellent, essentially free art programs at the City University of New York (CUNY). Here's what we see could be done. Get a degree at Hunter, Queens or Brooklyn College. By the time you graduate I'll be back at work, the twins will have graduated from Law School and both be working, and we'll send you for a graduate degree wherever you want to go."

Warren's first thought was how sorry he felt for his parents. "Dad, the tuition at the Art Institute is $9,000 a year. Including room, board and living expenses, it totals about $13,000. I figure it will cost $60,000 for four years and that would include transportation."

"I guess you've done some research—that sounds accurate to an old accountant."

Without comment Warren went to his room, where he located the top twenty-five sketches from his boyhood gallery outings. He had stored some in the original pads. Others were loose, safely stored between the pages of a large, coffee-table art book. Without comment he handed the package to his parents and before they could speak, Warren said, "Now you know what I was doing when I was wandering around those openings with my sketch pad. I wasn't drawing anything, but these artists were!"

Lillian and Jeffrey Wexler were speechless as they opened the books and Warren added, "You guys would know better than I what they are worth." He pointed to the backs of each drawing, where he had indicated the date and the event where the sketches were made.

Jeffrey answered, "It's hard to say—there's none here worth less than two or three thousand. The best ones may be worth $5,000. As a group they could be worth maybe $60–75 thousand!"

"Wow!" was Warren's reaction as his dad beamed.

"Why don't we take them to Leo Castelli? It looks as if most of the drawings came from his exhibitions. He'll love the story!"

Leo did indeed love the story and laughed uproariously. At first, Warren and his parents weren't sure of the paintings' worth or his interest, until Warren spoke up. "Mr. Castelli, I've been accepted at the Art Institute of Chicago—we're selling these so I can afford to go there."

"Young man, you're going! Why don't you and your mom wait outside while Jeff and I work out the details?"

The details turned out to be a check for $80,000, which Leo Castelli certainly recouped after the publication of his book, "Fifty Years with Leo Castelli," incorporating Warren's story and the drawings. The book actually made the New York Times Nonfiction Best Seller list fifteen weeks in a row…

"Warren, Warren! Wake up! Have some hors d'oeuvres and a drink before you go out—there must be another hundred people outside already, waiting to get into the gallery!"

The artist known as WW slowly worked his way through the crowd toward an attractive woman collector. She was standing enthralled in front of one of his largest paintings, entitled *Surprise in Blue.*

"Warren, I love this one—if it's under $500,000, you can put a red 'sold' spot on it right now."

"It's yours, Allison," he said as she gave him a joyful peck on the cheek.

He felt a pull on his trouser leg and looked down to see an adorable, blond pigtailed girl in an Alice in Wonderland-style dress. "Are you having fun?" he asked her.

Warren barely heard her response through the din. "Yes! Could you please draw something for me, Mister?" she said, standing on tiptoe to hand him a little pad and a crayon.

"No way, kid, no way! I don't do freebies."

THIRTEEN

Tiffany on Fire

C alvin Cooper, founder and CEO of United Global Partners (referred to as UGH-PEE by its detractors), was Skyping the London branch's managing partner of his international hedge fund.

The early dawn January sunlight reflected off Lake Michigan, making partial rainbows glint in other-worldly colors from the John LaFarge stained glass window. Dramatically suspended from the 20-foot ceiling, the multicolored glass bathed the artfully placed Frank Lloyd Wright furnishings in its reflections.

Cooper preferred his immaculately restored and highly important Wright residence overlooking Lake Michigan, north of Chicago, to his various homes in Greenwich, Manhattan, and Palm Beach. Architectural historians rated it, along with Falling Water in Pennsylvania, as a prime example of Wright's creative genius. Cooper had purchased the house fifteen years previously and spent the intervening years furnishing it with the finest examples of the master's works, incorporated with fine Tiffany lighting and metalwork.

From his accountant father, Calvin had inherited a facility for understanding complicated figures, as well as implacable stubbornness and perseverance. From his mother came the fine, fair looks and appearance of affability. Now approaching sixty, Calvin was often sought out to perform as a "talking head" on the financial cable channels; his views were frequently quoted in the Wall Street Journal. Calvin Cooper ranked just under Michael Bloomberg, long-time Mayor of New York City, on the billionaires list.

"Good morning, Calvin, it's a sunny day here, if you can believe that." Simon Gaines quickly added, "and a good day for commodities as well!"

"Keep your eye on platinum—the Russians are reporting they've discovered more in Siberia, so maybe we should short our position before the market closes."

"Noted," came Gaines' clipped reply. "More importantly, your daughter is doing really well over here with us on the corporate bond side and she has a boyfriend—a Brit, at that!"

"I'm not worried about Mara," responded Cooper. Since his wife Evelyn died ten years previously, Calvin had intensely overseen the education and development of their children. He knew that Mara's quick mind, Princeton undergraduate degree and Wharton School M.B.A. formed impeccable credentials for her success.

Calvin's son Peter, on the other hand, had followed his father to Cornell. Rather than enrolling in the challenging engineering program, Peter had matriculated in art history. Now just under thirty and with the help of his father's connections, Peter had worked as a low-level assistant in various Manhattan art galleries and museums.

Gazing proprietorially at the LaFarge window, Calvin continued, "Well, it's Peter I'm concerned about. Milton Burns, whom you probably know of—he's at Morgan Stanley—along with my money, got Peter into a partnership in New York with a firm called *Artiques*. They buy and sell mid-level vintage and antique decorative items worldwide."

Simon cut in, "Yes, I've heard about that outfit—they just opened a shop here on New Bond Street."

"It's a partnership where very rich people like us capitalize the business through monthly stipends and receive dividends on sales. I guess for some it would be a good way to launder cash of questionable origin, but that excludes present company, of course." Calvin laughed. "Peter tells me there are six investors so far. It's a way to keep their kids out of trouble and busy at something other than cashing their monthly trust fund checks."

"Well, that's a bit of an assumption that I hope is correct!" Simon quipped.

Calvin hid his annoyance. "Off the record, it's costing me $100,000 a month, but Peter and the other trust-fund babies get to travel worldwide, manage a few stores and buy and sell at the big antique events."

By the time the call ended, the entire room was enveloped in the golden morning light, so that the low-lighted Tiffany lamps and spotlighted art glass highlighted the golden oak Wright tables, Prairie settles and high-back chairs arranged in several seating areas across the 100-foot-long space.

It was not too soon to call Peter at his Chelsea loft in downtown Manhattan. He was an early riser, like his dad. "Peter, what's going on today?"

"Same old thing, Dad—getting ready for a show at the uptown Armory. We took a big space that cost us twenty-five grand, but the economy is improving and the guys on the Street will be getting their big bonuses again. So maybe we can sell some big-ticket items."

"Good luck! What's a big-ticket item for you guys at this show?"

"Well, we have a totally restored, 1935 Curtis Wright air-cooled engine that is re-chromed, with a heavy glass, beveled top and makes a great coffee table. We're asking $45,000. We also have assorted machine-age and transportation-related decorative stuff, deco jewelry and smaller architectural items. Eighty-thousand gross is break even for us, but we're hoping for the low six figures and at least a chance to get new customers to come to our shop."

Calvin privately considered these figures to be chump change. "Did you guys ever consider getting into Tiffany lamps and glass in a major way?"

"We sell the occasional lamp, but they are hard to find at a price that would give a decent profit."

"Son, that's the way of all business; the secret is you make money when you buy and that is how you succeed. Even in my business we look to make the markets for the assets we manage. We don't stint on the quality of people we hire and in the end it's the bottom line that counts!"

He went on, "Peter, as you know, I own lots of Tiffany from the Louis Comfort Tiffany period, spread about my four homes. It's the last category of great design still available at attractive prices. The Wright Prairie-style lamps are great. I own more than half of all those existing, but they don't hold a candle to the Tiffany product! Talk to your main guy about steering some of the monthly check I send into that area."

"Dad, I'm low man on the totem pole when it comes to choosing our purchases, in spite of the fact that your monthly check is the largest of all the investing partners. Dick Douglas, my boss here, doesn't really respect my judgment."

Dick Douglas was the founder of *Artiques* and a know-it-all who strode the aisles at antique shows trailed by his fawning retinue, uttering pronouncements about buying and selling, somewhat like a turn-of-the-century Austrian medical professor and his acolytes making rounds in the primitive hospitals of his day.

"I understand your predicament. You're the junior guy. Tell him that I'm prepared to make a more significant investment in Tiffany lamps, as well as in fine Handel and Pairpoint lamps of the early 20th century. Believe me, he will call!"

Two weeks later, Dick Douglas did call. "Mr. Cooper, how are you doing?" he opened in a self-important tone of voice, "Dick Douglas here. Peter suggested I call you. By the way, he's a great kid!" he added insincerely.

"I've always thought so," Calvin rejoined. "Look, if you are calling in response to the offer Peter transmitted, I'm in the City until Sunday and hope we three could meet at my club for dinner. Is tomorrow night at the Harvard Club at eight o'clock good for you?"

"Sure, Mr. Cooper, I'll cancel my previous appointment. Don't you have an M.B.A. from there?"

"Yes, I do and a Ph.D. as well."

Calvin left his 72nd Street and Fifth Avenue apartment a few minutes early to enjoy the brisk walk down Fifth Avenue along the Park, then west on 44th Street to the Harvard Club. Peter arrived with Dick Douglas a few minutes later. They both ordered a glass of red wine while Calvin took his usual Makers Mark with soda on the side. The ensuing small talk about the economy and gossip in the antique business filled the cocktail hour. A second round of drinks further eased the undercurrent of tension.

Once they were comfortably seated in a private room and the jumbo shrimp had been presented, Cooper began to talk business. "Dick, I understand that you sell the occasional Tiffany lamp at *Artiques* and recognize their uniqueness. Perhaps you don't share my conviction that they are magnificent examples of a timeless American era and that they will always be collected and highly valued. Unlike paintings, there will be no more of them. Even the finest reproductions are not close approximations of their beauty and craftsmanship."

"Calvin, if I may call you that, I do appreciate them, but there are dealers, such as the Weinbergs on Madison Avenue and a handful of other Tiffany specialists on Worth Avenue in Palm Beach and Rodeo Drive in Los Angeles who control the market in this country and, to a certain extent, internationally."

"I agree and disagree," Cooper said. "They buy and sell at the highest end, but there are many examples of lesser Tiffany under $100,000 in the hands of smaller dealers. These pieces come up at auctions and at high-end antique shows in this country and overseas. Even museums can be persuaded to part with a fine Tiffany lamp to enable their curators to fund a purchase of the latest overpriced abstract artist."

Calvin looked down at his just-served porterhouse steak and continued speaking as he contemplated where to make his first stab. "Here is my proposition. I will increase my monthly commitment to $500,000 and I'll tell Rich Cohen and Dirk Mauro to do the same. They are close friends and their sons are in the business with you. You should contact the other investors as well and at least let them know about the new investment strategy. I would like Peter to be the lead guy in this project, of course reporting to you and me on the progress of our plan."

Douglas was stunned by the amount of the new investment. He was even more insulted at how he was being pushed aside, but feigned enthusiasm. "Great idea, Cal. In painting there are the Old Masters, the Impressionists, Picasso and those of his ilk, as well as the modern masters like Warhol and Twombly. We are out of that league, but we could certainly compete in the under-$100,000 Tiffany arena and aim to be the top dealers in that genre of lighting. It is appreciated worldwide and never has nor will go out of style."

"Great! One more suggestion: even with my increased contribution and potentially more from the other investors, I would try to make most of the purchases under $75,000. You would have enough capital to purchase up to twenty items per month. Word will get out and the prices will go up somewhat, but in a couple of years you could own north of 500 examples. Even paying top dollar, the whole collection would be worth in the vicinity of $50 million. That is a tidy profit indeed. In the meantime, you can continue to sell your other inventory. The free publicity should attract lots of new buyers!"

The waiter's interruption with offers of coffee brought nods of assent from all. Cooper continued, "Peter, after you consult with the other partners and investors, get back to me with a formal business plan. Your sister, Mara, will help you with the format and details."

Douglas barely contained his annoyance at the last comment, but managed to thank Cooper somewhat graciously for the dinner.

A month later, Peter called his dad, happily declaring, "I emailed you the final business plan. Thanks to your help we're already taking in an extra $1.5 million per month!"

"Let's hope your partners also respect my knowledge of the Tiffany market. I have the best collection in the world! Look, son, as you know UGP owns and controls the Security Storage Corporation. It is the number one facility in the world with over thirty locations just in the NYC area. I'll make arrangements for storage of your inventory of lamps at the facility in the South Bronx. Just make sure you have excellent insurance coverage. I'll cover the tab and, of course, everything must be confidential. No loose talk!"

After hanging up, Cooper glanced out at his Central Park view and chuckled. "Now the fun begins!"

His next call was to Jane Weinberg, owner of the world-class Tiffany lighting store on Madison Avenue. Museum quality was their standard, as was their enviable client A-list. "Hi, Jane, it's Calvin Cooper. Hope you're well and keeping busy?"

"Thank you, I'm both," came the perky reply. "Actually, I was about to call you. I have a lead on a magnificent ten-foot-high, one-of-a-kind floor lamp that was in Louis Comfort Tiffany's personal collection. It's not catalogued and is coming on the market through a rather greedy dealer I know. I think it's worth over two million, but the pig will look for and possibly get three million. I'm sure you have space for it in your Wisconsin house!"

"Jane, do your thing. I want it—period. But listen, do you have some time to meet with me today or tomorrow?"

"Of course, drop over this afternoon and we can have tea in my office."

The "office" at Weinberg's Madison Avenue store was more like a period room at the Metropolitan Museum. The high tea that was served rivaled that at The Connaught in London. Though she was over seventy, Jane Weinberg could easily pass for fifty. Her slim figure, abundant salt-and-pepper, carefully coiffed hair, expert plastic surgery and regular Botox injections, as well as understated makeup, contributed to the illusion. Her forties Chanel suit and accenting jewelry were sartorially perfect.

After a polite exchange of family gossip, Cal said, "I'll come right to the point, Jane, because we're both busy. I want to invest in very high-end Tiffany, LaFarge and other outstanding examples of American decorative art of that period, including glass and metalwork. I'm thinking a bottom of $100–150,000 per item with no limit on the upper end. My funding for this entire project is unlimited and you will be sole agent in this endeavor."

Jane tried to feign nonchalance, but even her smooth, surgically perfected and Botoxed face gave her feelings away.

"It's simple math, really. Each time I seemingly overpay for an outstanding single lamp, I will increase the value of the cache, even if this project takes a few years."

"Well, Calvin, we're a little light right now in the type of super-premium material you are looking for. Although once word gets out, items from collections and estates may surface, though they often choose the auction option. Museums can also be urged to part with some things to fund what I call 'modern overpriced abstract crap.'"

"My sentiments exactly! Once word gets out, the sellers will be jumping to make a deal, just like hungry fish in an over-stocked mountain lake."

"I like your analogy. Let's talk about the details."

Over the next hour, Cooper spelled it out. "Jane, there are billionaires out there collecting all sorts of art. As you know, my shtick is the American icon, Louis Comfort Tiffany. Although in the end my entire collection might not fetch in dollars the same value as one blue-period Picasso, when people mention Louis Comfort Tiffany there will be a pause. Then my name, Calvin Cooper, the great Tiffany collector, will follow."

Jane Weinberg just stared as Cooper continued, "Jane, confidentiality is everything in this matter. Let me inform you that my son, Peter, is leading a similar Tiffany quest for his firm *Artiques* aimed at the under-$75,000 market. I'm behind this as well, but my motive, other than seeing Peter do well in this business, is to help shake out the entire Tiffany line and make my own quest even more meaningful. *Artiques* will eventually sell their holdings at what I predict to be a very substantial profit."

"If I can be frank," Jane said, "I am familiar with that outfit; they're trying to establish themselves with middle-of-the-road collectors in the international market. They've had limited success to date. The head guy, Douglas, if you'll pardon my vulgarity, is best described as a schmuck."

"Jane, your observation is as usual on the money and that's why I'll be helping my son, as well as myself in this matter."

Over second helpings of excellent tea sandwiches, they worked out the details. Cooper informed Jane that she had carte blanche in buying anything under $500,000. At any price above that, though he valued her judgment, he wanted to be consulted before any deal was closed. Calvin would set up an account to which she would have direct access with her signature.

"Jane, my level of trust with you financially and, even more importantly, esthetically, is that great. A twenty-five percent commission can be added to the cost. I think that is generous, but I am aware you will have to hire more staff not only in New York, but around the U.S. and overseas as well."

Jane picked up her cup to sip; her tremor caused the delicate china cup to shake and she carefully returned it to the saucer, hoping Calvin hadn't noticed.

"I think we've covered the outline of my plan," he said. "I'll deposit funds into the special account tomorrow. Although we won't need it for months, I'll arrange for a secure storage facility where you will take the purchases once they've been delivered to your store. The sellers will have no idea of the ultimate destination."

Calvin stood up, signaling the end of the meeting. "Oh, Jane, I saw some great-looking things on my way back here. Why don't we start doing business now? You're officially on the job!"

Jane's stammered reply, "It's a deal," betrayed her emotions at this totally unexpected windfall.

Back at his office, Cooper called William Kane in Chicago. He was the CEO of Security Storage Corporation. Calvin instructed him to have his Eastern manager call immediately. Within thirty minutes, Calvin's administrative assistant announced that Johnnie White of Security Storage was on the phone.

Calvin spoke to him firmly. "In the next few weeks you will be hearing from my son, Peter Cooper, about arranging storage in your

South Bronx facility for some antique lamps. Make sure he has an all-risk insurance policy with a first-class carrier and that it is in force instantly, as well as that all items are placed in temperature- and humidity-controlled storage."

"Of course, sir."

"I will need an additional storage facility nearby—within two to ten blocks maximum. One space will be dedicated for the storage from *Artiques*, my son's company, and the second will be in the name of the parent company, UGP." Calvin paused to make sure White was following. "I'm thinking 5,000–7,000 square feet each."

"Excuse me, Mr. Cooper, but we don't have anything that small."

"You have been told by the CEO of Security Storage Corporation, which I own, to comply with my instructions. Buy two small buildings in that area of Bruckner Boulevard or the Grand Concourse. If necessary, go up to 12,000 square feet. Do the necessary alterations. Put a company sign up and secure bars and alarms on the doors and windows, with the storage space above street level. Spare no expense. The contents of these facilities are confidential, as is this conversation. The second building will have no insurance, but will be staffed with round-the-clock guards. Ms. Jane Weinberg will also be contacting you. Consider all her requests as if they were from me."

"Of course, sir!"

"Try to complete the purchases within a few weeks. If you need off-the-record money to get building permits or variances or to pay off the unions, don't hesitate. Call the real estate people today. Overpay if necessary for the right property."

"Mr. Cooper, you've made yourself clear. We should be ready within a few months."

Two years later, both locations were overflowing with Tiffany treasures. When Calvin visited the UGP storage he was enthralled. Even the harshly lit open space could not hide the beauty of the cache of rare, historic Tiffany, Wright and Lafarge works. Large, complementary bronzes by St. Gaudens were scattered between the lamps. It represented over 100 million dollars-worth of museum- quality rarities.

By any criteria, at two different levels the Coopers had cornered the market. Rumors of Calvin Cooper's involvement had, as expected, loosened rare material from museums, who gladly sold their excess and un-displayed Tiffany items in order to make purchases of the current art market vogue, "Emerging 20th-century Modernists."

Jane Weinberg was thoroughly enjoying her financial success and the accoutrements that her twenty-five percent commission had brought as she sipped champagne from the front deck of her new weekend home in Southampton.

Peter informed his father that at current prices the investment by *Artiques* had tripled in value. "Dad, when can we start selling?"

"Very soon. I will let you know."

UGP managed $100 billion in assets worldwide. The company had experts on retainer to handle any type of delicate situation. Calvin did not delegate this job. He sought and found outside assistance through intermediaries, who were not on the books, but paid through a slush fund account listed as "Miscellaneous Business Expenses." He alone had access.

He found a party who specialized in undetectable arson. Calvin arranged to meet him at the Bushwhack Bar, conveniently located across the street from a stop on the L-line in Bushwick, Brooklyn. Calvin walked through the Western-style swinging doors under the flickering neon sign. He did not spot his target until his eyes adjusted to the dim light and there in a rear booth sat a nondescript, middle-aged man in a sports jacket and wearing a red bow tie.

Calvin slipped into the booth as he shook his hand. "I'll get right to the point. I understand you were once a fireman and specialize in accidental fires."

"Yeah, I used to be in the Bronx. Now I work all over, wherever I'm needed." The "fireman" added, "This is very simple. Just tell me the time frame and the address. Give me my deposit and it will be done: $100,000 now and another $100,000 when it is finished."

"I have it with me now."

"Use the bathroom before you leave. Put the package in the garbage can. I will go in right after you. After my work is done, I will contact you again in the same way we did and you will pay me the rest."

As he got back on the subway, Calvin thought how easy it was. He dealt in much bigger deals every day!

Ironically, the scheme ended almost three years to the day from that January morning. Calvin was again at the Wisconsin house and about to call London when the phone rang.

"Dad, did you hear the news?" Peter's voice was high-pitched and incredulous.

"No, son, I just got up."

"There was a huge fire in the Bronx in a storage facility full of Tiffany lamps."

"Well, didn't you insure everything?"

"Dad, it wasn't our stuff, it was a far more expensive collection. Can you believe it was actually in a storage facility just a few blocks away from ours?!"

"What! Are you sure?"

"Yes! Even worse, a guard was killed in the fire..."

Calvin Cooper dropped the phone and, as he collapsed backwards in the throes of what was later described as a seizure from a massive stroke, he toppled the LaFarge window, which crashed to the floor.

They were both now broken forever.

FOURTEEN

It's a Wrap

The questions from reporters directed at film star and now writer, director and producer Matt Fox came in bunches, as did his answers: "Although I didn't win here at Sundance, there was a lot of positive buzz!

"Look, I entered the film at Cannes and Venice and had good notices so, yes, we'll bring the movie to festivals at Tribeca, the Hamptons, Chicago and a few more places in the States, where I think the Arts and Crafts theme will be most appreciated.

"You asked me about the budget? Well under ten million—but of course, I'm not paying myself.

"Yes, I've had hard offers for national distribution from the majors—I'm told we could gross twenty-five to thirty million with cable rights—and that doesn't include worldwide distribution."

Fox finally broke away from the throng and found a seat at the rear of a trendy bar down the street. After knocking back his second Makers Mark, he began to relax and think back on the events of almost nine years earlier when this incredible story had begun…

In the fall of 1995, Craftsman Farms, located near Morristown, New Jersey, presented "Innovation and Derivation—the Contribution of L & J Stickley to the Arts and Crafts Movement." The opening cocktail party was attended by the usual cast of characters: local and state officials, curators and well-heeled collectors and dealers. They seemed to be there more to check out the crowd than the installations.

Prominent Greenwich Village dealer, Sam Taklee, was dressed in immaculately starched chinos, denim shirt, bow tie and tweed hounds-tooth jacket. He pointed out an unsigned Onondaga Couch, #732, to a scruffy furniture builder and restorer, William "Bud" Franks. "Bud, that's a nice original settle on loan. L & JG did a good job copying their brother, Gus. I know you're doing a great job yourself, knocking out good-looking Greene & Greene pieces."

"Sure, Sam—what choice do I have? I used to pick, restore and deal in the real stuff. Now the great furniture is in the hands of Hollywood types, a few rich collectors who were there early, and the rest is in museums like this one. Even the Grove Park Conferences have lots of dealers in reproductions." He grabbed an hors d'oeuvre from a passing server and continued as he chewed noisily, "I think there is big money to be made in building furniture that will pass as original—if it were made by a craftsman like me!"

Taklee sensed that the conversation would be better continued outside in private and gently guided Franks out a side door into the early evening country air. "Bud, people have gone to jail for building and passing fakes—you can't be serious?"

The builder replied, "I'm going to be in the city next week." The men then agreed to meet at Taklee's shop the following Friday.

Franks had been to the stylish shop on University Place near New York University many times. On this occasion he was greeted by an attractive woman he had not seen before. "Mr. Taklee is expecting you," she purred.

She guided him toward the back of the store. They passed rows of high-end Arts and Crafts furniture bathed in flattering yellow light, which also highlighted expensive lamps, pottery, copper accessories and paintings. In contrast, the back room where Sam waited was filled with a comfortable, old, overstuffed sofa and an armchair.

Taklee rose to greet Franks and said impatiently, "Bud, let's have the story—I have an appointment uptown in an hour and I can't be late."

"I don't blame you for being skeptical, but after you hear me out, I think you'll be more interested."

Franks began speaking in a confident manner that caught Sam off guard. "You, of course, have noticed the recent high auction prices for rare early Gustav Stickley large pieces. For example, tables and case pieces, especially those designed by Harvey Ellis, are breaking all auction records. In less than a year with Gus, Ellis must have been working very long hours to have designed so many pieces of furniture. Most of the furniture was produced after he died. There is absolutely no record of what was finally produced and exactly what the designs were like. I have extensively researched Harvey Ellis—he lived from 1852 to 1904 and died of a heart attack at age 52. He was an architect who was known to be associated with Gustav Stickley for less than a year. The Craftsman Magazine for 1903 has eight articles written by him, but he does not refer to any furniture designs and no designs for furniture attributed to him have ever been seen."

Bud paused and, seeing that he had Sam's full attention, continued, "You've been in my home and shop outside Toronto, but I don't think that you're aware that I grew up near Parry Sound. That's several hours north of Toronto on Lake Huron. One hundred years ago, there were great 'cottages' around the lake. 'Cottage' is a Canadian term for an Adirondack Camp. That is where the rich Canadian industrialists had their weekend retreats. Significantly, several were extensively decorated with important Stickley furniture. Well, I bought one recently, very cheaply because it was half fallen down. I can fix it up myself and equip it as a workshop."

"Look, Bud, I don't understand where you're going with this story, but please come to the point—I haven't much time."

Franks stood and took a deep breath. "I'm proposing, with your financial support, to build a house full of never-catalogued, big-proportioned Harvey Ellis case pieces. That would include bookcases, china cabinets, tables, secretaries, cellarets, bedroom chests and blanket chests that will be originals and not copies. The entire cache will be presented as a special custom-ordered-and-designed lot with historic implications. There would be 50-plus pieces worth altogether many millions of dollars. I'm also figuring it would take at least four years of uninterrupted work." Bud checked Sam's reaction: it was stunned silence, so he continued, "Here's the catch—I'm going to use real 100-year-old oak taken from generic furniture built in that era and even, if necessary, cannibalize low-end and middle-of-the-road Gus and L & JG material. Of course, the hardware may be a problem—but I can solve that using a lot of wood instead of iron and copper. After all, there was never a Harvey Ellis Catalogue. This is going to be a special order for Ellis-designed furniture that we have unearthed."

Taklee leaned forward and seemed to be tuned in for the first time. "Are you talking about spending one or two million dollars on vintage furniture that you will cannibalize?"

"That's about right—plus some real early pieces loaned by you and thrown in, so the picker who first reports on the find will figure it's all kosher."

Taklee walked out of the room and told his assistant to cancel the uptown meeting; when he returned he was carrying two cups of coffee.

Over the next hour, the two men worked through the procedure.

When the furniture construction was complete, Taklee would send his picker to Parry Sound to check out some unlikely rumors about the find. After the discovery, Sam would buy the lot from a shill who would represent himself as the descendant of an old Canadian Pacific Railroad Hotel executive. Eventually, they would sell the furniture privately to a few wealthy parties or put it up at auction, or a combination of both.

"Bud, this is wild—I've got to think hard about this. You are asking for two million or more from me over four years and then," he added with a chuckle, "if it doesn't work out, four more years in jail!"

The wily builder replied, "Naturally, but I've got one more idea that occurred to me last week at Craftsman Farms. My dream is to get some Hollywood celebrity to buy and then donate the whole lot to the Farms. Then they could get the State of New Jersey and other donors to build an addition to house the 'new stuff'. These movie types make two to twenty million and sometimes more per picture. In their tax bracket, they could write off the entire cost as a charitable contribution. Of course, they would love the publicity and their name would be attached to the whole deal."

There were many more meetings over the next several months. Their main concern was how to build the large unique pieces of furniture and have them pass as genuine. Bud pointed out that he had often been called upon to repair high-end examples of Arts and Crafts furniture that were 30–40 percent replaced wood or veneer by the time he was finished. They did pass as mint original finish. Finally, Franks stated confidently, "I'm the most talented craftsman in this area in North America. If anyone can pull this off—I can and I will!"

The other big problem was finding the right picker. He would have to be well known and respected by the Arts and Crafts community. The picker wouldn't be sent to Canada without the assurance that he could be convincing about the authenticity of the find when questioned by the experts. This meant a very generous finder's fee. The partners realized they might have an unwanted third partner if the picker had doubts about the authenticity of the furniture. They concluded that the $200,000 fee could be as much a bribe as it was a reward.

Almost five years later, the work was finished by Franks with the help of several local excellent cabinet makers. They had never heard of Gustav Stickley or Arts and Crafts and their outside interests were divided between hunting and the success of the Toronto Maple Leafs hockey team.

After months of sometimes acrimonious debate between Bud and Sam about which picker they would choose, they selected Walter Crowder. Walt was a middle-aged man from upstate New York with a history of some great early Adirondack discoveries. He had had few finds in recent years as the market dried up. Crowder was also well-respected in the antique furniture community. Further research revealed that he had two college-age children and could certainly use the money

Taklee fed out some clues to Walt based on local gossip as to where to look. Crowder called Sam right on schedule to tell him that he had made an incredible discovery. He could barely contain himself as he described the treasure trove to the appropriately "surprised" dealer.

In a well-rehearsed reply, Sam agreed to catch the next flight to Toronto and then drive north to Parry Sound.

Sam had never seen the property. When he pulled up to the curved driveway, he saw overgrown foliage and a dilapidated mansion. It barely retained a shadow of its former grandeur.

Inside, close to fifty pieces of furniture were spread over eight huge rooms and into adjacent hallways on three floors. Crowder bounced in and out of the rooms, proudly showing off the furniture.

Dust had been artfully applied and some of the furniture was in less than pristine condition. Taklee was overwhelmed by the quality of Franks' work and took pictures of everything. At the end of the tour, the shill, John Angus MacLeod, pretended to represent the estate of descendants of the deceased railroad magnate. He was formally introduced to Taklee by an ebullient Crowder. Sam told the "representative" that he would call him the next day with an offer as soon as he could arrange financing.

The entire cache, plus some of Sam's borrowed additions, was trucked to New York within a week to avoid any complications. They stored everything in a secret, pre-rented, climate-controlled warehouse in Brooklyn.

Instead of trying to sell the entire lot to one of his rich West Coast customers, Sam decided to leak the story using a well-known PR firm. Within a few weeks, the "Harvey Ellis Find" was all over the print and broadcast media, as well as the Internet. Boyle Auction Gallery publicized and advertised a special dedicated auction to be held six months later.

It all worked out perfectly, although there were skeptics. They were dismissed as negative and jealous. Taklee's reputation carried the day. Just as predicted years earlier, the Craftsman Farms Foundation mounted a campaign to have a famous person (read "movie star") buy and donate the entire contents of the auction to Craftsman Farms. The State of New Jersey and Morris County happily agreed to match any amount the Foundation could raise among donors. The goal was to build a compatible Arts and Crafts structure adjacent to the main house to display the Harvey Ellis Collection…

Matt Fox ordered another Makers Mark and recalled the phone call from Sam Taklee and Sam's trip to Malibu. At that time, Matt owned only six great pieces of furniture he had purchased from Sam. Taklee was carrying on about this "historic opportunity to preserve intact the last and greatest collection of Gustav Stickley furniture in America." Sam also pointed out to Matt the many benefits of being associated with this wonderful artistic and charitable cause. Matt Fox didn't need convincing. Three huge box-office hits in an eighteen-month period had left him with lots of cash and a large tax bill.

Matt recalled the auction as he took another sip. He had had to overcome some strong opposition for several lots—but in the end he'd captured everything for over thirteen million dollars plus 20 percent commission. His attorney and accountant assured him that, in addition to the benefits of the charitable deduction in his tax bracket, he was doing a wonderful thing for American art and culture. He was doing even more for himself and his net worth.

The positive publicity started right after the auction, with a final appreciation bash hosted by the Farms just three weeks later. What Matt wasn't aware of at that time was the war being waged between Walt Crowder and Sam Taklee. It had started right after the auction.

During a meeting at a nearby coffee shop, Crowder was livid. "Look, you got nearly thirteen million dollars for that phony stuff and I got a measly two hundred grand. I want a lot more, because if I talk, you're going to lose it all and spend a few years thinking about it in jail!"

Taklee laughed. "You're not upsetting me with your threats! The furniture is genuine, you've been well paid and you have no proof that it's not real. The Arts and Crafts community has voted with its pocketbook. Remember, this entire auction was vetted by the most critical minds in the business."

The picker interrupted, "I saw things in that house in Canada I wasn't supposed to see—old furniture in a back workshop that had been cannibalized to make those so-called Ellis pieces. I took pictures of everything. Someone's going to listen!" and he slammed out of the restaurant.

A few days after Matt had settled his account with the auction house, he received a call from someone named Walter Crowder. He identified himself as the picker who had discovered the furniture. Crowder demanded a meeting and, because he sounded so upset, Matt agreed to see him at his Tribeca loft the next day.

Matt was shocked at the appearance and demeanor of the unshaven, disheveled picker. Walt turned down all offers of drinks and began talking before even taking a seat. It took fifteen minutes of an uninterrupted emotional tirade before he finally completed his story and then he added for emphasis, shaking his finger—"Mr. Fox, you've been robbed!"

Matt asked the angry picker, "Before you called me I bet you threatened Taklee and asked for more money than he paid you originally?"

The picker slowly nodded. "Yes."

"Now you are figuring that with this information I'll sue Taklee, the auction house, the Farms and get my money back, plus damages? Then I'll gratefully give you the bigger cut that the others refused?" He glanced at Crowder, who nodded again.

"I believe your story, but you are wrong again. I want this deal to go through. Ground will be broken for the new building in a few months and the furniture will be installed in eighteen more months. My name will be all over the place. The truth will come out later in a way that will be very profitable for me."

Crowder managed a mumbled reply. "What do you mean?"

"Well, here's the kicker. Sure, I'm a movie star, but I want more. I'm going to be another Woody Allen. I will be the writer, director, producer and star of my own production. Now I've got a great plot and this movie will be the right vehicle. This story is true- it's a gold mine and Crowder, you are going to make money too—both as a consultant and an actor playing yourself in 'Reinventing Harvey Ellis.' We'll just throw in some sex and we've got a sure hit!"

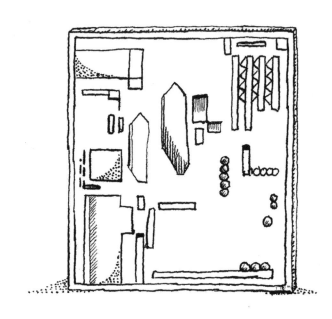

FIFTEEN

The Patron

Janet Lorraine Siegel was weeping. She placed the section of *The New York Times* open to the obituary page on the coffee table. *The Wall Street Journal* had a front page report of her dear friend Leland Purvis' accomplished life and his recent death. Her mind drifted back to the time of their first meeting a few decades ago…

After Janet's unpleasant divorce was finalized, an art gallery opening had seemed an appropriate first social event to attend. Still a young-looking forty-five, Janet was dressed New York stylish in her form-fitting black sheath cinched by a wide silver belt. Four-inch heels added significantly to her modest height. Her light, recently highlighted hair was coiffed in a high chignon and, with the vintage Mexican jewelry set of matching necklace, bracelet and earrings by Aguilar, she appeared to be more a patron of the Arts than the artist she was. The paintings displayed were highly forgettable, but the hors d'oeuvres were delicious, the open bar dispensing top-shelf liquors. She and Leland had reached for the same hors d'oeuvre, each laughingly insisting the other have it. Janet held a glass of neat bourbon in her other hand, which seemed to impress Leland.

"You're the first woman I've met in a long time who prefers whiskey to wine."

"Well, it sure works faster for me!" was her quick response.

Leland Purvis never needed to introduce himself. At that time in his early sixties, he was tall and athletic-looking, with his shaggy, now mostly gray, head of hair. A regular on the cable finance shows, his impressions and pronouncements on finance and the economy were sought after. Leland had clearly earned his credentials—first President and Founder of HCC (The High Compression Corporation), followed by directorships and consultancies with the most important Wall Street and banking giants. The President of the U.S. (then George H.W. Bush) had appointed Leland to head a commission overseeing international financial transactions. This took him to Washington and many foreign countries. Purvis's Bush contacts came through the Yale connection—although he had graduated many years after Bush Senior. Being a Yale undergrad, then graduating from MIT with a Ph.D. in Chemical Engineering gave Purvis gold-plated credentials, enhanced by an original and creative mind and entrepreneurial instincts. These served him well in developing the patents for more efficient distribution of natural gas and the formation of his company, HCC. Currently in the top twenty on the Forbes list of billionaires; his commercial record was not matched by marital success. Two failed marriages had nonetheless produced three children, all boys, all following his lead into the world of business. Their achievements were significant, with only a little help from their father.

Leland inquired politely about Janet's background, which was similar to his in three respects: two failed marriages; three children; and a love of great art. He suggested they continue their discussion over dinner at Nicola's, a restaurant in the east eighties just a few blocks away from the Madison Avenue gallery.

"That would be lovely!" she said. "Let me make a quick call and I'll meet you at the door."

Over dinner, Janet revealed that she was primarily a representational artist of New England landscapes, with a modest but enthusiastic customer base. She asked him how he had become interested in 19th-century American art.

"Several years after my graduation from Yale, the University wanted to expand their well-known British collection, including Turners and Constables. My financial support was a big factor. I believe that the American artists of the same period who portrayed the eastern and later the western areas of the country from the 18th to the 20th century are relatively unappreciated. Actually, although Thomas Moran and Thomas Cole were born in England and Bierstadt was born in Germany, they are known as American artists, as are the native-born Americans, Church, Durand, Kensett, Gifford and Cropsey. Their skill and talent in giving us the artist's view of America of those times deserves more recognition!"

"I am aware that your collections, gifts and loans are represented in all the major museums," Janet said. "Recently I attended an Eakins exhibition in Philadelphia and saw that you had loaned several of the major works." She added more emphatically, "The American wing of the Manhattan Museum would be a very different place without your contributions!"

He laughed. "Enough about me. I have the resources to buy what I want, but you have the ability to capture and create something. All the lessons by the best teachers in the world wouldn't help me do that."

Over dessert, he inquired politely whether he could call her, perhaps to attend the theater. They had discovered a mutual passion for theater, particularly Broadway musical revivals.

When Janet got home to her Flatiron loft, although it was almost midnight, she called her best friend, Sally. "Try and guess where I had dinner tonight—my first venture out after the divorce? Here's a clue: he's a billionaire and not named Bloomberg!"

After a few hints, Sally Cassidy—a fellow artist—ventured, "Not Leland Purvis?"

"Yes, Leland Purvis, and he's actually a very nice guy."

"Well, let's see how long it takes for your phone to ring!"

It took sixteen hours after that conversation. Over the next several weeks, the relationship developed. The first night Leland stayed over at Janet's apartment, she wondered aloud that he might be more used to having breakfast prepared by servants.

Leland chuckled. "Actually, every morning I'm in town I eat breakfast at a Greek diner on Lexington, a block away from my co-op on Park Avenue."

Janet insisted on treating him to the breakfast special at "her" Greek diner on Fourteenth Street at some later date.

Over the next year, Janet went on several trips with Leland to Washington and overseas. The tabloids, of course, made much of the relationship. Leland was extremely generous to Janet and seemed particularly interested in her artistic career.

On one occasion, Janet had blurted, "I love being with you and appreciate your interest in my art—but you could hardly call me a starving artist! My alimony and your generosity have allowed me to paint whatever I like. I believe I have real talent, but in a market that favors Abstract Expressionism or whatever is the current fad in Modern Art, I doubt that I could ever have any commercial success."

They both liked early 20th-century American art, especially the Ashcan school and Edward Hopper's work in particular. The new generation of collectors viewed all that as historically interesting, but not of the moment. Janet and Leland's relationship drifted in and out. Over the next fifteen years, they remained strong friends, though only occasional lovers. During the first few years of their relationship, Leland had helped arrange an exhibition of Janet's paintings at a top Madison Avenue gallery, over Janet's protests. In spite of faint critical praise, several paintings were purchased by Janet's admirers and Leland's friends. Since art sales are often the result of critical raves, "Janet Lorraine Siegel" did not become a household name.

About five years prior to that show, Leland and Janet had attended a fundraiser at the Guggenheim. As they strolled along the Museum's famous walk, hung with the post-war icons of the New York School—Larry Poons, Jasper Johns, Kenneth Nolan, Sam Francis, Kline, Rothko, Newman and Still—Leland asked Janet, "Could you paint shit like that?"

Janet was shocked at his choice of words; he'd become more outspoken and crotchety lately. "Yes, I could, but it would be a waste of canvas and paint, because the finished work would cost more to be hauled away unsold to the garbage than the price of the materials. On the other hand, my labor is cheap and I could knock these out in my studio in a jiffy!"

"Look, this is not supposed to be an accounting cost analysis. I'm really serious about my suggestion!"

"Well, Leland, what is your point? For example, would you object if the Manhattan Museum of Art incorporated a New York City wall covered with 1960's-style graffiti in their Modern collection?"

Purvis snapped back, "Well, that wouldn't have the historical significance of a graffiti fragment from the Berlin Wall, but I wouldn't mind so long as it didn't take up much of the gallery space." He continued, "What modern art has become on its radical fringes is an annoying minimalism. Artists' signatures are what the public is buying—autographs, if you will—and the rest of the canvas doesn't matter! It's very simple: most of the artists were once representational or impressionistic in their approach to painting subjects, whether in the studio or in nature. Most were competent at that so they paid their artistic dues. In New York after the War, these artists decided to take shortcuts in recording their emotions with slashes, stripes, spots and even blank canvases. It started over a hundred years ago with Picasso, Braque and their ilk. This was just the newest, weirdest wave."

"Leland, you never liked or bought any of this stuff and you could still afford to have your pick, so... where are you going with this?"

"The sad truth is that, from a market value point of view, this crap is worth more than my great Bierstadts, Morans, Coles and Churches. Even more disturbing, our great museums have been taken in hook, line and sinker; they would rather buy this modern stuff. Future art historians will determine what is more important when they judge by any rational measure."

"Well, the museums consider themselves purveyors of proper taste in art. They start with the Prehistoric, go through the Egyptians and end up with the Modernists—with space for everything else in between."

Purvis opined, "A comprehensive museum should prioritize their space. Modern museums can devote themselves to whatever they consider to represent appropriately the contemporary artistic era."

"But Leland, the Manhattan has an American Wing and they have lots of 17th- through early 20th-century art. Some of their best stuff is drawn from your collections."

They were sitting on a bench, facing each other. Leland raised his voice slightly, though not enough to be overheard by others in the gallery. "Look, Janet, we've known each other a long time; we've been good friends and more. I want you to consider this plan seriously: I'm not asking you to do anything dishonest. It will merely help demonstrate the fickle nature of the art establishment."

Leland's plan was quite simple: Janet was to produce twenty very large canvases over a six-month period, after which Purvis would arrange a huge exhibit. There would be tremendous worldwide advertising, marketing and public relations to promote the show. The catalogue would of course be available online and the actual printed catalogue would be a collectible work of art. Rich colleagues of Leland's, executives and friends, would be strongly urged to "invest" in the artist. Many owed Leland for big favors he had done them over the years. Much would be made of Janet Lorraine Siegel's previous representational style and articles would chronicle her evolution to the new imperative, Abstract modern art. Behind the scenes, Leland would make purchases through other parties. At his suggestion, the prices would range from $500,000 to the low millions.

And so it came to pass. Within weeks of the closing of the exhibition, all of the paintings were sold. Janet went back to work in her studio and within the year Christie's and Sotheby's were bidding against each other for the right to auction off her newer paintings. The prices realized were multiples of the former sales and Janet Lorraine Siegel was now hailed as the next Julian Schnabel—an American modern master.

At one point, Janet could not keep from asking, "Leland, I am bothered that our relationship and your machinations are responsible for the huge price run-up."

"But of course, my dear... and frankly, I don't give a damn! The money is useful to you and to me it just proves my point that the art itself doesn't matter."

"Look, I'm not under any illusions about my ability, but you've now proved your point. Is there something else here that I'm missing?"

"Please sit down, we need to talk." Leland looked at Janet unsmilingly. "We know how mercenary the art community can be. Now I would like to test the mettle of the museum community, from their money people to their curators. At my death, the terms of my will offer the Manhattan my very large collection of Coles, Bierstadts and Churches, many never seen by the public. Included will be over twenty Janet Lorraine Siegel Modern paintings, which my agents have been able to buy on the secondary market at huge prices. My conditions will be simple: if the Museum accepts a 19th-century painting, it must be on public view for not less than thirty-five years, except during periods when a gallery is being refurbished or the work is out on loan. No storage of any of my bequests will be permitted…"

Suddenly, Janet returned to the present, wiped her tears and picked up *The Wall Street Journal*, which covered the same biographical details of Leland's life. As expected, *WSJ* emphasized the business career and corporate connections of Leland Purvis. Having finished the front page, Janet turned to the continuation page at the back of the section. She was astounded at what she read, and then reread. "The **Manhattan Museum of Art** announced that they had received a bequest from Purvis with instructions that it be opened upon his death. It contained an offer of over forty important 19th-century works of art to add to their extensive Leland Purvis collection of 19th-century paintings now on exhibition in the American Wing. Due to a condition of the bequest, they regretfully turned it down. Over twenty contemporary works by his sometime companion, artist Janet Lorraine Siegel, were offered in the same bequest without similar conditions. These works have been gladly accepted and will find a new home in a large expansion of the Modern section of the Museum. The new wing will be named in honor of both, as 'The Leland Purvis and Janet Lorraine Siegel Gallery.'"

Janet could not contain herself as she put down the paper and the handful of wet tissues and laughed aloud.

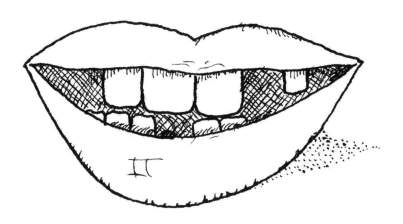

SIXTEEN

Filling Spaces

C harles Carlyle had a panoramic view from his desk at the rear of the shop of his gallery, which was stocked with outstanding examples of Arts and Crafts furniture and accessories. Seated on a rare Gustav Stickley office chair, he could see his only employee, Richard, outlined against the front window, blocking the double-C logo. The second-floor shop overlooked 57th Street near Madison Avenue.

Charles' oak desk had also been designed by Gustav Stickley and still retained its 100-year-old leather top and original tacks. It was one of the many fine examples of desks, chairs, settees, tables and case pieces in the shop. Most retained their original finish and had been produced in the early 20th century by Gustav, his brothers and other important contemporaries.

To while away the hours waiting for the first customer to appear, Richard was lovingly dusting the same table for the third time. Unfortunately, the recession had badly affected the antique trade and fewer people were finding their way to the shop. Even fewer were actually buying the beautiful, simply constructed oak furniture, or the lighting, pottery, rugs and hand-wrought copper work of the period, which so beautifully complemented the furniture.

Carlyle had been mortified when the landlord, sensing that the late rent checks were a symptom of an ailing business, suggested a move upstairs from the original street-level showroom. However, Charles was grateful to still be in business at less than half the rent and able to sustain the shop on fewer sales. Charles was still living well. He and his wife, Jane, owned a pre-war co-op apartment on the West Side and managed to keep and use their cottage in New Hope, Pennsylvania, on occasional weekends. In the early nineties, they had done very well and acquired a notable collection of Arts and Crafts furnishings, which filled both their homes. Their daughter, Gail, had two years remaining to graduate from Smith College. Enough money to cover all her tuition had been sequestered by Charles' father in a trust fund.

Charles occasionally and reluctantly sold a piece from his own collection in order to pay expenses in a slow month, but that was business—no place for sentiment. Besides, with his extensive contacts with pickers and special knowledge of the market, he was often able to upgrade to an even rarer piece.

In spite of the (he hoped) temporary softness in his niche of the antiques trade, Charles Carlyle was widely perceived to be in the upper tier in the Arts and Crafts establishment. He was mentioned prominently in the Arts and Crafts magazines and other media, and more importantly, his name and buying power were still a respected force in the auction rooms of L.A., Chicago and New York. Charles was often chosen, at a substantial fee, to front for a super-rich client who wished to be an anonymous buyer.

Charles said, after checking the time on an antique gold pocket watch secured on a chain to his English-style vest, "Richard, mind the store. I've a dental appointment and should be back before three."

He decided to walk the long mile to Dr. Alan Berkley's office on East 81st Street. Charles Carlyle was almost sixty, but with his tall, thin, athletic build and abundant hair he appeared to be ten to fifteen years younger.

An undergraduate degree from Williams College and a Master's in Fine Art from N.Y.U. were intended to lead him to a curatorship and then directorships and up and up the ladder of the hierarchy of museum administration. His late father, Charles Senior, had been in the antiques business in Larchmont, New York, where Charles Junior was exposed to the dusty atmosphere of the shop and the rich history of antiques on weekends and also on summer vacations from Williams. The business prospered. Later there were upwardly mobile moves—to a store in Greenwich Village and finally, fifteen years ago, to the street-level gallery on 57th Street. This last move to the "Gold Coast" by Charles Carlyle Senior occurred when Charles Junior was mired in a boring dead-end job as director of a regional western New York Museum. Ironically, at the same time, he read in the Alumni news that two of his classmates from Williams College had been appointed to positions as directors of major museums, one in LA County and the other in Chicago.

His wife Jane, then a kindergarten teacher and mother to nine-year-old Gail, was desperately unhappy to be stuck in the boonies. That settled it. They moved back to New York City and Charles joined the family business.

The museum experience was not without benefit for Charles. In his assignments in diverse locations, he found common behavior among the wealthy patrons of the arts. The openings, benefits and parties served as an internship for him in the social and financial attitudes of the privileged. They liked to be noticed, but more importantly, many of them recognized good taste in collecting and would pay handsomely to be in the forefront. Charles also learned that the rich preferred the sizzle to the sirloin, although the "meat" still had to be top quality. The thrust of this metaphor would serve him well later when he marketed and sold expensive items from his shop on 57th Street.

Coincidentally, the last unsuccessful posting near Buffalo was a venue that directed him to his specialty of Arts and Crafts. That part of the state was a rich source of supply for local dealers who were far ahead of the New York City crowd in recognizing and collecting top examples of that style.

After the death of Charles Senior, Charles moved rapidly from the general line in which his father had dealt to the Arts and Crafts genre. He was very proud of his strategy, having accomplished this maneuver in less than a year. First, he sold his father's stock to a couple of competitors at a modest profit, and used the proceeds to purchase middle-of-the-road basic items that were plentiful and not yet expensive, acquired through upstate auctions and estate sales. This provided basic stock. Finally, he did not try to compete with already existing networks of established dealers and their pickers. Instead, he bought rarer items from middle-end dealers who did not have the upscale customers who were attracted to Charles' 57th Street store.

During most of the nineties, these landmark early pieces, displayed with appropriate lamps, pottery, rugs and copper accessories of the period, sold quickly at huge profits. It did not hurt that Hollywood celebrities got on the bandwagon. Spreads of their homes and collections featured in *Architectural Digest* helped feed the frenzy for these top examples of Arts and Crafts. The major problem then was finding replacements.

Charles was nearing the dental office when he realized that it was, in fact, Jane's recent return to teaching that had prompted this trip. With Gail in college, Jane had lots of free time and her income and benefits package were very welcome. The dental plan was going to be utilized for the first time. Charles had some slight pain in his lower right jaw, some bleeding when he brushed, and a space in the rear of his mouth that might need to be filled by Dr. Berkley.

Charles' last dental experience was with his childhood dentist, Dr. Samuel Cohen, and that had been over five years ago. Dr. Cohen's demise ended those chatty annual visits to the Grand Concourse in the Bronx. The receptionist (Sam's wife, Rosalie) would fill him in on events and remark how cute he was when he was a little boy. He chuckled to himself as he remembered the couple and the old-fashioned office and equipment. Well, that was the past, and now it was on to the highly recommended Dr. Alan Berkley and his fashionable Upper East Side dental practice.

He entered the office and was struck by the pleasant and expensive scent and the sound of muted classical music, so different from the smells and sounds of Dr. Cohen's dental office—Lavoris mouthwash and the radio broadcast of the Yankee game. Charles' educated eye appraised the well-selected reproduction sixties chrome, glass and leather furniture. The decorator had picked subtle, warm, earth tones of green wallpaper to go with the beige patterned carpet. More earth-toned contemporary pottery with dried flower arrangements added color, but maintained the serene *gestalt* of calm professionalism. Behind the inevitable sliding glass panels sat two beautifully dressed and impeccably groomed ladies staring at computer screens. The office had the look of a very upscale brokerage office.

As he approached the window, one of the women said, "Mr. Carlyle, welcome! I'm Audrey. Please fill out these forms, indicate any insurance you may have, and the doctor will see you in a few minutes."

Charles was impressed. Right on time he was shown in to Dr. Berkley's office. From his seat, he could see rows of diplomas, letters and certificates covering the walls. On the free-form Nakashima-style desk, a silver-framed picture of Dr. Berkley and family on a ski holiday was displayed. Charles noticed that the sixties theme of the waiting room was repeated, but this time with original prints, including a late-Picasso signed and numbered graphic behind the desk. A few minutes later, the dentist came quietly into the office and closed the door. He reached out a firm hand and introduced himself. "Alan Berkley—I'm pleased to meet you."

"Our mutual friend, Dick Johnson, recommended you. He works with my wife, Jane, who will also be coming to see you."

Dr. Berkley was in his mid-forties, which Charles thought was perfect—a dozen years of experience, but still young enough to be up on all of the latest dental innovations.

The dentist was of average size and build, but his outstanding features were his very blue eyes, fair skin and straight blond hair, styled fashionably to fall just slightly over his ears. With his Greenwich accent, he was the perfect uptown society dentist.

He glanced briefly at Charles' health history and said, "I'm going to have our hygienist, Lila, X-ray your teeth today and give you a thorough cleaning. Then we'll set up another meeting to go over your situation after I've examined you and have studied your X-rays. In the meantime, is there any pressing problem you would like me to check or discuss now?"

"No, thank you, I'll wait for the consultation."

Ten days later, Charles lay back on the ultra-modern dental chair with a view through the window that included most of the main span of the Triboro Bridge. Dr. Berkley expertly picked at his teeth while staring through surgical telescopes mounted on his glasses. A probe had measured gum pocket depths in millimeters and automatically recorded them on the computer. Dr. Berkley explained that twos, threes and even an occasional four was acceptable, but elaborated jocularly that, as in golf, fives, sixes and sevens were like double bogeys and needed to be eliminated!

A few minutes later they were back in the private office, and Dr. Berkley asked Charles if he would like coffee.

"No, thank you," Charles responded nervously, as if the caffeine might further heighten his anxiety.

Dr. Berkley had prepared for the meeting with X-rays displayed on a large flat screen monitor, along with a computer printout of the gum assessment and a printed description of the treatment options.

Dr. Berkley cleared his throat and said, "Well, there are some problems in your mouth. Some are of immediate concern for your dental health and require treatment as soon as possible. Other conditions can be addressed later on and there are a few treatment options that are available. The first concern is your periodontal situation. Ideally, you should see a specialist for this, because in some areas surgery may be required. You may recall some of the numbers that were measured were very high. In the case of one of the teeth, even the periodontal care may not be able to salvage the tooth."

He stopped and waited for a reaction from Carlyle. Seeing none, he continued. "In the area of restorative dentistry, you need several crowns and a bridge to fill the space in the back of your mouth on one side or an implant and several crowns. On the other side, you have no upper back teeth with a large empty space and a couple of implants would be the state-of-the-art way to correct the situation. I see also that at least one and possibly two root canals need to be done." Again, the dentist glanced at the patient waiting for a question before continuing. "Naturally, you will want more details of the proposed treatment plans. I emphasize the plural, because there is more than one way to deal with most problems—dental and otherwise."

At this point, Charles knew a response was expected and he replied simply, "Of course."

Dr. Berkley pressed on. "We'll meet again in a week or so, if that's convenient. I will have a very detailed analysis of your problems and proposed solutions, including names of specialists, time required and of course fees."

Charles replied with a little hesitation in his voice, "I wonder whether you could get me some ball-park figures for these options. Of course I won't hold you to them, but it would give me something to consider until we meet again."

"Well, that's a little tricky," replied Berkley with just a slight edge to his voice, "but I'll try—understanding, naturally, that they are preliminary rough estimates."

Charles nodded his approval.

"Okay, the Hollywood answer for the best of everything to resolve your problems and fill those spaces including specialist fees would be about sixteen to twenty thousand dollars. The second choice—no implants, a fixed bridge to fill the space, fewer crowns, root canals where needed, but still the periodontal services—would run ten to twelve thousand dollars. Finally, the simplest approach—cleaning up your mouth, some fillings and extractions and placement of a removable partial denture to fill the spaces—would come to, say, four thousand dollars. I should add that you can do the basic as a first step and then upgrade to another option at a later date."

Dr. Berkley offered his hand. "Audrey will reappoint you and next time, once we agree on a plan, I can even leave time for us to get started." He paused and then added almost parenthetically, "Don't expect too much from your insurance, but you'll get something back after treatment is completed. Audrey will discuss office payment procedures with you."

Audrey stopped Charles at the desk as he was leaving. When she suggested he might like to set up an appointment, he replied that he would call from his office after checking his schedule. He did not glance back, as he knew he would not return.

Charles reflected on his walk back that the fees were probably in line with today's technology and standards, but he didn't like the concept of options. Dr. Cohen had never presented treatment plans, specialists or multiple consultations. He talked to you in the chair and told you what he was going to do as you looked out the window onto 173rd Street and watched the kids playing stickball in the street. Then Charles would pay his wife, Rosalie, directly as he left. There was no dental insurance to consider—or reject as Dr. Berkley had as hardly being worthy of consideration. Charles had read the benefit plan. He and Jane had annual coverage each of $2,000-worth of dental benefits. Times weren't great and a few thousand bucks would come in handy if Gail decided to go to graduate school. The sixties furniture and Picasso print were great touches, but why should he finance the dentist's art collection? Yes! He had decided. He would call the Teachers' Union benefit office and get someone who fully accepted the insurance plan.

About three weeks later, Charles was sitting at his desk at the back of his showroom, having just made an appointment to see the Union dentist. As he replaced the receiver, he could hear Richard at the front discussing the purchase of an item with a customer. They were just out of view, but Charles knew the piece and the sales pitch well—he had coached Richard exactly in it. The settle was a beautiful Gustav Stickley with original finish that he had purchased for $5,500 about five years earlier at a country auction—it was a bargain even then, reasonably priced because the auction had not been well advertised. Since it was near his New Hope house and his competitors were at a Christie's auction held on the same day, he had snagged it. Charles had originally priced it at eighteen thousand and had regrettably turned down an offer of fifteen thousand a few weeks later. Now, in this more sober decade, the price tag said twelve thousand

and he would happily take ten—or even less for cash. In fact, if he didn't move it soon he would test the market and his luck and throw it into an auction.

Charles sensed some reluctance on the part of the customer and he was happy to hear that Richard remembered the next part. "Now, this is a special, signed, all-original Gus—an investment piece. We do have a similar unsigned, refinished settle that we can positively attribute to one of Gustav's brothers—that is on sale for 5,200 dollars."

Again, Charles judged from the silence that there was more resistance and he thought he might now join the conversation. Richard tended to be ineffectual at times and Charles could discreetly turn up the pressure a notch or two to help close the sale.

However, the young salesman was not giving up. "The advantage in buying the unsigned piece is that it will allow you to trade up to the better settle if you want to go with Arts and Crafts, but don't want to spend more money now." Richard hesitated for a moment then continued, "This is a great start-up piece, but you could also keep it to use some day in a second home."

From the customer's continued silence, Richard was apparently judging there would be no sale, as he added sarcastically, "If you want a sofa for watching television, you can buy a decent contemporary couch from Bloomingdales for around three thousand dollars."

The potential buyer continued to admire and stroke the beautiful Gustav settle, which was illuminated by warm reddish spotlights that enhanced its beautiful oak grain and finish, along with the buttery soft tan leather seat and cushions. Next to the settle, on an early L & JG Stickley table, a copper-and-mica Dirk van Earp lamp contributed to the appealing glow—it all should have been quite irresistible to anyone of taste.

The customer spoke firmly and without apparent indignation. "This is a great piece of furniture! I love it. The price is fair for its quality and rarity. Unfortunately my business is off right now so it is out of the question. I couldn't in all conscience choose something less just for the purpose of filling a space."

Charles Carlyle strode in to the main gallery just in time to catch a glimpse of Dr. Alan Berkley leaving the shop.

SEVENTEEN

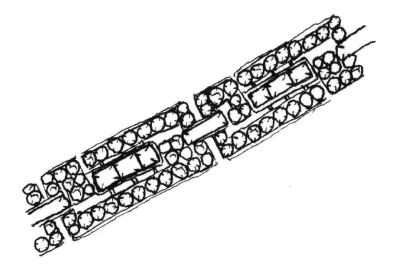

A Steal at the Thrift Shop

O n the drive home to Darien, Connecticut, after viewing the Van Cleef Exhibition at the Cooper Hewitt Museum, Jan and Drake Hudson thought about their own Van Cleef and Arpels diamond, ruby and sapphire platinum bracelet and the other four pieces in their collection.

While perusing the exhibit catalog, Jan turned to her husband, Drake, who was driving north along the West Side Highway bordering the Hudson River, and said, "It's been almost four months since we moved the five pieces of jewelry I inherited from Grandmother Abbott from the safety deposit box at the bank to the big safe you brought home from work." Drake was a senior partner at the venerable law firm of Johnson Miller & White. After the office renovation was completed, he'd brought home one of the large document safes that were going to be thrown out.

"The idea of the safe was to make wearing those gorgeous pieces for special occasions less of a chore."

Up until now, the five signed VCA pieces—a platinum and diamond watch chain, a small, gold, *necessaire* purse, a cabochon emerald brooch with matching earrings and the bracelet—had rarely been worn in the twelve years Jan had owned them. Jan had been the beneficiary of her Grandmother Hazel Catherine Abbott's fine jewelry collection. All five items were from the mid-thirties, made with the invisible mystery jewel mounting, a patented Arpels device. All were signed "VCA" and had a combined insurance estimate of $410,000 as of the date of Grandmother Abbott's death.

Jan said, "Dear, I love wearing the paste copies Grandmother had made and if someone asks, I usually tell them that they are top examples of Chanel, Dior or Trifari. Life's short; we're in our fifties, so now—maybe I'll wear the REAL bracelet to the annual spring golf party at the Club."

"I agree, but I guess I didn't tell you that I took all the VCA jewelry off the insurance rider after we got the safe installed," replied Drake, adding, "Ironically, that paste copy is the one piece I sent with Bernice to the thrift shop."

He was referring to their housekeeper, Bernice, and his response to a charitable drive to benefit the Darien Hospital (where he was a trustee) Expansion Fund. "I recall after she came back from dropping it off, she told me that the guy at Acquisitions in the back said it was the best piece of costume jewelry he had ever seen. He even told her to put a value of $1,800 on it for tax purposes, since he thought it was a piece of early Chanel, unsigned."

Six weeks later, and probably forever, Jan would recall the moment when Drake helped her put on the bracelet. She felt it was somewhat lighter on her wrist than she remembered. The beautiful deco design, rectangular bracelet had a cross pattern with ovoid rubies and sapphires, interspersed throughout with lines of diamonds.

"Jan, since you haven't seen or even tried this on for years, how could you remember the weight? It sure feels plenty heavy to me."

"Take it off! I do remember that the copies Grandmother had made did not have the Van Cleef or Platinum marks and they were not initialed HCA for Hazel Catherine Abbott," Jan blurted in a panic, "and get me a magnifier—it's in the top drawer of the desk on the right side."

With mounting feelings of horror, they took turns checking and re-checking, determining that the bracelet had no signatures and therefore had to be the paste copy.

"Oh, Drake!" cried Jan, "How could you have mixed up the two boxes?"

"Calm down. I'll go over to the thrift shop in the morning. They are open on Sunday."

"Drake, that was weeks ago! I'm sure it's gone," cried Jan.

"It might still be there; they may be asking a very high price for a so-called piece of costume jewelry," Drake replied hopefully—but from the tone of his voice, he clearly did not believe his own words.

Needless to say, they skipped the party at the golf club and stayed home that night, both unable to sleep.

The next morning they drove the short distance to the thrift shop in silence. No one there could even recall seeing the piece—of course, it was long gone. There was no record of any sale or even of its acquisition. Their quest to recover their Van Cleef bracelet had reached a dead end...

Jerry Lester, like Drake Hudson, commuted to Manhattan every day from the much less upscale city of Norwalk, a couple of stops further from New York City than Darien. Jerry's previous job, pushing penny stocks in a boiler room atmosphere at Atlas Securities, a low-end stock firm, had evaporated during the dotcom bubble. Now he had made a small niche for himself in the jewelry trade, barely surviving by dealing in lower-end resale jewelry. His propensity for picking slow horses kept him constantly in debt. On weekends, he would hit the area flea markets and occasionally venture to the City to buy and sell in the markets there. At first, he was content to show up early at the local Connecticut thrift shops, where some of the rich people dumped their excess "stuff." Their reward was contributing to good causes, and of course, there were the little contribution slips that were universally inflated and offered to their accountants to help enhance their bottom lines by contributing less in taxes to the government.

Jerry's favorite thrift shop was the Darien Hospital Resale Shop, located in an out-of-the-way store front just off the Post Road. Although he usually made it his first stop, he invariably heard from one of the volunteers, "You should have been here when we first opened—you just missed the Stickley end table" or "the Sloane etching."

The idea of becoming a volunteer struck him as being obviously the best way to get an edge. He was not going to dust the shelves or ring up purchases—instead, he would volunteer at the acquisitions counter.

Jerry quickly demonstrated to the thrift shop manager that he was skilled at repairing items, including jewelry, in the acquisition back room where donors brought their merchandise. The items became more attractive and valuable before being released for tagging and displaying.

Jerry would never forget the morning that the plump, uniformed, middle-aged woman came in with a magnificent pre-war designer bracelet. Not wanting her to think the piece was special, he quickly handed her a blank slip and suggested that she tell her boss that it was worth $1,800. At the same time, he was picturing how quickly he could sell it at his tiny rented space in the back of a jewelry arcade on 47th Street in New York City. Alternatively, he could offer it to one of the Russian dealers at the 25th Street Garage that next weekend.

The bracelet went into his pocket immediately. He wanted no

one to spot him examining the bracelet with his jeweler's loupe. He would do that at home. Claiming a stomach upset, he left immediately.

On the short ride up I-95 to Norwalk, it occurred to Lester that perhaps he was getting ahead of himself. What he had might only be a very good piece of vintage costume jewelry with a wholesale value not more than what he had told the maid in uniform. He turned into his apartment complex and parked in his usual spot. His rented garden apartment was set too close to the Interstate, because when it had been built fifty years earlier, the previous road was more like a busy lane. Now even a noisy fan running day and night could not drown out the sound of the traffic.

What he saw when he examined the bracelet with his loupe left him almost paralyzed in his chair. The familiar "VCA" was there on the back, with a tower inside a diamond-shaped outline with a platinum mark and the engraved letters, "HCA." What to do? Certainly, he had better not return to the Darien Hospital Resale Shop under any circumstances. He would inform them that he needed surgery and would be out indefinitely. But the bigger issue was that this was certainly not a $100,000 bracelet that was donated as a charitable contribution, but rather a major error by the owner. If the owner of the bracelet really wanted to be so charitable, he would have auctioned the piece or sold it privately and given the contribution directly to the hospital. It was obviously a HUGE mistake, and the owner would eventually notice—so he would have to unload it quickly and quietly.

At this point, Lester found his Jack Daniels stash and poured himself a triple. After a couple of swallows, he answered his own question. The answer, clearly, was no. If he put the bracelet in a high-end auction, it could possibly be noted by the former owner. He would wait at least six months and sell it on 47th Street where it would not stand out as much because similar pieces were not unusual.

On the other hand, if the mistake were noted in the next several weeks and was traced to him by the insurance company, a grateful owner would be satisfied with its safe return with the explanation that he was carefully cleaning a piece of vintage Chanel. He would probably get a huge reward…

Well, of course, none of that happened because there was no insurance company out there asking questions…

Fall came and Jan and Drake Hudson had not quite put the sad loss behind them. The four remaining Van Cleef pieces and one not-quite-matching copy would remain in the safe, not only for obvious reasons of security, but to keep "the death of the departed" out of sight and hopefully, eventually, out of mind…

The Wednesday matinee of Cole Porter's *Anything Goes* fit right in with a late morning dental appointment for Drake at 49th and Madison. Then they took a walk west to the theater district with time for lunch at a Turkish Restaurant on 47th Street between Sixth and Seventh Avenues. The stroll toward the restaurant took them past the stretch of 47th Street that is the "world famous jewelry district." Here, virtually every specialty of the trade is available, along with fabulous diamond displays in the windows. Passers-by are routinely accosted and asked if they want to sell gold or buy a beautiful diamond ring. About halfway down the block, Drake remembered that he needed a new watch strap for his Patek Philippe watch and, while passing one of the Arcades, he inquired of the guard at the front whether there was a dealer inside who could supply that. The guard pointed toward the rear of the store, where close to thirty dealers had rented small spaces to ply their various specialties.

"Drake, we have barely an hour left for lunch if we are going to make the curtain."

At that exact moment, Drake noticed the bracelet. He gently guided Jan away from the booth and said, "Don't turn your head, but

I think I might have seen our missing bracelet in the case we just passed on the left."

"Are you sure?" was the excited and hushed reply.

"No, and that's the point—let me deal with this and don't say a word."

Drake and Jan casually wandered back and pretended to be interested in another item on the shelf immediately below the bracelet.

Jerry Lester noticed the well-dressed couple and said, "Hello, I'm Jerry Lester; may I show you something?"

Drake pointed to an ugly pinky ring made up of several small diamonds mounted to give the appearance of a larger stone.

Lester quickly retrieved it and placed it on a purple velvet display pad. "A great-looking ring with a total diamond weight of three carats—and only $4,200."

"Can I borrow your loupe?" After examining the ring, Drake casually remarked, "That's a nice old bracelet on the shelf above it— what is that?"

"Oh, that's a wonderful Deco Van Cleef and Arpels piece from the thirties—it actually came from a Darien, Connecticut, estate."

"May I see it?" asked Drake, his calm voice not betraying his rapidly beating heart. Jan was also beside herself, but remained visibly in control. Drake, still holding the loupe, said, "Do you mind if I examine it closer? I'll be careful—it's gorgeous!"

Lester quickly sized up the couple as being substantial and replied, "Yes, of course—what are you doing here?"

"Oh, we're up from Philly for a day in the city and we're going back tonight."

As he spoke, Drake turned the piece over to check for the VCA mark and Jan's grandmother's initials. They were both there. Drake remained calm and planned his words carefully. "Please tell me if you have an appraisal?"

"Yes, I do. It's for $122,000. Here it is with the photos and details, but if you have a serious interest I can make you a good deal."

Drake gave Jan a quick glance and said, "We'll have a conference—if my wife agrees she wants it, maybe we can negotiate a number we can both agree on."

Without waiting for Lester's reaction, Drake gently pushed a trembling Jan toward the next aisle.

"Yes, it's *the* bracelet!" he said. "You must be calm. Involving the police could take months, with no guarantee that we would get it back in the end. After all, we stupidly gave it away. If we ask any questions about how he got it, he may get suspicious. I have a different plan."

Drake quickly outlined his plan to Jan. "To make this look legitimate, we'll haggle for the best deal. He will insist on cash or its equivalent—a cashier's or bank check. I will agree to that. I don't have time to tell you the entire plan now, but—trust me! We are going to get that bracelet back."

The couple returned to the counter and Drake began the negotiating game. "Let me get this straight—up-front. I've seen the photo appraisal and I accept that, when I pay you, the sale will be final. Just give me your best cash price and I will bring you a cashier's check if we agree."

Lester was conflicted between making a deal that would get him the maximum price and not asking such a high price that it would discourage the buyer. "I'll sell it for $88,500, which is close to my cost."

Drake answered, "Make it $82,000. And we have a deal." Lester put out his sweaty hand and Drake grasped it with relief. "I'll go to my bank in Philadelphia tomorrow morning and bring the check. I'll grab a cab from Penn Station and should be here by early afternoon."

"I'll see you then," said Lester happily.

As Jan and Drake left, it occurred to them that some lucky people standing in the back would get their fourth row center seats at *Anything Goes.*

Back in the car, this time taking the less scenic but faster route on I-95, the couple was back in Darien within an hour. They spent the short ride and the rest of the day working out the details of their plan for the next day.

Before the Hudsons had even left the street, Jerry Lester was on the phone to his bookie. "Hey, Johnny Q, this is Jerry Lester—I'll have the fifty G's for you tomorrow—stop by after four."

"What about the rest you owe me, pal?"

"Actually, I can make it sixty—I'll see you tomorrow."

Jan and Drake Hudson slept very little that night. They had rehearsed their plan—it seemed like more than a hundred times. It was about 2:30 p.m. the next day when they arrived at the 47th Street arcade and Jerry greeted them with a cheery, "Right on time! You are practically stealing this at $82,000. You could auction it for a lot more."

Drake said, "Well, we are not going to do that." As he stood close to Jan, Drake asked, "I'd like to examine the bracelet one more time." He reached into his jacket pocket and took out a Chase bank envelope and placed it on the counter.

Jerry opened the display case and carefully withdrew the bracelet, placing it on a velvet tray and then handing it to Drake for examination. At that precise moment, following the script they had practiced so many times in Darien, Jan's knees buckled as she murmured, "I'm going to faint." Lester reached out instinctively to break her fall, his attention diverted from the bracelet. He had come from behind the counter and bent over Jan, who was now on the floor. Drake quickly pocketed the bracelet with his right hand and, at the same time, pulled the previously positioned paste copy with his left hand from his other pocket, placing it in the tray on the counter. He quickly followed this by retrieving the bank envelope and returning it to his right jacket pocket. The entire operation took less than ten seconds.

Both men leaned over the prostrate woman. Drake said, "Mr. Lester, I think she will be all right—too much excitement probably, but let me get her outside into the fresh air. We'll be back in a few minutes to complete the sale."

Jerry checked the tray and saw that the bracelet was safely back. "Get her some water or coffee—I'm sure she'll be okay."

"We'll be right back—maybe you can find us a nice box while we're away," suggested Drake, trying to maintain an even tone.

With great restraint, the couple walked very slowly toward the exit, feeling Lester's eyes on them. Once out on the street, they walked quickly to Sixth Avenue and hailed a cab, which dropped them off at the parking garage ten blocks away. Less than ten minutes after leaving the Arcade they were jubilantly driving home, their treasure safely in their possession.

One hour later, Jerry decided that Jan was really in charge and had changed her mind. The deal was dead.

At 4:30 p.m., a short, portly man accompanied by two large, muscular thugs came to the booth. "I hope you got the dough!"

"The assholes backed out—the lady wears the pants and couldn't part with the money—so I don't have the sixty G's we agreed to, but actually it works out better for you. I got an appraisal on this bracelet for $122,000—photos and all and you can keep the change—which I figure will leave us even."

"Gimme the piece and put it in a box, so it don't get damaged."

"Of course."

"Lemme tell you this, pal—if this bracelet don't check out with that appraisal, you're gonna get so damaged you'll end up in a box too!"

As if on cue, the two accompanying thugs smiled, the light glinting off the gold caps on their front teeth.

EIGHTEEN

Gambling with Antiques

The Pier Show set-up in New York City is always a crazy day for dealers. For some, it is also the ultimate buying opportunity. They run through the aisles, watching other dealers unload their trucks. As the bubble-wrap drops away it might reveal some wonderful fresh merchandise they can grab before a retail customer gets it.

For Pete Robinson and his neighbor Carol Grant, neither unpacking nor early buying was their priority. They had been neighbors through several previous Pier Shows. Making their space attractive with the stock they had was all the challenge they needed. In Carol's case, the merchandise was mainly Arts and Crafts accessories: hammered silver flatware and hollow-ware, copper, pottery, tiles, lighting and smaller pieces of furniture. Pete set up across the aisle with his American regional impressionist paintings facing the strong natural light streaming through the windows of Pier 92 at the Hudson River.

They were both single. Carol was currently unattached because of the death of her 20-year-older husband eighteen months earlier; Pete was single by choice, having been divorced many years previously. In their early fifties, they had maintained a rather flirtatious relationship. So far it had not extended beyond the venues of the various New York area antique shows they did together each year. However, during the last few shows they had shared Saturday night dinner and discussed possible future dates, since they lived near each other in the Chelsea area.

Robinson's collection of early 20th-century California and regional paintings was actually very complementary to her Arts and Crafts objects. In the heady days of the 1980's and early 1990's, when the works of Gustav Stickley and his contemporaries were hot, he had done very well with his paintings and had maintained a successful gallery in Soho. But the dot-com bust, followed by 9/11 and the still ongoing recession after 2008 had changed everything in that market. Selling antiques and collectibles was much more difficult today than it ever had been.

Carol interrupted his musings, "Pete, can you help me position this small settle?"

"Of course!"

It was a simple task for six-foot-two and 200-pound Pete to move furniture. "Your booth is really shaping up. Do you know what would look good here? That Leon Dabo oil I just leaned against the wall over there."

"Let's try it," Carol agreed enthusiastically.

Pete pulled over his ladder and Carol admired his strength and craggy good looks as he easily scampered up the step ladder, painting in hand. He brushed back his longish, graying, blond hair so he could see where to place the nail.

"Looks perfect to me!"

Carol Grant was petite, with a heart-shaped face, Cupid's bow mouth and abundant dark hair. She could easily pass for early forties and until a few years ago had regularly been "carded" in bars. For the last six months she had been irregularly dating a twice-divorced finance guy, Todd Wilson, who loved the Vegas and Atlantic City scenes. Todd did very well on Wall Street. Clearly, part of his attraction for Carol was the stark difference in personality from her recently deceased high-school principal husband, Glenn Grant. Glenn had thought that anything more than buying an occasional lottery ticket was the sign of a degenerate gambler. Todd could be very charming, but after a few months of exciting dates, Carol noticed that when Todd drank too much he developed abusive behavior.

By the end of the day, both Carol's and Pete's booths were ready except for some small finishing touches they would complete before the show opened the next morning. They agreed to have an early dinner together.

All that day of set-up, dealers were buzzing over the Gambling/ Antique Fair two-night cruise that was scheduled to depart Monday from the berth next to Pier 92 and return on Wednesday. Selling antiques shipboard was not a new idea, but tacking it on to a gambling casino-style cruise was definitely a novel concept in New York.

As an incentive, the gambling cruise company, Lucky Liners, had offered a great package to the first fifty dealers who signed on. Besides a very reasonable rent of five hundred dollars for the cruise, they offered help in moving their stuff directly from the show and on to the ship at the close of the regular Pier Show on Sunday night. In addition to this, the dealers would get a complimentary cabin, meals and wine with dinner! The only additional requirement was that, besides their set-up in a large public space secured by guards, they would have to be available for casino patrons who wished to shop at odd hours. In other words, customers would have access to around-the-clock gambling and antiquing—what could be better?

Carol and Pete spent most of dinner discussing their prospects for the Gambling/Antique Cruise. Fewer than forty dealers had taken advantage of Lucky Liners' offer. As far as Carol and Pete were concerned, they would have a captive audience, so the fewer dealers the better.

When the baklava dessert of their *prix fixe* dinner at the Turkish Kitchen arrived, Carol said, "I've got two important ideas to discuss with you."

Peter, now pleasantly high after two generous Pomartinis said, "Let's start with number one."

"You recall I've mentioned Todd Wilson to you a few times. He is a gambler and he is going to be aboard this cruise; however, he and I are history as a couple, so don't form any wrong impression if you happen to see us talking together."

"Well, I'm not in charge of your social life at this point, but maybe that might change," he responded with a twinkle in his eye.

"Never can tell! But more importantly, I have just received some substantial insurance money from my late husband's estate. I've decided to open a shop in the Meat-Packing District." She was referring to a section running along the Hudson River in West Chelsea and part of the West Village.

"Do you have enough inventory to stock it?"

Carol replied with a definitive "no" and after a long pause continued, "And that is the second thing I want to discuss. With the real estate downturn and considering the space that furniture takes, what I have in mind is including in my stock American paintings of the type and period you deal in. They would combine beautifully with my Arts and Crafts accessories."

"Sounds like a reasonable plan."

"Well, here is my idea—I'd like to buy all the art you brought to the Pier Show. Are they for sale as a group?"

After a momentary pause, he replied excitedly, "Of course, I'm sure we could work out a deal! At the show tomorrow, I'll check my costs and listed prices and hopefully I can come up with a number that would be agreeable and fair for both of us."

Robinson made sure that he got to his booth a full two hours before the show formally opened. The total retail price for all the art works he had brought came to $528,000. As is the usual case with stock acquired over a period of time, some had been obtained at a bargain price; some were stale and in stock for over two years. In retrospect he had overpaid for some. His actual cost basis came to $210,000. Just to sell them as a group with the chance to have a pile of cash in hand to start over and be very selective about what he bought was a wonderful opportunity. When Carol arrived, he had his list ready and suggested $350,000 for the entire lot. Any sales at the current show would be hers.

Carol thought about it for a few minutes while looking at the paintings and glancing at the inventory list and then offered her hand and said simply, "We have a deal!"

The first day of the show there was only one painting sold, but it was a good one. At the very beginning of the show, a California collector in New York on business bought an Orrin White, 20x24-inch, 1912 Sierra scene in the original frame for $11,500. As the buyer left with his carefully wrapped painting, Peter commented to Carol—"Well, that painting is going home."

That evening, Carol took Pete out to dinner at *Marinella* in the Village to celebrate their deal. He thanked her and after dinner they headed back to Chelsea. When he dropped her off, they exchanged a rather serious kiss and embrace. "Maybe I'm for sale now, too," Pete joked.

Carol laughed and Pete replied, "Maybe I helped pay for this celebration because I forgot to include in the inventory list four large and rather common Picasso prints I bought in the parking lot yesterday during set-up from a hard-up-looking dealer from Ohio. The frames are probably worth more than the prints. I left them in the truck, but I'll bring everything aboard tomorrow night when we go on the ship. I paid two hundred dollars for all of them and that should cover our dinner. He did look so desperate, buying them was like charity."

Carol kidded, "I'll have a medal struck for you!" She added, "We can have our picture taken by one of the other dealers to commemorate the marriage of our collections, enlarge it and have it put in one of the frames when I open the shop." They both laughed and hugged again.

Privately, Pete thought that the cruise, with Carol in her present mood, had great possibilities and of course, selling more antiques was not what was on his mind.

Sunday was a good day for Carol. Her total sales for the show, excluding the painting, totaled $31,200. After figuring in show expenses and cost of goods, the net came to $19,000. It was not like the old days, but considering the economy it was okay-plus.

Pete Robinson had hoped for a better show, but he ended with only the one sale. Nevertheless, they were both in a good mood and hoping to have more success in Part Two of the event—The Lucky Liner Inaugural Gambling/Antique Cruise.

The breakdown and transfer of the material in their booths turned out to be more of a chore than they anticipated. It was well after midnight when the two dealers, exhausted, parted ways for their respective cabins.

The stateroom was about what Pete had expected. He found space for a few of his—or rather her—paintings, not all of his stock having been set up in one of the spare dining rooms. This was in anticipation of the after-brunch crowd who would perhaps be anxious to see antiques after gambling most of the night away.

The first day of the cruise, Carol and Pete sat next to each other, concluding that the concept was not working. Before it was over, they hoped that some of the gamblers who had made a big score would want to take home an expensive object—maybe some silver or a painting. That concept often worked in Atlantic City and Vegas. At six p.m., they headed back to their respective cabins to shower and change, ready to meet for a late dinner at nine p.m. at the Dolphin Bar.

Pete had actually brought a vintage "Cruise Suit" that was a 1920's tux with accessories and wondered if Carol would get dressed up also. He fortified himself with a generous shot of Blanton's bourbon from his private stock and then headed toward the bar at 8:30 p.m. The large, painted wooden dolphin suspended over the entrance was a definite clue.

Carol looked gorgeous, wearing a contemporary designer, full-length, crimson velvet gown, her hair high on her head and crowned with a vintage tiara. Pete's initial pleasure was immediately spoiled by the presence of a tall, bald man in a light poplin suit, who held her hand. Both held cocktails, probably Manhattans, in their free hands.

It was obvious they had both had a head-start on the cocktails and were way ahead of him. "Oh, Pete, meet Todd Wilson. Todd, this is Pete Robinson. Todd will be joining us for dinner."

Both men nodded warily at each other. Pete thought if this was a broken-up relationship it must have been very hot when it was on.

After an uncomfortable dinner together, Pete mentioned that he was tired, ignoring their insincere request that he stay. He excused himself before dessert and coffee and went back to his cabin. After throwing himself on the bed and entertaining depressed thoughts on this unexpected turn of events, he rationalized that he should not have assumed anything more than friendship with Carol. Besides, he still had a good deal in the sale of his paintings.

A knock at the door at 11:30 p.m. roused him from a half-sleep. "Carol?"

"No, my name is Jason Kindall; I'm a buyer—is it too late to come in?"

"All right, come on in—it's the rules."

A distinguished-looking older man warily entered the cabin. "I went by your booth this afternoon, taking a break from the crap tables. I'm sorry to bother you—I could come back tomorrow. I was wondering if that small Edgar Payne painting is still available."

"Yes, I have it marked $48,000, but if you are really interested, we can talk and I would entertain a serious offer. I do have the provenance, as well as auction records and an appraisal for it."

"Well, I had a very good day at the tables. I am interested—so I'll come by tomorrow and have a closer look. Sorry to be so late, I sort of lost track of time, which you do on these gambling cruises."

As he turned to go, he noticed the four large Picasso prints leaning against the wall near the door. "What do you have here?"

"Oh, I just picked those up recently."

Kindall replied, "Can I see them in a better light?"

"Of course. I'll bring them out to the big room tomorrow so you can see them better when you are checking out the Payne. You do see that they are not numbered." Robinson was going to offer to let Kindall take them to his cabin to examine if he would only leave and let him get some rest.

Jason Kindall seemed very excited by the prints and lifted one towards a lamp to view more closely. "Where did you get them?"

"Oh, they came out of an old Ohio estate."

"What do you need for the lot of four?"

"I guess I could do three hundred fifty for all of them."

Jason exclaimed, "That's a really reasonable price; someone must have practically given them away!"

"Look, it's late—could we meet at nine a.m. in my booth if that's not inconvenient for your crap game schedule," said Pete, barely hiding his sarcasm.

"That's fine. I'm going to look up recent auction records for fine Picasso drawings like these. To my recollection, a much smaller one with a similar subject went for over $100,000 plus buyer's premium at a recent auction in London. I did extremely well today, but not that well. If I had $350,000 on me, I'd grab all of them now!"

He opened the door, repeating "See you at nine" twice.

Pete Robinson did not sleep that night after all. Would Jason Kindall really try to buy one or more of the Picasso drawings? Was he obligated to take $350,000 for the drawings or could he withdraw his offered price? More importantly, would Carol even notice that the Picassos were not included, since they had not been on his inventory list? Then he could negotiate privately and sell them before he transferred everything to her. Well, they would not leave the cabin. On the other hand, if he told her what had happened would she allow him to keep the major share of any proceeds from the sale of the Picasso drawings?

He was still dressing at 8:15 a.m. when he heard a knock on the door and Carol calling his name. "Come in!"

Carol looked distraught and Pete sensed some unpleasantness coming. "Look," she said, "I'm sorry about last night and I'll get right to the point. Todd and I have decided to see if we can make things work for us. You and I can certainly continue to be friends, but there is something else. Todd is a finance guy and he wants to help me handle the insurance money, starting now. So, I've come here early to tell you that our deal is off. Todd says selling artwork is not a good financial investment and since we only shook hands on it and have no written agreement it is not binding in a court of law. The one sale is yours now—I hope you can forgive me and we can remain friends!

I know this must be extremely upsetting for you!"

Pete Robinson, to Carol's surprise, smiled broadly and replied very cheerfully, "I'll get over it!"

NINETEEN

Adirondack
Camp

I t was the First Annual Gala Garden Antiques and Collectibles Show and the crowd was thinning out at Madison Square Garden on that late Saturday afternoon in September.

Jim Custer, sitting on one of his unsold V-backed side chairs, glanced at his cardboard show sign, Custer's Last Stand, thinking how aptly his business was named. The show had not been a total disaster. In the first six hours, he'd sold a Roycroft library table, a Handel floor lamp with original shade and a large collection of Craftsmen magazines. Nevertheless, the rent and set-up costs associated with the show were even stiffer than those at the uptown Armory. The promoter had stated in the show application: "Madison Square Garden is the most famous arena in the world is and may be expensive to rent, but the cost will be offset by the throngs of eager buyers."

So far, those "eager buyers" were not much in evidence. He would have to do a lot better on Sunday to justify the additional expenses of moving heavy merchandise to the City from his upstate home in Saratoga Springs, not counting the cost of Manhattan hotels and restaurants.

Custer looked toward the ceiling of the arena and caught sight of a massive banner that proclaimed the New York Rangers the 1994 Stanley Cup Champions. He was reminded that fifteen years earlier, while an undergraduate in Fine Arts at Syracuse, he'd played in a hockey game at the Garden. In fact, he guessed that his booth corresponded very closely to the location of the penalty box and he had occupied it several times during that game. He mused that he was still, figuratively, in the penalty box, but this time more because of his major in Fine Arts than his hockey misbehavior.

Jim rose from the chair and strolled toward the adjacent booth. At six feet tall and 180 pounds, Jim retained his boyish athletic looks. Only his thinning blond hair and element-weathered skin suggested a progression toward middle age. There were half-a-dozen other Arts and Crafts dealers in the show if one counted only the dealers who sold "wood"; more if you counted the sellers of pottery, copper and silver. Most were located along the same aisle.

Custer, from past experience, predicted that one dealer would boast that he had sold out to the walls. At the other extreme, another would report no sales and an intention to quit the business. The rest, like him, would comment on a "soft" show.

Ralph Costa saw Custer approach his booth and said, predictably, "How's the show going?"

"Well, I've sold a few things, but not enough to cover the rent."

"What about that gorgeous Gus bow-arm? If you weren't asking fifteen thousand firm I'd buy it for my own collection."

Costa was referring to a spectacular early oak chair with bow-shaped arms, in original mint condition and including the original leather seat. In fact, it was even slightly larger than the catalogued illustration, which suggested that it had been built to order. Custer had acquired it through a complicated arrangement with his Adirondack picker, Judd Banks. Judd had sole access to a magnificent "Camp" that was alleged to have the largest remaining cache of undiscovered Gustav Stickley furniture in the country. Even more enticing was Judd's report that this chair was not even close to being the "pick of the litter."

The Camp or Lodge, he'd said, had over fifty pieces of original, rare (many one-of-a-kind) items of furniture, as well as wonderful lighting, rugs, copper, photographs and books.

Judd Banks had been employed as handyman by the owner for almost twenty-five years. He was one of the few people who had *entré* into the huge house. The owner was Walter Newington, an elderly recluse in failing health. He was the sole surviving heir of the original builder, who had made his fortune in the early 20th century in the railroad freight business.

Purportedly, Newington, a bachelor, had not left the property in forty years, except for medical emergencies that had occurred only in recent years. He had no friends and lived off the income of a very large portfolio of bonds and securities that a local Lake Placid bank managed for him.

Judd Banks' continuing access to the house derived from the old man's affection for the handyman's twelve-year-old son, Todd. Newington insisted that Todd accompany his father whenever possible. The boy suffered from a congenital heart problem that he was not outgrowing and that would require surgery within the next year. Newington helped financially by overpaying for Judd's often inept house repairs; nevertheless, Banks had the good grace to be embarrassed by the barely disguised largesse.

One day, Banks suggested a possible source of more independent funds. Newington objected at first to selling the bow-arm, but one look at the ashen-faced, sickly youth changed his mind. Anticipating the picker's venality, he said that this sale would be the only exception to his policy of not selling anything out of the house. Furthermore, Newington insisted on one condition—he demanded ten thousand dollars cash, with no written record of the sale. The money was to be delivered directly to him by the dealer who would sell the piece for Judd and at that time Banks would receive his commission. This arrangement made it clear to Judd that the old man did not trust him, but he secretly hoped that Newington's love for the child would result in his giving up all of the proceeds as a generous gift to be applied towards Todd's future medical expenses.

Banks later related this background to Custer, leaving out some of the details, including Newington's insistence that this was the only item he would sell. In the scheming scenario, Jim Custer would be tempted to offer Judd an additional up-front commission in hopes of gaining access to the treasure trove of material in the camp.

Costa and Jim's conversation was interrupted by Jane Wilkes, who had a booth a little further down the aisle. "Don't stare, Jim, but you've got a live one in your booth."

Jim turned slowly and could see the back of a man leaning over and carefully examining the bow-arm chair.

Wilkes continued, "That's George Lawson, the famous horror story writer. He hasn't done anything lately, but he *has* written a dozen or so novels. Half of them were made into movies. The last one, a few years ago, called *The Vortex*, was a real blockbuster."

Custer was impressed. "Sure, I've read his stuff and seen some of his pictures. I hear he gets at least a three-million-dollar advance on each book!"

"And that doesn't include pre-selling the movie rights," Jane interrupted, "or doing the screenplay, or points on the picture's gross. He just sailed past my booth. I've heard he's got a great early twentieth-century collection in his New York digs, but I wasn't aware he was particularly focused on Arts and Crafts."

"That's true—I've been told he practically bought out a few booths at Modernism at the downtown Armory a couple of years ago," remarked Costa.

Jim started back toward his booth. "Thanks for the information. I wouldn't have recognized him, even from the front."

In the few moments it took him to return to his booth, Custer debated whether Lawson was the type of celebrity who liked to be recognized. Deciding quickly that he was, he said, "Hello, Mr. Lawson, I'm Jim Custer—it's a pleasure to meet you."

The successful writer could be best described as "New York Hipster"—fiftyish, average height, with dark curly hair and mustache and wearing a denim work shirt, pressed jeans and hiking boots. Lawson turned from perusing the chair and offered his hand. "Beautiful chair you have here. I know it's rare and all original."

Using his new-found information, Jim replied, "Yes, you're right, it is. I've been told you are an expert in 20th-century design."

"Well, thanks for the compliment. I'm hardly an authority, especially when it comes to Arts and Crafts, but I do read a lot and keep up on the sales, shows and auctions." Lawson glanced again at the chair. "This chair is really a prize! Where did it come from? Is there any more furniture of this quality available?"

"Well, Mr. Lawson, it's a long and complicated story; however, the short answer to your question is that the chair came out of an Adirondack Camp and I'm not sure what else—if anything—is available."

Lawson didn't wait for any further explanation. "I'll take this at your listed price on a couple of conditions. First, that you deliver it to my loft after the show closes today; second, that you agree to stay and have dinner with me and promise to discuss the more complicated version of the story, especially with regard to the Adirondack Camp."

He paused for a moment, looked back down the aisle and added in a soft voice, "One more thing—obviously, some of your colleagues have recognized me and will assume that I purchased the chair. That's okay, but I want anything else that should transpire between us to remain confidential. Is that agreed?"

He handed Jim a card with his address and wrote a check for fifteen thousand dollars, made out to Custer's Last Stand.

"Of course," replied Custer enthusiastically.

Jim happily hung a red "Sold" sign on the chair and spent the remaining hour of the session hosting the curious dealers, all of whom predictably asked the same questions: "How much?" "What else is in his collection?" and "What other stuff is he looking for?" Jim answered truthfully that the price was fifteen thousand and he didn't know the answers to the other questions. He thought it best to keep his dinner date a secret.

At six-thirty, Custer's van was on its way to Lawson's apartment, a short, ten-minute drive south through Greenwich Village, Soho and into Tribeca. He was lucky to find a parking spot directly in front of the writer's nineteenth-century converted loft building on Duane Square. Lawson had instructed him to ring and he would come down and assist him with the chair.

"Hi, Mr. Lawson," Jim said as the writer opened the door.

"Jim, please call me George. I hope we will become friends."

The chair fit easily into the large commercial elevator that stopped at the top floor. Although Jim was expecting to see a beautiful loft, he was overwhelmed by the size and scale of the area that appeared when the elevator door opened directly into the space, which occupied the entire floor. The multi-level design was accommodated by seventeen-foot ceilings.

Jim estimated the space at 6,000 square feet on the main level.

Through the huge arched windows on four sides, the furthest window was more than a hundred feet away. He could see the gap where the twin towers of the World Trade Center had been and the silhouette of the new building, as well as the lights of the Verrazano Bridge twinkling in the gathering dusk. There were original columns throughout. The room was painted white with contrasting pastel accent panels on the walls that divided the space into functional areas. Jim spotted paintings by Mondrian, de Chirico and Matisse. A large Calder mobile hung near the entrance over a Ruhlmann Macassar server. On it were displayed sculptures by Archipenko and Brancusi. Further inside the loft he could see a large poster by Paul Colin overlooking a grouping of Aalto bentwood chairs. The effect was that of entering a museum containing the finest examples of 20th-century art and design.

"George, I'm overwhelmed, to put it mildly. This is breathtaking!" Jim literally gulped as he said this.

"I'll give you a quick tour. I hope you'll return again for a more leisurely viewing, but I must apologize, I didn't expect to see you tonight. I have a standing appointment so we'll be served a light dinner in a few minutes. We can discuss our business while eating."

The quick tour revealed an equally spectacular view of the midtown skyline, including the Empire State Building bathed in the last shimmers of the setting sun. As they proceeded through the impressive open space, the dealer was impressed by examples of exquisite furniture by Mackintosh, Breuer, Mies van Der Rohe and Josef Hoffmann. There was lighting by Tiffany and Handel casting shadows over a beautiful Art Deco rug designed by Delaunay.

Turning a corner, Jim was struck by large oil paintings by Dali and Braque, which appeared much at home with a more modern Deco revival table signed by Michael Graves. On the way to the dining area, they passed an oil painting, either a Kandinsky or a

Klee—Jim wasn't sure and decided not to reveal his ignorance by asking. The only element of Arts and Crafts design in the entire space was a unique Harvey Ellis-designed secretary in an alcove, next to which the two men placed the bow-arm chair.

Sitting at the previously set Wright dining table, Jim said, "I'm trying to imagine you writing about ghosts and terror and wondering where in the loft you work at that."

George laughed and replied, "Actually, I do some imagery and plotting here, but almost all my writing is done in California at my West Coast home in Pacific Palisades. Although New York is still the publishing capital, I can email all my stuff back here. Occasionally I have to be available for rewrites or screenplay conferences."

He stopped for a moment then added apologetically, "You may know that lately I've had a bit of writer's block and I'm troubled by this dry spell. Almost all artists and writers go through phases, including some whose work you see represented in this loft."

Their conversation was interrupted by a uniformed woman, who served the first course of cold gazpacho in a colorful Clarice Cliff bowl. When Jim picked up his soup spoon, he recognized it as a rare hammered silver 14th-century pattern produced by Shreve & Company of San Francisco in the early 20th century.

Over glasses of chilled Premier Cru Chablis, Lawson offered a toast. "May our friendship be mutually profitable."

Jim clinked in approval. "Candidly, I'm surprised you invited me here, because your décor is certainly not Arts and Crafts. Do you have a collection in California?"

"Like some famous stars and directors? No, I don't." Lawson laughed. "I'm a purist and believe that Stickley belongs in up-state New York near where it was made, in a circa-1900 Adirondack Lodge. Most of the great things you see here fit style-wise in an urban space with a view of a great modern city in the early 21st century."

The two men continued their conversation as the main course of hot poached salmon with dill sauce over wild rice arrived. An arugula salad with warm sourdough rolls accompanied the fish.

"Jim, I want to get to the point quickly because, as I've indicated, I'm short on time. I have very happy memories of going to summer camp in the Adirondack Mountains as a boy more than forty years ago. Although I've never been back as an adult, I'm determined to buy a large lodge there and I would decorate it with the furniture of Gustav Stickley and his contemporaries. I've furnished this loft with appropriate 20th-century artists and designers. Since you are from Saratoga Springs, I thought perhaps you could advise me."

"Well, yes, I do travel there frequently. I've never actually seen the lodge at Crescent Lake where the bow-arm originates, but I'm sure there are always a few properties for sale at any given time."

Lawson cut him off sharply. "Did you say Crescent Lake?"

"Yes," replied Custer. "The camp or lodge is at the north end. Do you know the lake?"

"I can't believe the coincidence!" Lawson exclaimed. "My summer camp was called 'Crescent Lake Mountain Camp.' I'm sure we're talking about the same place!"

He paused for a moment, took a long drink of wine, and said, "Look, Jim, I'll be very up front. I want you to tell me all you know about the owner of the property, the camp itself and, of course, the furniture that's in it. I'm going to cancel my previous plans for the evening."

By the time Jim had related all he knew, including his financial arrangement with the picker, coffee, sherbet and cookies were served.

"Jim, I'm really excited," Lawson said. "It's no secret that I'm a very rich man. I want to see that property and buy it if it suits me. It wouldn't be a big deal for me financially. Some of the paintings you've seen here are undoubtedly worth more than even a fabulous lodge.

I'm going to ask you to help me in a rather unorthodox way."

"Wait a minute, George. I'm happy to assist you, but I don't think Walter Newington will sell even if he's dying."

At Jim's acceptance of an after-dinner Remy Martin, George picked up a Baccarat decanter from the ebony-and-rosewood bar and poured large portions into two huge snifters.

"Here's the plan: you and I drive up there with the ten thousand bucks in cash. You explain to Newington that your vision is failing and I've come along as your driver. We will get a view inside-and-out of the house and the grounds. You can do a quick inventory of the furniture while we're inside."

Shocked by Lawson's impetuousness, Jim asked, "You mean, if you like what you see you'll simply make him an offer?"

"No, not exactly," replied Lawson. "If *we* like what *we* see, *you* are going to tell him you want to buy the property using a recent inheritance. He is aware that you are a dealer from up-state who knows the Adirondacks and who has spent his adult life involved with the furniture. In any case, he's a lot more likely to sell it to you at a realistic price than to one of America's richest fiction writers." George laughed as he thought about his self-description.

Custer asked for a refill and while George poured he answered, "Okay, I agree in principle, but how would we work out the finances?"

George replied with barely a pause, "That's just boilerplate for my bankers, lawyers and accountants. I'll front the money—all cash—and for your advice and appraisal of the property I'll give you back ten percent of the purchase price at closing as a finder's fee. We'll wait a month or so and you will sell the property to me. My people will minimize your tax consequences and I will reimburse you anything you owe the Government. Is that acceptable?"

Jim stared at Lawson, at a loss for any words except, "Yes." He sensed the meeting was over when the writer stood up.

"I'll call you in Saratoga Springs next week," said his host. "In the meantime, you can set up a date to see Newington. At best, I'm going to own the finest surviving camp in the Adirondacks and at worst, we'll get to see the leaf-change at the height of the season."

While driving back to his hotel, Jim contemplated his situation. After eight years on the antique show circuit, he was barely making a living. If it weren't for his wife's nursing job, with benefits, he would probably have given up. This could be the breakthrough of his career! From his hotel room, he called home.

"Pat, it's me."

"How's the show going?"

"Great! Is Allison okay? How's your mom?"

After getting the domestic details sorted out, Jim finally blurted, "Look, Pat, something unusual and wonderful has just happened, so sit and listen—this may take a while."

Ten minutes later, Jim stopped talking. Pat sounded just as excited as he was. "Unbelievable! That commission could be two hundred thousand or more dollars if the deal goes through—plus a great new customer."

"That's right," said Jim excitedly. "I'll see you late tomorrow night—don't spend the money yet, though."

He was about to hang up when Pat asked, "Is there a Mrs. Lawson?"

Jim chuckled. "I didn't ask—are you interested?"

Pat just laughed and said goodbye.

Ten days later, Lawson picked Jim up in Saratoga Springs. As they drove up the Northway, they worked on additional details of their plan. Both would ask to use the bathroom at the Lodge as soon as they arrived. The success of this plan rested on the fact that typically, even in a large camp, there would be only two bathrooms, one upstairs and one on the main floor.

About two hours later they reached Lake Placid, a resort village filled with tourists enjoying the fall foliage. They continued westward for about eight miles to Saranac Lake, almost missing the poorly marked right turnoff to the north that Judd Banks had described. Another fifteen minutes of slow uphill driving brought them to the southern end of Crescent Lake. The late afternoon light reflected from the brilliantly colored autumn leaves growing along the steep ridges on the lakeside onto the deep, blue-gray water.

"Stop here," said Lawson suddenly.

Jim thought he wanted to focus on the view, but instead George was peering intently at some long-ago abandoned cabins falling down on the lake shore. "That's my old camp—49 years later. What a strange feeling!"

"Do you want to get out and look around?" asked Jim.

"No!" replied Lawson sharply. "Let's get there. According to the map, the lake is about six miles long. We should reach the other end in ten minutes or so."

Custer glanced at Lawson and noticed that his mood had suddenly darkened. "Is something wrong? Are you nervous about confronting Newington?"

"No, but you are perceptive. I'm remembering something terrible that happened during my last time here many years ago, but I don't want to get into that now."

The ride along the narrow winding road that skirted the lake was spectacular. There were sparkling lake views alternating with thick bowers of trees; suddenly, the lodge came into view. To the left of the entrance gate they could see a beautiful curve of sandy beach, with a vintage mahogany Chris Craft bobbing near a boathouse at the far end. A stand of mature white pines partially obscured the main building; however, its twin peaked roofs and upper windows reflected the afternoon sun. The rough log walls were stained a pale golden shade, which contrasted dramatically with the dark brown window frames and the maroon roof shingles. The smell of pine and fruit wood smoke coming from the chimney was marvelous.

They drove through the gate onto a stone gravel courtyard and noticed what was undoubtedly Judd Banks' pickup truck parked a respectable distance from the main entrance. The two men pulled their vehicle in next to the truck and walked to the house. Judd was waiting at the open door, probably having been alerted to their arrival by the sound of tires on the loose gravel.

"Howdy!" was the greeting from the middle-aged rural handyman, a scruffy figure out of Central Casting, complete with unkempt beard and workman's bib overalls.

Custer peered past the bulky figure and observed the huge chimney fifty feet away. It was massive, reaching thirty-five feet to the peaked roof line. On either side of the entrance were mirror-image, 60-foot-long wings with screened porches at each end. The windows would be replaced with insulated windows in the winter, but in the warmer months they allowed for black fly- and mosquito-free breezy comfort.

Period furniture was everywhere, all obviously Gustav Stickley by design, proportion, oak structure and original leather finish with tacks. This was not furniture that had ever appeared in a catalogue—it was custom-made for the space. There were two settles of monumental proportions, case pieces with straps and hardware, the copper patinated to the color of ripe chestnuts. A banquet table that could easily seat thirty people was the central focus of the room with three massive copper fixtures hanging over it. The geometric-patterned rugs remained brightly colored considering their age. The furniture must have been waxed regularly and the leather kept supple by careful attention, probably by Judd Banks.

Jim was amazed to find large framed photographs of Gustav Stickley supervising construction of the lodge, including several in which he was shown helping to install the built-in bookcases near the hearth. On the porches, they found wicker furniture in excellent condition.

The interior walls were made from original natural logs. Around the fireplace, the bookshelves were filled with rows of volumes in custom hand-tooled bindings. Pottery pieces in groups of two and three were spread tastefully on side tables and pedestals and included work by Rookwood, Van Briggle and Grueby. Floor and table lamps were mainly from the Gustav Stickley catalogue, with a sprinkling of lamps with Tiffany shades on Grueby pottery bases. Jim's view was that this Adirondack camp was a monument to Gustav's true vision and genius and far beyond the examples that were displayed at Craftsman Farms.

George whispered, "I want it, whatever the price."

As Jim was wondering how he could get upstairs, they came upon the old, white-haired man and Judd sitting in what must have been a smoking room. "Hi, Mr. Newington, I'm Jim Custer."

The elderly man did not respond or stir. An old pipe was balanced awkwardly on one side of his mouth, as if he had palsy or permanent damage from a stroke. Spittle oozed out of that side and he made no attempt to dry it.

"Mr. Newington is having a bad day," murmured Judd, who seemed to feel obligated to speak for him.

Custer responded, "I don't see well enough to drive at night, so Lawson here was kind enough to help me out."

Newington squinted at Lawson for a long moment and said, "Ever been up this way?"

"Almost fifty years ago, sir. I was a camper down at the south end of the lake. I haven't been back till today. When we drove by the old campsite, I was reminded of a terrible tragedy that occurred at the end of the last summer that I was here, about 1960."

The old man nodded for him to continue.

"At the end of August, just before the camp closed, I was one of six boys, all ten years old, who were qualifying for canoeing badges by doing a solo trip around the lake. We started out at intervals late in the afternoon of a hot day, all wearing life preservers, with counselors accompanying us in separate canoes.

"A cold front unexpectedly came through. There was a severe summer squall. Those steep ridges funneled the wind right at us. I'll never forget how high the waves got and the spray made the visibility zero. All the canoes capsized and in the confusion I lost my life preserver and was holding on to the canoe for dear life. My closest friend from home, Jack Wells, an only child, ended up next to me and told me to hang on and he would swim to shore for help. Tragically, as it turned out, we were all rescued except Jack, who was never found.

"The State Police dragged the lake and scores of volunteers searched the woods for weeks, but no trace of him was ever discovered. I assumed that he was buried in the mud at the bottom of the lake or that he was lost in the forest and his remains consumed by animals."

He continued, "Naturally, my parents never allowed me to return to the camp or any other camp for that matter."

George paused for a moment to gather his thoughts and then added, "Fifty years is a long time, but, truthfully, I think of the beauty of this place far more often than I do of that tragic event."

Newington stared with watery eyes at Lawson before saying, "You're a pretty good storyteller for a man who ain't been around these parts since you were a kid." He continued to gaze at George, his flaccid features seeming to harden in anger. "What did you say your name was?"

"George Lawson, sir."

"Well, I remember that summer too, Lawson. Damn State Troopers poking around here asking a ton of questions and tramping through my property. Took my gardener near a month to clean up after them."

There was a long silence before Lawson remembered to ask to use the bathroom. Judd pointed in the direction of the kitchen. Jim announced that he also urgently needed to use the bathroom; fortunately for their plan, Banks motioned towards the stairs leading to the second floor. Jim quickly checked the six upstairs rooms and found that the chests, beds and night tables had a special quality of design and finish that he had never seen before. He had always felt that the bedroom furniture of Gustav was inferior to his more celebrated living and dining room pieces, but now he would have to re-think that assessment. He waited at the top of the stairs until he saw the bathroom door open below. Then he rushed downstairs and confronted Lawson.

"It's a museum upstairs! I figure the furniture plus all the other stuff is worth at least $2.5 million. The main lodge is pristine and, of course, there are guest cottages, a boathouse and other buildings on the estate. Add to that 140 acres and 800 feet of lakefront and I'd say fair value up here would be at least four million. So let's offer two million."

When they arrived back in the study or smoking room, Newington was coughing and looking annoyed. "Do you have the ten thousand?" Judd asked expectantly. Custer pulled out an envelope and began to count out hundred-dollar bills.

Newington picked up on Judd's impatience and mumbled, "Quiet, Banks! You and I will take care of business as soon as these men leave," he said, giving special emphasis to "leave." He added in a raspy voice, "Now, gentlemen, as you can plainly see, I'm a sick and tired old man, so if you don't mind…"

Jim quickly interrupted him. "Sir, there's something else. I've recently come into an inheritance. Now that I've seen this wonderful camp, I wonder if you might consider selling it to me."

He stopped speaking for a moment and, hearing no reaction, continued, "I'm a man who is very familiar with these furnishings. As you may know, I grew up in Saratoga Springs and have spent a lot of time in the Adirondacks. I'm a person who would preserve what you have created and keep it intact for future generations."

Newington looked quizzically at the dealer and said, "You've certainly done a lot of running around trying to sell one chair for a few thousand bucks profit considering you have a rich relative or friend ready to leave you enough to buy the whole store."

Custer wasn't sure how to respond to the old man's acute observation so he decided to ignore it. In the meantime, Newington caught his breath and wiped his drooling mouth with the dirty cuff of his shirt. For the moment he seemed to ignore Custer's proposition.

Pointing vaguely down the hall, he said, "You probably noticed the framed photos of Gustav that were taken here years ago. Well, my father told me that Stickley actually lived up here while the place was being constructed. I also have specifications for the custom furniture he built for my dad. They stayed friends, even after Gus retired."

He coughed painfully and continued, "A year ago I'd have thrown you out of here if you dared suggest that I sell you even a single *Craftsman* magazine. But a lot of bad things have happened to me in the past few months. The doc tells me my mouth cancer has spread from my tongue and neck down into my bones. Nobody needs to tell me I don't have long. I have only one relative: a rich great-nephew who lives somewhere in England. I get a Christmas card from him every five years if he can find a stamp. When I die, he'll probably contest my will and if he wins he'll dump all this stuff in a yard sale."

As he spoke, he waved a bony hand in the direction of the furniture. Then he mumbled on, "I guess after a big court fight some developer will knock everything down and put up some junky condos around the lake. They'll fill up with disgusting people from the city. Yes, I just might sell to you, move to the village—where I can be closer to the doctor, the hospital and the cemetery."

No one spoke for almost a minute and then Custer said, "Well, Mr. Newington, what might be your asking price?"

The old man yelled angrily in a surprisingly strong voice, "Don't give me that crap! My father was a great business man and he always said—'Never give a price, let them make you an offer.' And listen, don't low-ball me and try to bargain. Give me a serious offer and I'll give you my answer. I'll tell you right now—if you come up with some insulting number, I'll have Judd just plain throw you out of here!"

Everyone looked at Custer. "Mr. Newington thanks for being so direct. I'm prepared to make a generous offer that would include everything within the boundaries of your property except, of course, your personal effects." He paused and then said, "Two million dollars."

Newington coughed nervously and answered, "My daddy taught me something else—whatever offer somebody makes, they are prepared to pay more. I know you figured I would ask for more, probably two point five, but you're wrong. I want three million, plus another hundred thousand for the books, pictures and memorabilia. You can take it at that price or leave now, I ain't bargaining with you!"

Jim glanced surreptitiously at Lawson who nodded, almost imperceptibly. "Okay, Mr. Newington, we have a deal!" and he reached over to shake the old man's cold and bony hand.

Newington barely acknowledged the gesture and in a calm voice said, "Now that you've left me with nothing but my dirty laundry, you should know that my estate is going to the County Hospital and

I'm going to direct that the proceeds from this sale go toward building a new children's wing. One other thing, Custer: this is a cash deal so get it done quick. I'm not going to last much longer and I don't want any goddamn bank appraisers poking around this property."

Newington motioned to Judd to escort the two men out. They turned to leave, understanding his gesture.

"Don't call here, Custer. Just leave your address and phone number and my lawyer will set up the details for the contract and closing." His voice softened. "I don't expect to see you again. My attorney will have full power. Please take care of this place—it has been my whole life."

Jim nodded. "Of course, Mr. Newington, you can depend on me."

As it turned out, the old man was right. When the closing occurred about a month later, he was in a coma in the hospital. A few days later, he died. Only a small announcement in the Lake Placid weekly newspaper noted his passing.

Lawson and Custer conversed frequently over the phone. George thought it best to wait at least another month before the property was transferred to him. Jim didn't care—he already had his $300,000. The week before Thanksgiving, George called Saratoga Springs and asked if he could borrow the lodge. Jim laughed and answered, "Well, maybe just this one time."

The Friday after Thanksgiving, George left the city at seven in the morning and reached the camp just before one. Jim had arranged for Judd to leave the gate and door open, but not to be present over the weekend. On Sunday night, he was to return and secure the property.

It was a clear, crisp day in the North Country and George was glad he had packed a picnic lunch. He sat at a table near the beach. Behind him, the property quickly climbed beyond the rear of the main lodge to a ridge below the high hills. The lake's surface was ruffled by the wind and the stragglers of geese who had not yet flown south were honking at the lake's edge. Toward the southeast, the higher peaks were already snow-covered. Lawson believed that there were few locations in the world that would suit him so well—how fortunate he was to own this! The penetrating cold finally drove him into the house.

He took a slow tour of the lodge, savoring all of it. An Eastwood chair near the fireplace was particularly inviting and he collapsed happily into its huge dimensions. He glanced up at the books that Newington had left, per their agreement. George noticed a half-full bottle of Scotch that had not been written into the deal and decided to take advantage of this unexpected bonus. As he was lifting the bottle and preparing to pick up a suede-bound Roycroft book to browse, he noticed a modern volume in a red dust jacket that, even in the poor light and at a distance, looked familiar. As soon as he pulled it off the shelf, he recognized that it was one of his more recent novels, because his portrait on the back cover still resembled him. The book had been a tremendous commercial success—and was now a successful movie, entitled *The Entrapment*.

George's first reaction was to smile and salute Newington's good taste. He was about to replace it next to the Roycroft books when a bunch of faded photographs that had been placed in that book fell onto the floor. Maybe more Gustav photos, he thought hopefully. He replaced the book, gathered the dozen or so photographs and the Scotch, and returned to the chair. As he flipped through the dozen photos quickly, he gasped with apprehension, barely able to look more closely.

The photos clearly showed his childhood friend Jack Wells, who had disappeared from the camp, in various grisly poses. Some showed his hands tied behind his back, mouth gagged; others were of his back with visible deep red welts. There were pictures of a prison-like room and, worst of all, of a gravesite certain to be somewhere on the property, because he could glimpse the main camp gate in the background. Lawson shuddered as he considered that Jack might not be the only victim buried on the grounds.

Lawson threw the book in his overnight bag, with the pictures inside it, ran out of the house and threw up just outside the door. He didn't bother closing the door, but jumped into his car and accelerated quickly, the loose gravel banging loudly against the undercarriage of his Mercedes. The noise jolted him out of his state of shock as he swung the car into a hard right turn down the lake road.

A real life horror story! Only he knew the facts. Jack Wells' parents had died years ago and there were no siblings or close relatives. It had happened half a century ago. Newington was dead—so there was no point in reporting it to the police. Nothing would be gained by making the story public now.

By the time George reached the south end of the lake, he felt calmer. He stopped the car at the abandoned summer camp and realized that he could never again go to either end of Crescent Lake. Then another revelation hit him.

Newington had recognized him and knew all along who was the real buyer! The pictures in the book had been planted by that sick, evil man, whose revenge from beyond the grave was to have him live in a murderer's house in which his best friend had been tortured and died!

George half smiled. There would be one more twist Newington's warped mind had not contemplated. What was done was done, but here were the ingredients for a blockbuster novel and movie. He would call his agent in the morning. He knew the advance would more than cover the cost of the house and his earnings would probably be fifteen million from the movie's distribution. More importantly, he would never live at that Adirondack Camp.

There was the matter of disposing of the property—but that

wouldn't be a problem. Technically, he didn't even own it. He would just let Jim keep the title in his name.

Jim Custer would never know the true story—after all, Lawson had the only real evidence and he could destroy it. Besides, why question a three-million-dollar gift? The collection would stay intact. It was generous and serendipitous, but it was through Custer that he had gotten out of his long, creative dry spell. This was really not a gift, it was a good investment. He gagged suddenly as he thought of the county hospital's new children's wing.

Lawson picked up his cellular phone and was happy when Jim answered on the third ring. "Jim, listen carefully. I'm not going to buy the camp."

"What's wrong?" came the startled reply. "Is there something wrong with the camp or the furniture?"

"No! Please don't interrupt me. It's strictly personal. That means I'm not going to talk about it. I'm rich and I can afford to change my mind. You get to keep the property on a few conditions: one, send back the original agreement that spelled out the legal transfer to me; two, never, never mention our deal to anyone and do not try to contact me. Incidentally, don't concern yourself about Judd Banks. He doesn't know who I really am. Finally, please keep the camp and furniture intact. I'll keep the bow-arm as a souvenir. You can say for public consumption that you bought the camp with an unexpected inheritance. Do you agree to these conditions?"

Jim managed, in a shaking voice, to say, "Yes, but how about the $300,000 commission that I have already deposited and partially spent?"

"Keep that; invest it so you can maintain the property and pay real estate taxes. My lawyer will call you in the morning to arrange details. Don't ever call me again!" Lawson hung up without waiting for a reply.

Jim called to Pat who was in the kitchen cleaning up after Thanksgiving. He quickly related their good fortune and said, "I guess he's crazy or at least crazy rich. We'll never know the true story."

Pat hugged him as he spun her around with joy. Then she stepped back and joked, "Maybe he saw a ghost—he probably believes the stuff he writes!"

A few minutes later, Lawson reached the turn onto the main road back to Lake Placid, pleased that he had given his chauffeur the weekend off. He kept both hands on the wheel to control the big Mercedes through the sharp turn and, when the car straightened out, reached with his right hand and pulled out his miniature tape recorder.

He held it close to his mouth and began to speak: "It was the First Annual Gala Garden Antiques and Collectible Show and the crowd was thinning out at Madison Square Garden…"

TWENTY

Whatever Happened to J.L. Spratling?

A stroke of genius! That was the consensus of the public relations community. Bill Van Edy of Picken Press had booked the famous Oak Room at the fabled Algonquin Hotel for the press conference. The cachet of the Algonquin has been unabated in the literary community since the "Round Table" gatherings of the twenties and thirties.

The purpose of the press conference was to announce the publication of the new novel by J.L. Spratling. One December morning, after tough negotiations with the event manager, he'd rented the cabaret space just off the hotel lobby for two hours on a Tuesday afternoon for $14,000. That price included all room arrangements, moving the piano to the side, an open beer-and-wine bar for the first hour—but not the world-famous Algonquin lobby cat.

The ghosts of H.L. Mencken and Dorothy Parker seemed to hover and shimmer over the crowd gathered to celebrate the first publication by J.L. Spratling in twenty-five years. Spratling's last book, *Low Key*, had been an enormous success, as was the subsequent Hollywood production by the same name, winning the Academy Award for Best Picture of 1988. During the seventies and eighties, J.L. Spratling was known as "the other Stephen King". He had published five hugely successful novels, two of which were adapted for the movies, including *Low Key*. Then J.L. Spratling had seemed to vanish into thin air as mysteriously as a character in one of his genre ghost novels. It was a saga of reclusiveness following success in the manner of J.D. Salinger. Reported rumors had him living in seclusion, possibly in Mexico, Norway, the U.K., Idaho or Canada. Had he achieved the ultimate seclusion—death? That was never confirmed.

Van Edy sent invitations to the publishing, media and showbiz giants. Anyone who could fit into the Cabaret Room or the adjacent lobby would be welcome. About a half-hour into the press conference, a seventyish, tall, erect man strode confidently into the room from the service entrance of the kitchen. Thick, straight, iron-gray hair fell over his deeply furrowed forehead, stopping just short of his heavily lidded eyes of indeterminate color. J.L. was tieless and jacketless, with an open-collared, blue oxford shirt tucked neatly into tailored blue denim jeans. His only accessory was a pair of half-moon reading glasses dangling from a woven string around his neck. He carried no briefcase or papers and looked neither to right nor left as he stepped up to the lectern, flanked on one side by publicist Van Edy and on the other by Janet Cohen, his editor at Picken Press. The generally younger journalistic audience gave a sprinkling of light applause, unsure of the identity of the recent arrival.

"Let me start by saying thank you to all of you for remembering me and coming here today."

There were murmurs throughout the crowd and a voice at the back rang out, "Welcome back, J.L.!"

"I'll only make a few remarks and I won't be taking any questions."

The hum in the crowd muted and then totally quieted.

"*Dark River* was conceived and largely completed twenty-five years ago. This was pre-computer days and if any of you are old enough to remember that time in the publishing business..." Spratling paused for the laughter to subside. "Writers and editors in those days actually mailed chapters, ideas and manuscripts back and forth for review and suggestions. A 500-page book involves lots of editing and rewrites. Today it can be done in minutes through the Internet. My very capable and gifted late editor Karen Chase and I would have exchanged packages at least twenty times over a two-year period! Each new version would have annotations, red pencil deletions and comments all over the manuscript."

Spratling continued, "All that time I was living in a cabin along the Mira River in Cape Breton, Nova Scotia, Canada, with no need or desire for a telephone. During these past twenty-five years, I have experienced a very long drought of writing creativity often referred to with dread as writer's block."

When the author paused, many hands in the crowd were raised. "Again, I remind you that I will not be answering questions today; however, I do have more to say."

Spratling pointed toward the rear of the room. "I'd like to acknowledge my dear friend, Dr. Howard Harris, who is here today and it is through his efforts that a late draft of this novel was uncovered and ultimately re-worked and published as *Dark River.*"

The old man, Van Edy at his side, stepped away from the podium and disappeared through the door to the kitchen.

Dr. Howard Harris smiled, finished the last of his wine, placed his glass on a tray and ignoring the questioning looks around him headed through the lobby into the fading December light of West 44th Street. He was reminded as he strolled of the famous Paul Harvey line: "...and now for the rest of the story..." He hoped that when the rest of the story was told in the book he was working on, it would make an even bigger splash than *Dark River*...

Two years earlier and exactly thirty blocks south of the Algonquin, also on a Tuesday, Sylvia Klaff bounded through the entrance of the McBurney Y on Fourteenth Street. An unattractive and overweight gym rat, she kept rigidly to her daily, early morning exercise routine. After scanning her ID card at the front desk, she headed downstairs to the women's locker room and made her daily stop at the single half-bookcase, which was the Y's unofficial and casual lending library. However, Sylvia was not a reader; she would peruse the new stack of books, attempting to determine which of the soft and hard covers might have some retail value. She "borrowed" them with no intention of returning or exchanging them.

The nearby Strand Bookstore on Broadway and Twelfth Street is the largest in the world. Available is everything in print, fiction and nonfiction, and the store also features a famous rare books department. Their buyer purchases used hard and soft cover books of all types. Sylvia was often able to cover her monthly dues at the Y with the books "borrowed" from the lending library. Only a few months before, she had picked up a first edition of *Schindler's List* with dust jacket, which had netted her $225. This Tuesday morning there were lean pickings, with only about six dog-eared paperback Harlequin romance novels that Sylvia knew had no re-sale value.

As she was about to turn away, she spotted an oversized, cardboard-bound, thick volume, on the cover of which were the words "working title," handwritten beneath "The River" and the initials, "J.L." She picked up the heavy package and rapidly leafed through some of the 400-plus typed pages. Many pages contained red pencil markings with additional handwritten comments on the reverse side.

To her thinking, this was either an abandoned pathetic attempt at a first novel or a draft for a doctoral thesis. Well, spin class was starting soon, so if it was still there later she would take it to the buyer at the Strand in hopes it might have some value.

A week later Sylvia, pulling a roller bag filled with her Y acquisitions, stopped by the Strand. Most days the Strand is jammed with New Yorkers and worldwide tourists, all of whom share a love for the miles of books. Sylvia found the book buyer sitting on a high stool just inside the entrance. She pulled out her collection, which he quickly and professionally examined, noting the titles and condition. He extracted the two books in which he had an interest, deftly sliding the rest back to her. "I can give you eight dollars for the two John Updike short story collections."

Sylvia nodded her approval and reached into her roller bag. Awkwardly, she handed him the heavy *River* manuscript.

The buyer glanced through the thick volume and pushed the package away. "I have no interest in this either."

"What do you think it is?"

"Judging by the yellowing of the pages, I would guess that it is someone's long-ago attempt at writing fiction." The buyer glanced beyond Sylvia and found a line beginning to form. He hurriedly wrote her a voucher for the eight dollars and said, "You can redeem this at the cashier."

On the way out of the Strand, Sylvia looked around and then dumped the heavy manuscript of *The River* onto the outside dollar-per-book sale table. She slunk away, the roller bag squeaking behind her...

Howard Harris, M.D., had lived in the East Village on Ninth Street near Broadway all through his psychiatric residency at the NYU Medical Center. He developed a regular routine of walking up

Broadway to Union Square, where he would take the Number 6 train to 33rd Street and then walk east to the University Hospital or Bellevue, wherever his rotation was. On cold days, such as this December morning, he favored his red-checked Woolrich hunting jacket. The bulky but tailored coat emphasized a youthful athletic build. He had a full head of longish, straight blond hair and with his pressed chinos he typified his Poconos, Pennsylvania, rural upbringing. His routine took him by the Strand, where he loved to shop for books matching his varied interests. He was particularly attracted by novels dealing with subjects of rage, duplicity and revenge, because they reflected his focus in psychiatry. However, today he was in a hurry to get to Grand Rounds in time to hear a visiting scholar, Sir Alastair Betterich of Oxford University, present "Psychiatric Implications of Genetic Metabolic Disorders."

As Howard rushed by the sidewalk dollar table, he noticed a bulky book that had fallen to the ground below. He stopped to pick it up, noticing the title *The River* and the initials "J.L." After a glance at his watch, he leafed through the bound manuscript, wondering whether this could possibly be a draft of a published J.L. Spratling novel. He made a quick decision and reached into his pocket for four quarters and a dime to cover the tax as he rushed inside to the cashier.

The young woman flipped the book over looking for a price sticker. "Where did you find this?"

"Just outside on the dollar table."

"I don't see a price anywhere," she said. She called across to the buyer in the almost empty store, "Jim, this guy says he found this outside on the dollar table but it's not priced."

Howard was getting anxious that he might be late to rounds but was determined to have the book. He could not afford the chance that it might disappear into the Strand's rare book system, so he pondered how much he'd pay to have it now.

Before he could express his offer of more money, the buyer called out, "Oh, I know that book. Some woman brought it in to sell about twenty minutes ago and I rejected it. She must have used the sale table as a garbage pail!" He laughed. "It really is garbage. He found it—he can have it for nothing!"

Without waiting for further conversation, Howard grabbed the book, stuffed it in his backpack and raced toward the subway with the prize.

Howard Harris had spent almost eight years at the New York University Medical Center, first as a medical student, then an intern and the last three years in the residency program in psychiatry. The field of psychiatry had many years ago shifted emphasis from any type of talking therapy to drug management of psychiatric diseases. The theory was that, with so many drugs available to treat symptoms, the psychological aspects could be muted or made to disappear. Howard's thesis for presentation at the residents' research day had been "The Pharmacologic Management of the Neurologic and Psychological Aspects of Acute Intermittent Porphyria." This rare genetic disease was known to cause severe physical pain, as well as red skin and purple or red urine. Other symptoms included confusion and paranoia. Once appropriately diagnosed, pain is managed with opioids such as morphine and symptoms can be significantly abated with the drug, Hematon.

Dr. Betterich's lecture, well received by over fifty physicians and nurses, covered several genetic diseases including porphyria. At the call for questions, Howard raised his hand. "I'm sure you have seen the movie, *The Madness of King George*."

"Yes, I did and I enjoyed it."

"Well, Dr. Betterich, with the drugs we have today, can we effectively cure our patients diagnosed with acute intermittent porphyria?"

Dr. Betterich laughed. "Yes, we might if properly diagnosed and

I think our current politicians would offer a large reservoir for potential study."

Later that day Howard returned to his East Village home, a remodeled studio apartment on the second floor of a 19th-century townhouse. Even before removing his jacket he perused his bookcases, pulling out his collection of J.L. Spratling novels. The five paperbacks were lined up on the lower shelf and there was no "River" in any of the titles. He decided to put off a more detailed examination to see whether there were similarities with parts of the five novels and reminded himself that J.L. could be the initials of a completely different author. Besides, with his on-call schedule and the planned visit of his girlfriend Jan, a law student at Northwestern in Chicago, he would be tied up until Monday.

The following Monday at two p.m., Howard rushed home and sat at his desk with a pad and the manuscript. He noted the typed manuscript and the two different sets of handwritten notations, quickly establishing them to be comments of author and editor. Based on the subject and writing style, and the fact that the editor addressed the author as J.L., Howard was convinced that he was examining an unpublished J.L. Spratling novel. Besides, "J.L." addressed his comments to "K.C." and the editor at Picken Press who had handled J.L. Spratling's novels exclusively was Karen Chase. He knew she had died ten years previously. For Howard, the most exciting discovery was the full-page comments written on the inside cover in a shaky hand. "K.C., I can't finish this novel. I'm not well. I'm in terrible pain. My skin is angry at me—it has turned red. Everyone is trying to take advantage of me and stealing my sentences. Please don't send this back with any more comments. You are part of the literary conspiracy against me. Leave me alone! Destroy this manuscript! In spite of your duplicity, we did have positive experiences in the past, so I can only wish that after you leave me alone you will be okay."

It was signed "J.L.S." and there was one final comment: "As one last favor to me, please keep my Mira NS address to yourself."

It was almost midnight; Howard was exuberant as he put down the thick, unwieldy manuscript. He slept very little that night. Putting all the available facts together, the writer's block of J.L. Spratling represented symptoms of acute intermittent porphyria as described by Dr. Betterich in his lecture and as Howard had researched for his presentation on the last residents' research day. There were no dates on the manuscript and no mailing envelope, so he had to find out whether Spratling was still alive and if so, where was he?

A Google search over the next hour incorporated the rumored J.L. Spratling locations in Mexico, Canada, Australia and the U.K. Howard determined that "NS" could stand for "nuevo something" and "Mira" certainly sounded Spanish; or "NS" could have something to do with Australia and New South Wales. As he headed to the fridge for a late-night snack, a silly idea popped into his head: NS—could it be related to the smoked salmon from the deli that they advertised as Nova Scotia salmon? That represented a province in Canada, one of the rumored locations of J.L. Spratling.

Back to Google Maps: he quickly located the Mira River outside Sydney on the Island of Cape Breton, part of the province of Nova Scotia. A name search for J.L. Spratling in that area was fruitless.

Three days later, after much searching online and over the phone, Howard located a helpful postal supervisor in Sydney, Nova Scotia, to whom he explained that he was trying to reach his elderly uncle, J.L. Spratling. After a long wait, just when Howard was about to hang up, the supervisor picked up the line. "Yes, I've located the agent who does the twice weekly rural mail delivery to Mira, which is quite remote. He says there is an old man by the name of Jay Sprat who has been there the whole time he has worked that route—twenty-two years."

"Thanks so much! How do I address mail to him?"

"Jay Sprat, Mira, NS, Canada B1K1L3."

"Thanks again!"

After considering the letter-writing ploy, Howard rejected it as likely to be unproductive. A letter from an unknown person—even if Jay Sprat turned out to be J.L. Spratling—would be resented and ignored by a man with paranoid ideation. No doubt the best course was an uninvited visit and a direct meeting.

About a month later, Howard flew to Halifax, changed planes and landed in Sydney, a city on the northeast coast of Cape Breton Island across the water from Newfoundland. Directions provided at the Avis counter took him on a thirty-minute drive to the sparsely populated Mira River Valley. The gently rolling hills and quiet beauty of the evergreens were interspersed with views of the winding, dark Mira River as it snaked toward the Atlantic.

A solitary biker gave him directions to the little convenience store, Burke's, mentioned by the Avis agent. When he announced that he was looking for Jay Sprat, the fortyish, dimpled, plump, blond woman stared at him for a moment, then stepped outside with him and pointed to a house high on the opposite river bank. Passing over the shaky one-lane bridge proclaimed by a sign as Albert Bridge, Howard was at the simple, faded white, green-trimmed, shake shingle cabin in five minutes. Rather than knocking on the door, Howard walked around to the river side, where a screened porch overlooked the dark Mira River. There he found an old man, seated in a wooden rocker and staring at the water.

"Who are you? What do you want?"

Howard was taken aback by the strength of the voice coming from the bent, seated figure dressed in jeans and a baggy gray sweat-shirt.

"Mr. Spratling, my name is Dr. Howard Harris—I'm a physician."

"I didn't call any doctor."

"No, I know you didn't, but I've come all the way from New York City because I know you're not well."

"Well, you're correct in that—but I've been sick for a long time and will remain so until I die, which I figure isn't too far off."

The old man struggled to his feet and faced Howard. "Look, who told you I was sick or where I live—was it that bitch Karen Chase?"

"No, Mr. Spratling, she died about ten years ago."

"Oh… that's too bad."

Howard took the manuscript out of his backpack and related how he had found it and the fact that, ironically, he had attended a seminar just a few hours later where a disease called acute intermittent porphyria was discussed. Howard handed the manuscript to J.L. Spratling.

"Yes, that's my work and if you've come up here to get my approval to publish it you've made a long trip for nothing—the answer is NO!"

"No, what caught my attention was your description of your mental condition and physical symptoms, which probably prevented you from making the final corrections."

Spratling put on some bent metal reading glasses held together with a safety pin. Howard pointed to the inside cover.

J.L. slowly read his comments. "Well, these words were written in the late eighties. I had moved here a few years earlier to get away. I was sick then and I'm still sick." He took off his glasses. "I'm always depressed and in pain. The red skin is not from the sun—there sure isn't much here—and my urine is the same color. Mostly I feel angry about everything. So thanks for making the long trip up here. If you still respect me you can keep the book, but don't publish it or sell it to anybody!"

"Mr. Spratling, I more than respect you—I'm a huge fan of your writing. But as a favor to a doctor, please give me a few minutes to discuss the disease I think you have."

The few minutes became an hour, during which Howard discussed the genetic background and symptoms and signs of porphyria, its treatment and prognosis. J.L. gave Howard his full attention. When Howard finished, J.L. left him sitting in the chair while he went to make coffee for his uninvited guest.

"J.L., before coming I did some research on facilities available here to treat your condition. Dalhousie Medical School based in Halifax has a satellite center in Sydney. I would be happy to spend a few weeks with you as you see the doctors there, have the appropriate diagnostic tests and begin treatment."

"I've been sick so long I don't think anything will work, but I'm feeling so rotten I'm willing to try, if you will take care of the details."

The treatment, after diagnosis was confirmed, was both chemical and psychological, augmented by exercise and a healthier diet. The exercise involved long walks through the woods and roads of the beautiful countryside.

Six weeks later, Howard posed a question to J.L. in front of his team of treating physicians. "Well, J.L., how do you feel?"

"I think you can all go home."

The doctors looked at each other, feeling very let down.

"I mean that if I didn't like it so much here I would be ready to go back to New York—I feel so much better!"

After the conference was over, Howard gave J.L. a restrained hug. "Well, I have to get back. I'm leaving tomorrow—I've used up all my vacation and my research elective time."

"Thank you and please take the manuscript; it's yours for being so helpful. As a fan, keep it on your shelf next to the other published novels."

"No, J.L., I hope you will pick it up again and finish the project. It is still timely and could be your most important work…"

A year later, Dr. Howard Harris was a full-time attending physician at the busy psychiatric service at Bellevue Hospital. In the mail one day came an official invitation to the publication party at the Algonquin. He smiled as he read the handwritten note below the engraved invitation: "The author has specially requested that you attend."

Howard smiled even more broadly as he scanned another note below written in a different, firm hand.

"Please come—without you there would be no book and I would be dead… J.L.S."

TWENTY ONE

De-Signs of New York

A picture-perfect modern beach house sits high behind a dune overlooking the Atlantic Ocean. From the rear deck, Long Island is visible on a clear day, six miles north across the Great South Bay.

Bruce and Barbara Case, a childless couple, were the new owners of the home. They were a fit, diminutive pair, who enjoyed their daily five-mile run along the beach to the Lighthouse and back at low tide. They sparkled with positive energy.

The summer community of Dunewood, Fire Island, is one of a dozen spread along the coast of the thin, thirty-mile-long barrier island. Only sixty miles from Manhattan, the island is a wonderful escape, with its no-automobile, bicycle-only, casual atmosphere tradition. The social life revolves around sunning, swimming, sailing and tennis, and when day is done, gourmet eating and drinking. Sharply contrasted is the summer scene in the Hamptons, seventy traffic-congested miles further east on the Long Island Expressway at the tip of Long Island. There, one's senses are accosted by the mansions of the super-rich, the society sweethearts, media stars, entertainers and wannabes to all of the above. Even a reservation at the overcrowded and overpriced restaurants is a marker of the pecking order.

Barbara's background was in industrial design, her credential a degree (cum laude) from RISD (Rhode Island School of Design). Bruce had enhanced his degree in general studies from Columbia with an executive MBA from Fordham University, earned on weekends while he was employed at a dead-end job in the shoe industry. Their eight years as marriage-and-business partners had been more than eventful…

The *Island Maiden* ferry from Bay Shore pulled into the Dunewood dock on a perfect, cloudless, early summer day. Bruce's parents, Jack and Claire, waved enthusiastically from the rail of the upper deck, clearly looking forward to their first visit to the Fire Island home.

"Welcome to Dunewood!" the younger couple shouted in unison.

It was a very short walk across the two-block island's width to the beach house. Bruce pointed out the local landmarks. "On your left is our little yacht club and on the right we are passing the tennis center—two well-maintained composition courts."

"Wow! What a great location and house," was Jack Case's first awed comment as they turned the corner on the beach path and Bruce pointed to their summer home.

After a timeless and classic day at the beach, the cocktail hour found the two couples sitting on the broad front deck overlooking the darkening sea and the blue haze on the horizon.

"I hope you're insured for hurricanes," was Claire's subdued reaction.

The grill was heating and the on-shore breeze had dropped the temperature into the sixties, necessitating light jackets. Bruce appeared with the tray of gin and tonics as Barbara passed the hors d'oeuvres.

"Happy Fourth Annual De-Signs of New York barbecue!" Jack toasted and they raised and clinked their glasses. The sound of the breaking waves on the shore seemed to second that comment.

The drama of the sprawling layout of the house was accented by soaring windows all around, vaulted ceilings and impressive natural light. At night, stage spotlights highlighted heavy, vintage enamel signs suspended artfully from ceiling supports and wall mounts. All of the signs were from New York City streets and subways of the early 20th century. The street signs were "turtle back" in shape, with white lettering on a deep blue cobalt background. The subway signs, some over six feet horizontally, were in white enamel with black lettering. All were in good condition, considering their age and long exposure to the elements. Any visible wear was an important part of their charm. Some still had their original cast-iron frames or hangers.

At first glance at the historic Manhattan locations represented by the street corner signs, one felt in a time warp: Times Square (Broadway/West 42nd Street); Union Square (Park Avenue/Fourteenth Street); The Metropolitan Museum (Fifth Avenue/East 83rd Street); The American Museum of Natural History (Central Park West/West 79th Street); Greenwich Village (McDougal Street/Bleecker Street); Plaza Hotel (Fifth Avenue/East 58th Street); Wall Street (Wall Street/Broad Street). The large subway signs included those for Times Square, Herald Square, Grand Central Station and Penn Station.

On the conference-size oak dining table, the New York signage theme was continued on the fine quality, unusually shaped and designed dishes, tableware, glasses and napkins. Bruce and Barbara served the dinner wearing white canvas aprons decorated with the images of the blue cobalt New York street signs.

The corks of the perfectly chilled Perrier Jouet champagne brought by Jack and Claire popped with a satisfying *thonk* as more toasts were proposed for success, happiness and more summers at the beach house.

"Let's not forget the first De-Signs Day barbecue in New Rochelle just four years ago and everything we owe to Mom and Dad," Bruce added…

July 12th, 2006, was a great Saturday for a barbecue—seasonably hot and not humid. Bruce and Barbara had just moved into their two-bedroom condo on the Upper West side, two blocks from Central Park and their daily six-mile running route. Unfortunately the condo, although bright and quiet, had no outdoor space for barbecuing. The cook-out invitation to his parents' New Rochelle house was happily accepted.

Bruce, an only and much-loved child, enjoyed his parents' company. Barbara was warmly welcomed into the family arms as their long-awaited daughter. Jack Case had just retired from his accounting position in the New York City Highway Department, where he had risen to Associate Director. Claire, a math teacher at Larchmont High School, took her retirement after thirty years at a job she had thoroughly enjoyed. Claire and Jack had to remind each other to refrain from pressuring Bruce and Barbara to produce a grandchild for them to dote on.

Barbara's Toyota SUV pulled into the driveway of the 1930's Tudor-style home, well-situated on a half-acre. Tall privet hedges obscured the large flagstone patio and carefully tended garden with an area devoted to a serene, Japanese-style stone bridge.

The younger couple both accepted cold Beck's beer in the bottle as they sat on comfortable Adirondack chairs the older Cases had purchased in upstate New York twenty years previously.

"How's your new dish business going?" Claire asked with interest.

"Oh, Mom, it's actually much more than that."

"I know, dear, I was just using an expression."

Claire was referring to the business venture Bruce and Barbara had bought and were now developing and expanding. They had just signed a long-term lease on a 2,200-square-foot showroom at Eleventh Avenue and the West Fifties in Hell's Kitchen, a booming area that the real estate honchos now referred to as "Clinton." Car dealerships and run-down buildings were being replaced by trendy restaurants and new residential buildings, whose draw was their proximity to the Broadway theater district.

They had purchased an existing restaurant supply business then immediately sold off the stock to accumulate more capital for the business, *Gotham Ware*. Barbara looked at the "foodie" craze as a growth industry, where the new signature and theme restaurants needed designers and suppliers to give them an edge in promoting their unique character. Using Bruce's business skills, they developed a website offering consulting services for new restaurant designs. Although the owners might have the finances, the food concepts, chefs and locations, they needed advice and counsel to succeed in making dining a special experience for their customers.

"Son, would you please pull the grill out of the garage?"

"Sure, Dad, no problem."

The gas grill had apparently not been used for a long time, because access to it was blocked by two very large cartons. Bruce attempted to lift them out of the way, but their weight and clinking metal contents discouraged him. "Dad, what's in the boxes that are blocking the grill?" he called back to his father.

"Oh, just some old New York City street and subway signs."

When Bruce came out of the garage, Jack continued, "Bernie Black gave them to me when I retired. He told me they might be valuable someday."

"Why does he think so?"

"I'm not sure. I only glanced at them at the time. They are 50 to 75 or more years old. He described them as 'the pick of the litter.'"

"Can I have a look at them? If I take some out of the boxes, they'll be easier to move."

"Sure, Bruce, let's have a look. I'm curious myself why he gave them to me." Jack thought and added, "Actually, Bernie kind of owed me. Please don't repeat this. Well, he had and still has a drinking problem that led to some accounting errors or worse. Anyway, I covered for him; he weathered the crisis and kept his job. I told him that his sincere thanks were enough. His department controlled sign replacement and these vintage signs were for some of the prime locations in the city."

"Okay, Dad, I'll take them out and lay them on the grass."

In all, there were twenty signs from some of the most famous street and subway locations in Manhattan. Laid out as a group, they looked amazing.

Barbara commented, "That's quite a collection! You could easily sell them on eBay." She added thoughtfully, "Actually, they would look great in our showroom. After all, 'Gotham Ware' is a New York themed and based restaurant supply and design business."

"They're yours! Now, let's get the fire going and keep the cold Becks coming."

Bruce installed the signs in their showroom, giving the Broadway/42nd Street sign prime billing at the front of the shop. Most customers noticed the signs; a few wanted to buy them.

One day, two Brits, touring New York steak houses in preparation for opening their own restaurant in London, dropped in on their way to the Triple Pier Antique Show on the nearby Hudson River Shipping Piers. They had already been to *Smith & Wollensky*, *The Palm* and *Peter Luger*. The Brits were attracted by the 42ⁿᵈ Street/Broadway sign in the *Gotham Ware* window.

Ken Dawes, one of the partners, gave them the ultimate British superlative compliment. "These signs are brilliant!" He and Arthur Wells, both just less than six feet and trim, with their round, gold-rimmed eyeglasses, looked like twins. Only the mustache and van Dyke beard that Arthur sported distinguished them. After further conversation, it was apparent that their interest in surveying the steak houses went beyond the food. Arthur and Ken discussed their plans over the lunch that Barbara and Bruce ordered in from the nearby deli.

Ken spoke first. "Before we had dinner in Brooklyn at Luger's, we spent the day checking out the scene in Williamsburg and Bushwick. The look and feeling there is very much like East London."

Arthur interrupted and added, "I see the same type of young upscale crowd as we see in East London coming there to eat and live. We think there is a great opportunity to be the first with a New York-themed steak house in East London."

Ken commented, "Most of the steak houses in London have a Scottish look."

Bruce asked, "What do you mean by that?"

"Sort of your London club member meets the Scottish uplands in feeling and décor. We think that an 'Olde New York look', not only in the design of the restaurant and bar but in the dinner plates, glasses and tableware, would be huge and unique to the London dining scene."

Arthur added, "We've already leased a warehouse in East London that could accommodate a 300-seat restaurant. Our financing is in place—in fact, we're close to making a similar deal in Brighton. It will be a 200-seat satellite of the London operation."

Barbara responded, "You guys must be excited! It seems you've hit on a great business concept."

"We're about six months away from opening in East London. That will be perfect timing because we aim to be in operation next spring in Brighton as well and pick up the seasonal crowd there," Ken enthused.

Bruce said, "Well, it all sounds super. What can we do for you?"

Ken replied, "You might design lots of things for the restaurant. We could use your décor suggestions and designs and most importantly the china. We really love your stuff!"

Barbara suggested, "Look around the store. Check out our website—we have a lot more listed there."

Arthur raised his hand to get their full attention. "In six months, could you supply us with a thousand place settings of ceramic ware with the New York Street and subway signs prominent in their design?"

Barbara replied, "If we can agree on the terms of the contract while you're in New York, I can do the preliminary artwork and email it to you. Adjustments can easily be made online and our lawyers can work out the financial details. If we do it quickly, it will give me the lead time to have everything ready in six months."

Bruce brought in their favorite champagne, Perrier Jouet, when they signed the contract the day before the Brits left. Along with the contract came a substantial check, which Barbara needed for the down payment to the production company, Utica China, in Utica, New York.

"One last request, guys," Ken said.

Barbara responded, "What can we do for you?"

"We'd like to buy all your New York signs—just name the price."

"Sorry, they're not for sale."

"But they would look so perfect hanging in our restaurant," Ken pleaded.

"Tell you what," Barbara interjected, looking at Bruce for his agreement, "If Bruce approves, we could loan them to you for the opening and you could have them for six months."

Bruce smiled as he nodded yes.

"Make it a year instead and we'll fly the two of you over the pond for the opening and a great vacation week in London."

"You're on, mates!" was their happy reply.

The restaurant progress photos emailed by Ken and Arthur did not prepare Barbara and Bruce for the opening throngs and hubbub inside and outside the converted warehouse, located just two blocks from the Aldgate East Tube stop. The area did indeed remind them of rapidly gentrifying Bushwick, Brooklyn. Over the main entrance was a twenty-foot replica of the Grand Central Station subway sign.

Their engraved invitation got them by the bulked-up, tattooed, shaven-headed security guys. After pushing their way through, they noticed that Ken and Arthur had indeed given their signs the most prominent position, suspended by invisible wires from the high ceiling illuminated by klieg lights and over the American-style oak paneled and stained glass bar. At the far end of the restaurant was the huge open hearth for grilling the steaks. Scores of smaller spotlights focused on groups of well-framed vintage New York City scenes that the Cases had also loaned from their collection.

Arthur Wells spotted them and as he hurried over shouted, "This is what success looks like!"

The crowd was diverse: financial types, hipsters, beautiful models, media and rock stars. Arthur pointed to a more sedate couple, indicating, "Minor Royals."

Seated at their table was a formally dressed, late-fortyish couple. They rose simultaneously at the introduction by Arthur.

"David Drake and his wife, Karyn—the Cases, Barbara and Bruce, who did these wonderful designs—look at those dishes!"

Drake was known as "the British Ralph Lauren." His well-designed and fitted suit nicely camouflaged his middle-age spread and somewhat fleshy neck. His longish blond hair and visible athleticism projected enthusiastic energy. By sharp contrast, his wife Karyn was petite, dark and pixie-like.

"Great job!" was Drake's response as he looked at the dishes that carried decals of three signs along the rims. In the center was a larger version of the Broadway/42nd Street camelback sign; below it "Crossroads of the World." The theme was repeated in the rest of the tableware.

Drake displayed more than polite interest in Bruce and Barbara and their design business. They were amazed at the breadth of his knowledge, interest and enthusiasm. He had clothing lines, as well as furniture and bedding, appliances, sporting goods, even wine labels and baby carriages, and decorative objects that his company marketed in their own signature emporiums, as well as in dedicated boutiques in major department stores. Drake Enterprises even had their own signature restaurants, emulating the Tommy Bahamas concept in the USA.

As the Drakes excused themselves and stood up to leave, explaining they were heading to an art show opening, David Drake requested their business card.

As she handed him the card, Barbara commented, "This is our old card; we've just renamed our business *De-Signs of New York*."

"Great name! I get to the States frequently and I hope we can get together to talk more."

"We look forward to that."

The rest of the night was a blur of too much food and drink. But the rest of the week was memorable for fine London meals, meeting with the delightful friends of Ken and Arthur, shopping and West End theater. The highlight was the trip to Brighton with Ken to see the progress of the other Grand Central Station restaurant. Its central location just north of the famous shopping area, *The Lanes*, appeared to be a great choice. From the state of the construction, the April opening looked optimistic. They checked out Brighton's shingle beach on the English Channel. Bruce remarked in an aside to Barbara that the Long Island Beaches didn't have to worry about competition from Brighton!

Back in New York, business for the Cases was definitely picking up. Their real estate agent was scouting Brooklyn for another location for *De-Signs of New York*. Meanwhile, the Brits reported they were looking for another restaurant location in Oxford. Though smaller in scope, it would require another large order from their business, which they formalized after the lease was signed.

The first sign of concern occurred in August when labor problems with the Brighton project delayed the opening until November. Ken and Arthur assured them that the Christmas crowd and the New Year would get them off to a great start. Disastrously, none of that happened. The Brighton restaurant opened on November first and closed for the season on January 15th, 2008. Bad weather and the economy were blamed. The banks were not patient.

In February, an urgent email arrived telling the Cases to cancel the Oxford order. Zoning variances were refused; the investors had pulled out and decided to put their venture capital in shoes. Unfortunately, in anticipation of the opening, the Cases already had the dishes manufactured, delivered to their storage facility stacked in packing cases, along with the unpaid invoices.

Then worse news arrived—the Brighton property had been seized by the bailiffs in order to pay creditors and was closed. All of the contents had been auctioned by the bank. Although the London operation was still successful, it could not possibly cover the financial losses of the other failed locations.

In a long tearful conversation, Ken and Arthur suggested that the Cases accept a fifteen percent partnership in the London restaurant to compensate them for their large unpaid bills. They were optimistic that prospects would improve after the current European financial crisis passed.

Ken said, half-jokingly, half-hopefully, "When the recession is over, businessmen from all over the continent will jet to Heathrow, get in limousines and come to Grand Central Station before they even check into their hotels."

It wasn't funny to Bruce and Barbara. Their attorney told them that they had no choice but to accept the small partnership stake. Practically, he said, even if they were successful in their suit for the more than $150,000 they were owed, a judgment would be difficult to enforce and only his British legal colleagues would make money.

When the office phone rang about three weeks later, the number indicated was a British area code. Barbara figured she had heard enough bad news from there and chose not to pick it up.

A minute later, the phone rang again.

Bruce said, "Look, we can't keep our heads in the sand forever—so let's just pick it up." He put the phone on speaker so both could hear, "Is that Bruce? David Drake here."

"Hi, David, how are you doing?"

"Actually, I'm very well, and I have news for you—I bought *Grand Central Station*!" Drake continued without waiting for comment. "The laws are different in the U.K. than in the States. Your small minority share was written in such a way that I was able to purchase it without your agreement when I bought out the majority owners. My attorney says that I owe you over $200,000."

Barbara and Bruce replied almost in unison, "Well, that is great news for us!"

"Rather than wiring you the money, I'd rather see you and deliver the check in person since I will be in New York next week."

Barbara replied enthusiastically, "Super! Call us when you get in and know your schedule. We would love to have you stop by and see our operation."

"One other thing—I really wanted to keep all the New York signs but I was informed by the former owners of the oral loan agreement and I will honor it. They're on their way back to you by DHL and should be there in a few days."

The following Tuesday, David Drake arrived at *De-Signs of New York* at the appointed time. After an effusive greeting, he noticed the signs were back in the shop. He reached into his pocket and pulled out a check made out to their corporate name for $227,000, along with a legal document requiring their signatures.

Bruce commented, "We're very happy to get the check and I must confess that we actually came out ahead. Our bills have been more than fully covered."

David asked for a tour of their facility and then the three adjourned to *Nello,* a trendy restaurant nearby, for lunch.

After they were seated and enjoying cocktails, Drake asked, "Do you have any idea why I wanted to see you besides a friendly reunion and to present you with a nice check?"

"Not really—but we're very happy to see you anyway."

"Actually, this is a genuine business lunch and I have a proposition for you."

Half seriously, Bruce suggested, "You want permission to copy our signs and use them in your stores?"

"No, when it comes to that type of display, I prefer to have the real thing." He put down his drink and in a very serious tone, said, "I'm starting a U.S. branch of *David Drake Enterprises International.* It's something I've thought about for a long time. However, meeting you guys in London spurred me to go forward. I'll want dishes and many, many other American-themed items in my stores in the States. I'm actually starting with the restaurant concept."

The conversation stopped while the waiter took their orders.

"What I'd like you to do is to gather real vintage signs from all over America. Then we'll have *De-Signs of LA, Chicago, Dallas, Miami, and Boston* and of course, a similar restaurant design project will start for each city."

"Sounds like an idea that hasn't been tried before," was Barbara's kidding comment.

"I guess you've forgotten about London now that you're ex-partners."

David added, "Here's the bottom line. You did a great job in the London project and my team has checked you out. Like they say on Broadway—you got good notices!"

Smiling broadly, Bruce replied, "That's very generous of you."

"Bottom-bottom line is this. I want to buy out *De-Signs of New York* and incorporate it into my American operation."

"I believe I speak for Barbara when I say we would certainly seriously entertain your offer."

"Please also consider, while you are thinking, that the offer would include your appointments as Senior Vice-Presidents of *David Drake Enterprises (USA) LLC...*"

Barely, one year later, the Cases exercised some of the stock options given to them as part of their employment agreement. Thanks to their design and business skills and the David Drake Empire behind them, the NASDAQ-traded *David Drake Enterprises International (DDEI)* had tripled in value.

It was time to purchase the beach house...

TWENTY TWO

The Hidden Room

S enator and Mrs. Claude Harmon's red-brick home off Massachusetts Avenue in Washington, D.C., had been built just after
World War I. The corner lot allowed generous outdoor space
and the boundary privet hedges provided privacy from snooping
neighbors and passersby. The gracious house was the base for the
happy childhood and adolescence of their twin daughters, Elise and
Amanda. Both daughters subsequently moved to Cincinnati, Ohio.
Their father had ably and profitably represented Ohio for thirty-four
years: two terms as Representative and five as Senator. The twins'
young children (four grandchildren, two of each gender) occupied
the girls fully; visits to D.C. and the house off Massachusetts Avenue
were infrequent.

For the past five years, Claude had been the powerful Chairman
of the Foreign Relations Committee. He was to retain that position
after the recent re-election to the Presidency of his party's candidate.
The party had also kept control of the Senate…

Elaine Harmon sat across from her husband in their cozy den. Attractive, with her short, curly, blond highlighted hair and trim figure, she could easily pass for ten years less than her biological age of sixty-two. It was six p.m. and the Harmons were drinking Makers Mark Bourbon Old Fashioneds. "Claude, I think the kids would come visit more often during school breaks in the spring and even a few weeks in the summer," she said, "if..."

"What's the 'if'? If we take them to Disneyland?"

"No, if we build a swimming pool at the side of the house. We hardly ever sit on the patio out there because it is so hot in Washington in the summer."

Senator Harmon could have satisfied a casting call for a typical Kentucky Colonel, with his huge white moustache, Vandyke beard, full head of white hair and casual outfit, complete with bolo tie. "Look, even with my connections, getting a variance for permission for a 32-foot pool fenced off would be difficult for that space in the side yard. That doesn't even take into account the space needed for a pool house with pumps, filters and chemical storage."

"Well, dinner's ready. Let's talk or fight about it another time. After dinner I'll call Elise and Amanda and see if the pool idea is really a ticket to seeing our grandkids more often."

The housekeeper/cook, Carmela, served them a not fancy, but delicious dinner of baked chicken and grilled vegetables, carried in on magnificent Majolica serving dishes. Their china was elegant 19th-century Minton set on the 1920's mahogany and ebony Jules Leleu designed dining table. The table and the Baccarat crystal chandelier above had been gifts from the French ambassador. The chandelier had arrived after the Foreign Relations Committee approved the sale of the latest anti-missile armaments by the Ambassador's brother-in law's company to the US Defense Department. The Minton china, totaling almost 150 pieces including serving dishes, had come from the stores of the Queen of England. The crates packed with china had arrived after the signing of a successful and favorable mutual defense treaty. The large colorful antique rugs were Turkish, also a gift—from an Istanbul "businessman" with whom the Senator had "worked" to complete yet another successful deal with the U.S. government. A more complete tour of the house would reveal that almost everything was foreign in origin, acquired during Senator Harmon's tenure as Chairman of the powerful Foreign Relations Committee. The only thing genuinely American was the Federal Revival house itself and the modern appliances. Senator Harmon's diplomatic skills were clearly evident in the elegant decorations in the house. In addition, the contents of a large safe secured to the concrete floor in the basement were a testament to the Senator's highly valued skills. It was overflowing with valuable jewelry and *objets* that he had received as tokens of appreciation from grateful foreign leaders and businessmen. Senator Harmon was often heard to say to his colleagues with a chuckle, "Isn't diplomacy wonderful!"

After being assured by both Elise and Amanda that the pool would certainly be a way to encourage family visits, the Senator put his mind to work on the project. His first call was to Art Eagle, a one-man home improvement service. Art had, in recent years, upgraded bedrooms, bathrooms and the kitchen in a beautiful, efficient and economical manner. Senator Harmon respected his taste, judgment and workmanship. The fact that Art worked alone and was very discreet kept outsiders away from inspecting the Senator's treasures and secrets. This was a highly important motivating factor in selecting Art. Claude Harmon wanted to check on Eagle's availability and get his recommendation for a reasonable and reliable pool contractor.

At their first meeting, the pool company designer made careful measurements of the side yard as he and Senator Harmon toured the outdoor space. They then sat in the den to discuss the details.

"Frankly, Senator, it's going to be a tight squeeze to get a 32x16-foot pool out there. I sense that something smaller would not satisfy you."

"I anticipated that, so I have something else in mind. Come downstairs into the basement." Claude Harmon pointed out the site of the main water supply and the foundation wall that faced the proposed pool site.

"In the original plan for the house, which I will show you, a large section of the foundation wall was earmarked for a future expansion of the house. Therefore it was constructed to be not load-bearing. It could now allow a large opening to be built to an underground area adjoining the pool that would house all the mechanicals and the pump. That would eliminate the need for that space in the yard for the pool house."

"I see your point! If we excavate the yard right to the house line and leave space for a room that will connect directly to the house then we can put a metal cover over it and pavers over that, and that would make room for a pool after all! The pool would be placed about twelve feet from the house and the underground room for the tanks and pumps would have dimensions of 16x12-feet and possibly seven feet high. The pool equipment could be easily serviced through your basement and the opening you described."

"In your final design, if you would, put the mechanical stuff in one corner and I'll find a use for the rest of the space."

Within a month the plans were drawn. Senator Harmon made a few calls to the "right people" he knew in the DC bureaucracy and within ten days the plans were approved and a variance granted. Construction began in early February and was completed in time for the grandkids to come visit for the Memorial Day long weekend.

As soon as the children left, Harmon called Art Eagle and asked him to stop by.

"Your recommendation for the pool construction was great. I'm very pleased with the result," Harmon said when Art arrived.

Eagle thanked him.

The Senator gave Art Eagle a tour of the installation, landscaping and beautiful poolside pavers and furnishings. "I think you'll agree they did a great job, but most importantly, I want you to see the underground pool room."

Art nodded his approval at the well-lit and ventilated 12x16-foot space.

"Now, here's where your work begins. At my direction, they placed all the mechanical stuff in one corner of the space. Even if you leave a wide corridor to that equipment from a cellar door for servicing, you still have more than half the space to work with."

"What do you have in mind?"

"I want you to construct a hidden room with a carefully concealed doorway that will operate both mechanically and electrically. This will be done in secret by you alone and we will not file any plans with the district."

"I need to think about the mechanical details. It can certainly be accomplished; however, the volume and weight of any part must not exceed what I can personally handle in order to ensure the secrecy you demand."

The Senator nodded. "Let's sum it all up. There are three big considerations. First, I trust you, because no-one can know about this hidden room. Two, the wall must look like it abuts the outside so that nobody would even suspect that there is a space behind it. Third and finally, the design should be such that you won't need outside help."

Six weeks later, Art Eagle's work was completed. The sliding walnut-paneled walls were operated by a small motor whose switch was carefully concealed at the foot of the kitchen stairs in the cellar. Behind the wood panels was a layer of impenetrable steel panels and

soundproofing material. Within the hidden room was another mo-
torized switch, as well as a concealed mechanical switch to be used in
case of emergency. At the Senator's request, inside the room Art had
constructed an entire wall of glass-covered lighted showcases and
cabinets to display the Senator's valuable objects. The room resembled
a small but expensive jewelry store that could have been located in
the lobby at the Mayflower Hotel.

Although Elaine was aware of the construction, she took no special
interest in its progress and purpose. Decades as a politician's wife had
taught her not to be too curious.

Harmon called upstairs. "Elaine, we're finished in the cellar.
Please come down so I can show you how to operate the hidden
room opening."

When she saw the completed space she asked, "What will we
store there?"

"Some of the valuable treasures we acquired overseas, as well as
the stuff we've jammed in the safe and in cabinets scattered around
the house. Now that you've learned to operate the mechanisms, I
can't stress enough that we must keep this a secret. When we get
older we will tell the twins, but there is no reason now to burden
them with this secret!"

Ironically, a year later almost to the day, Senator and Mrs. Harmon
were dead, victims of a plane crash into the Black Sea while on an
official government mission to the Ukraine.

The grief-stricken twins, Elise and Amanda, came to Washington
one last time for the well-attended memorial service and to remove
the things they had selected to keep among the furniture and decorations. They turned the sale of the house over to a top real estate
broker who also helped to arrange for the sale of the remaining contents of the house at an auction.

Late that fall, the house sold for a strong $2.1 million, the DC market being almost recession proof. The buyer was a 41-year-old real estate developer, Jason Fornow. He had a shady reputation and had lived previously in nearby Chevy Chase, Maryland. Fornow's flat face, with his bull dog like appearance and aggressive attitude matched his industry reputation as a pushy go getter. Totally opposite in appearance and personality, Vanessa, his wife of six years, had agreed with Jason's decision not to have children so they could pursue their careers. Jason and Vanessa decided that the "Harmon House" would offer a better location for their ambitious desire to be a "power couple" on the Washington scene.

Fornow's niche in real estate involved investing in questionable neighborhoods, with heavy support from local governments who subsidized mortgages for unqualified buyers. They would then get out before there were any personal or financial repercussions. Vanessa worked as Director of Human Resources for a start-up internet company called *WayTrips*. Their specialty was selling coupons for discount travel experiences. Her company had recently opened a branch in Bangkok, requiring frequent travel on Vanessa's part. This allowed for separations, which gave both an opportunity to fool around. Nevertheless, when they were together they enjoyed the challenges of furnishing and fixing the new house.

One evening, just after the closing but before they were scheduled to move in, they toured the house, carefully inspecting every room.

"Vanessa, I think the kitchen and bathroom appear to have been upgraded fairly recently. I found a plaque inside one of the built-in cabinets with the name of the guy who did the work. It says 'Art Eagle Home Improvements: I work alone for your security and privacy.'"

Vanessa commented, "I like his work. Do you think we could hire him to break through the wall in the master bedroom to make it larger and more up-to-date? Maybe we could add some built-in closets? The old-fashioned pantry could be incorporated into the kitchen space, making an eat-in area. Then we could share the den for home offices if we constructed a double-sided partner's desk and added more wall shelves."

"I agree. Instead of the cheap work from the firms I use, with their undocumenteds swarming all over the house, I'd rather pay a little more, take a little longer and get some quality work."

At the time of the tragedy of the Harmons' sudden deaths, Art Eagle had noted the passing of his former customers. He felt badly, especially for their daughters and grandchildren. Art was surprised when Jason Fornow called to inform him he had bought the Harmon house and discovered the company plaque. He asked Art if he could come by to discuss further improvements. The minute Eagle entered the familiar house, Jason's first question was, "Do you still work alone?"

"Yes, I do, although occasionally I use a plumber or electrician for a complicated final hookup. However, all the design, dry wall, carpentry, tile work and installation of appliances I do myself, and also minor electrical and plumbing work."

The three walked through the still empty house. Art noted their preferences and offered suggestions. He agreed to return with preliminary plans and estimates. Two weeks later, just after Vanessa got back from a ten-day trip to Bangkok, they looked at the plans and the estimates for everything. Inclusive of appliances and all finishes the total came to $82,500.

For obvious reasons, Jason did not discuss his shaky finances with Art. His annual mortgage and tax bill for the Harmon house totaled $120,000. His company held the mortgage for him on their books, although their monthly balance statement consistently showed they were operating in the red. Furthermore, since he was holding out for his high listed price, the Chevy Chase house was still unsold and also heavily mortgaged. Vanessa's position helped. She did have excellent benefits, though a small salary. Vanessa had been promised a huge salary and bonus once *WayTrips* completed a successful IPO. As previously mentioned, her frequent long absences allowed Jason to participate in the Washington club scene, enjoying alcohol binges, cocaine parties and casual sex.

"Art, I think I speak for Vanessa too when I say that, at first glance, we like your plans. I can go over minor changes with you by phone and email."

Eagle replied, "Just to get this out of the way, you should be aware that I work at an hourly rate, plus the cost of materials, for which I will provide statements. You will benefit from my tradesman's discount. I would prefer that you pay these bills directly. Once we agree on a final contract, I expect 20 percent down—say $15,000—the balance to be paid as the work proceeds."

"That will be no problem!"

Twelve weeks later, the job was completed. Vanessa and Jason shook Art's hand and promised to refer many friends to him. Vanessa added as she headed out the door, "I'm on my way to Dulles on a long business trip to Australia and New Zealand, so this is a going-away present for me!"

After she left, Art said, "Jason, I've been informed by my lumber and tile suppliers that you have a large balance with them and they have only tolerated late payment because I am such a good customer."

Jason replied angrily, "Yes, I do. It's less than $20,000 and you can assure them that Jason Fornow is an important real estate developer in the District and they will get paid!"

"Actually, I'm more concerned with the balance of $18,200 that you owe me. I don't usually let that much debt accumulate since I work by myself and need the cash flow."

"Of course you'll get paid. I'm waiting on a check for $240,000 for a building upgrade my firm completed recently. I'm also on my way out of town on a two-week trip to the Coast. I'm close to making a deal on a big old office building in downtown LA—we're talking seven figures! Let's make a definite date for you to come back in a few weeks when Vanessa and I will both be here and we'll clear up the balance then."

Art realized that he had been foolish to let this creep get so far behind and should not have finished his work without final payment. As he gazed at the newly finished door leading to the basement, an idea came to him. "Mr. Fornow, I know you're a substantial person and will pay me in two weeks."

"Great! I appreciate your confidence. Now, I have to get going to catch my flight."

Art continued, "There is a hidden room in this house, known only to myself and the late Senator Harmon and his wife."

"Where is it?" Jason demanded.

"Well, I promised to maintain its secret. Now they're gone and I'm the only one who knows."

"I own this house. The room is mine and I demand you tell me where it is!"

Art replied calmly, "You can take me to court or you can pay me what you owe in two weeks and then I will show you the secret."

Jason reached for his checkbook. "Okay, you win—I'll write you a check for $9,000 now. Even better, I'll have it wired to your account. Show me the room, you'll have the rest in two weeks—deal?"

After Art nodded his approval, Jason said gaily, "Lead on, Macduff!"

Art said, "Call the bank first."

As soon as Jason had complied, Art said, "It's off the pool room in the basement."

Jason ran down the stairs and was in the pool room before Art had gone two steps. "There's nothing here!"

As Art reached the bottom of the cellar steps, he pressed the concealed button and remained there. Meanwhile, the door rumbled slowly open, giving Jason a startling view of the vast treasure trove not visible to Art from his position on the stairs. Jason quickly returned to Art, grasped him across the shoulders and began pushing him up the stairs. "Okay, I'll see you in two weeks and you'll definitely get the balance. Now I've got to go to the airport."

"But Mr. Fornow! Before I go, I must show you how the opening and closing mechanism works electrically and on the timer and mechanically both from outside and inside the room."

"Thanks—but you can fill me in on the details when we meet in two weeks. Goodbye!" Jason said as he pushed Art out the front door.

Two weeks later when Art returned, he was met at the door by a very distraught Vanessa.

"What's wrong? Where's Mr. Fornow?"

"I don't know! I texted and called him on his cell several times from Australia, but he never answered!"

Art volunteered, "Well, maybe he's still on the West Coast and his phone isn't working?"

"No—he never got there, according to his office and his friends. He just disappeared. He never even contacted the LA office to say he wasn't coming!"

"Calm down—there may be a simple explanation for this."

Vanessa asked, "When did you last see him or have contact with him?"

"I left the house perhaps fifteen minutes after you," Art said, recalling the last few minutes of their meeting. Pausing thoughtfully, he added, "Look, I hope I'm wrong, but it just occurred to me what might have happened."

"What are you talking about?"

"Just before I left, I showed him how to access a hidden room I had built for the Harmons and I'm wondering..."

Vanessa screamed, "Where is it? Show me!"

Art hurried to the kitchen, opened the door to the cellar and ran downstairs, Vanessa at his heels. He pressed the concealed button on the wall at the base of the stairs and the door to the hidden room slowly whirred open. Together they rushed to the opening of the space. The sight they encountered was a completely trashed room, with broken shards of glass and metal, and the scattered glint of colored gems and diamonds. In the corner of the room lay the bloated corpse of Jason Fornow, still clutching an exquisite Faberge egg in his swollen claw-like hands.

TWENTY THREE

When it Snows in the Bronx and Rains in Hilton Head

My name is Sy Green. I own a large and successful uniform rental and laundry business in the South Bronx. My hobby is restoring old discarded things and making them into useful and attractive items. If you are a collector, investor, appraiser or dealer involved with antiques, you may find this interesting.

About one year ago, I was leaving the plant for home on a snowy evening in January. I was driving the company panel truck since my Jag was in the shop. Snow was quickly accumulating, so I turned the radio on to AM 1010 for the traffic and weather report. There was an accident on the Bronx River Parkway, my usual route to Scarsdale; therefore, I decided to detour through the West Bronx via Kingsbridge to reach the Saw Mill River Parkway going through Yonkers and onward to Scarsdale. How serendipitous that change in route would turn out to be!

The Kingsbridge section of the Bronx, though changing, is still mainly German and Irish and has been since before the turn of the

20th century. Somewhere just west of Broadway in the vicinity of 230th Street, I stopped for a traffic light. I recall looking first at a street light and seeing the falling snow in the glare. Glancing left, I noticed a wooden cabinet dumped at the curbside, awaiting Saturday pickup by the sanitation truck.

As I mentioned, my passion and hobby is restoring discarded things: furniture, lighting and toys. Interestingly, this compulsion is heightened when the object is abandoned. I pulled over to take a closer look. I'll admit this behavior is eccentric, but in the course of several years I've acquired many wonderful things: rare books, Art Deco lighting, original player piano rolls, an early phonograph with horn and a fine old violin—just to mention a few.

At first glance this corner cabinet, perhaps a china closet, did not look like a keeper. It was a little on the plain side, of clumsy proportion and heavy in appearance. Even in the dim light, it was obviously made of oak, and appeared to be easily moveable. That quality, plus having a company van with a rear-loading ramp, enabled me with a little huffing and puffing to shove the cabinet into the truck.

During the rest of the ride home, I planned how I would overcome the expected objections of my wife, Hope, by suggesting that she use the cabinet in her studio to store paints and other art materials.

Hope is a wonderful companion. She is my wife, mother of two wonderful college-age sons, an excellent chef, a marvelous entertainer and a talented, abstract figural artist who has had many successful shows, commissions and sales.

As I approached our home, a large, stone, English-style Tudor dating from the 1920's, I parked the truck in the side driveway, planning to take the cabinet directly into Hope's studio. The house was originally designed with a separate entrance into a side wing; early in its history, it was configured as a physician's office. Several owners later, we had gutted the inside rooms and created a large studio space for Hope. I managed to wrestle the piece out of the van, through the door and into the empty corner near the door. I paused, caught my breath, felt no coronary coming on and proceeded through the inside door into the house proper.

Hope heard me enter, rushed up and gave me a big kiss. Then she backed off a few steps and smiling wryly said, "I recognize the expression—what did you pick off the street this time?"

"It was a rough ride in the snow tonight. I had a long trip."

She giggled. "Don't change the subject."

"I'll show you the find after dinner. To tell you the truth, I haven't given it a good look in the light yet."

"But what is it?" she insisted.

I convinced her to have a vodka tonic first and then we would check it out. As we walked into the studio Hope gasped. "Are you serious? This is an awful-looking thing!"

The "thing" turned out to be a double-door, oak corner china closet less than five feet high. The upper section had three shelves and eighteen panes of glass, several of which were cracked or missing. The lower portion had a two-door cupboard, each side containing a pair of weathered-copper strap hinges that were both decorative and functional.

I looked at my wife and asked, "What style or period is this?"

"*Early Bronx*, made in a shop in the Mission style; probably—and fortunately—one of a kind." She continued, "Mind you, there are some very fine pieces of Arts and Crafts furniture around; it's very much in vogue, but this is not a good example."

"Well, it has its original cobwebs," I replied. "Even the elements couldn't loosen them. I added hopefully, "It could sit right where it is and hold your paints and supplies."

Hope did not reply, but turned and headed back toward the kitchen. I decided, discretion being the better part of valor, not to pursue the issue.

As I mentioned earlier, we are very happily married. That, plus exercise, prosperity, relative youth (we are still in our late forties) and mostly good luck, have left us in glowing health. People describe us as a very assured, attractive and warm couple.

Over dinner, we discussed our forthcoming golf holiday at Hilton Head in early March. Our dining table is a double-pedestal, Sheraton-style centennial reproduction with matching chairs. Hope's contemporary artwork contrasts sharply with the 18th century-style furniture. This variance between period furnishings and modern art extends throughout the house; the effect is dramatic and it works. During dinner, Hope mentioned the cabinet only once and said she would keep it if I promised never to bring home any more junk…

One Sunday morning in early February, Hope was out driving golf balls in preparation for our vacation. I had barely glanced at the cabinet in the six weeks that it had been in her studio. Being at loose ends, I decided to plan some restoration.

I looked the cabinet over carefully; it was definitely solidly built and still dirty. I measured for new glass and applied a few coats of wax after carefully sponging the superficial dirt away and lightly cleaning it with very fine steel wool soaked with furniture oil. The hinges badly needed polishing, but in Hope's absence I couldn't locate the copper cleaner. The cabinet had mortise and tenon joinery, as well as wooden pins throughout. The mitered mullions supporting the panes of glass were beautifully constructed in matching pieces of oak. Nevertheless, I decided that this type of clunky furniture was an acquired taste, like scotch whiskey. I preferred the latter and was enjoying the same when Hope arrived home.

"I'm ready for the Hilton Head Links. I actually drove a couple of balls over two hundred yards! What have you been doing?" said Hope.

"I've been cleaning up the china closet—it's really not bad. Would you consider putting it upstairs in the den?"

Hope's eye-roll and abrupt about-face telegraphed her answer.

We arrived at Hilton Head the first day of March. The less I say about the resort, especially the weather, the better for everyone, including the local Chamber of Commerce. It rained so hard that not only was golf out but all other activities, including even the mandatory real estate sell, which was canceled. Finally, on the fourth day Hope suggested we drive into Savannah and check out the town and a French restaurant mentioned in *Town & Country*. On the way back to our car after lunch, we happened upon a cluster of antique shops on the next block, in buildings that dated from the early 19th century.

"I'm really not in a shopping mood—I'm tired and a little drunk," I said.

"In that case," Hope replied, "you'd better sober up a little before we drive back. I promise I'll look only in this one shop." The shop was named *Huneycutt's*.

The main gallery occupied about a thousand feet, including the adjoining building. The low period ceiling made the space charming. The collection was classic 18th- and early 19th-century American and English furniture and accessories. There were no early American painted colonial things, folk art or common Americana: they sold strictly good furniture that had been made in England, New York, Philadelphia, Boston and the South.

The proprietor introduced herself as Anne Davidson. She appeared to be on the sunny side of sixty. Anne, as she preferred to be called, spoke with a cultured accent. She wore a ruffled silk blouse decorated with a large Victorian cameo brooch in a gold frame. Her A-line pleated skirt was a perfect accompaniment. Apparently, the blue-hair look was still a few years off. When she offered her assistance, we gave her the "just looking" disclaimer.

Hope and I saw the pair of chairs at the same moment. A small sign, discreetly written in a neat script, described them as important chairs attributed to Thomas Chippendale. The price was $35,000. Hope is very knowledgeable about Chippendale, Heppelwhite and Sheraton. She goes regularly to museums and lectures and at the very least would be considered an educated lay person.

Hope whispered, "I'm in love with them" and said aloud, "Excuse me, Anne, the chairs are exquisite and appear quite genuine—do they have a formal provenance?"

"Yes, of course. If you are interested, I'd be happy to show you a large file on them. They're really museum quality!"

Over cups of very good coffee that was graciously served, we studied photographs, certificates of authenticity, old bills of sale and an auction record. Hope commented, not too diplomatically, that the price seemed very reasonable for a pair of such important chairs.

Anne asserted, "To be perfectly frank, we obtained these chairs from an estate at a remarkable price. We almost sold them to a museum in Boston, but unfortunately, during these difficult economic times, institutions are de-accessioning, not buying. I think they are a great buy at $35 thousand and at $30 thousand, which I'll accept now, a steal!"

We were both hooked. I make a very good living and can afford an occasional splurge, particularly when I see it as a good investment.

We went through the usual looking and checking. The chairs were mahogany and intricately carved in the manner of Chippendale. Of course the upholstery was more recent, but first rate. I agreed readily to the price, but insisted that I have, in writing, the right to authenticate them as attributed to Chippendale. If they did not pass a recognized authority of my choosing, who would also be acceptable to her, I would have the right to return the lot. Mrs. Davidson agreed, saying my request was reasonable, but she believed, unnecessary. We arranged the details of shipment. I wrote a check and we left the store on a little cloud of joy and headed back to Hilton Head and the rain.

Two weeks later, the chairs arrived in Scarsdale. When I got home from work, Hope was sitting on one, waiting for me to sit on the other. On the lamp table between the chairs were a bottle of Cristal champagne and a dish of caviar. A memorable moment and, reader, a place where I wish this story had ended. It would have if Hope had not at that instant reminded me, "Darling, they're superb, but let's invest a little more and get them authenticated!"

"Hilton" and "Head," our pet names for our new purchases, occupied a conspicuous area of the living room. Above them, Hope hung a large abstract painting of a hand holding a teacup entitled, *Cream Tea*.

Friends were shown the chairs and told of our luck in having that rainy holiday. We didn't discuss price, but said they were very reasonable.

In the meantime, I queried retail dealers, museums, auction houses and appraisal associations for names of experts. A few names came up repeatedly and I finally decided upon Duncan LeMar. Before hiring him, I called Savannah: Anne Davidson kept me on the phone several minutes while she did her own checking before approving of him. She was polite, but a little short. "He's fine. Please send me a copy of the report for my records."

Then I called LeMar, described the chairs and their provenance and asked him if he would come out to the house. He was all business, told me his fee was $650 and that he expected payment at the time of inspection.

Ironically, the day he came was a rainy Saturday afternoon. Hope and I sat in the living room like parents nervously and apprehensively waiting to meet a prospective daughter-in-law for the first time. We listened to the sound of each car coming down our street, wondering if it would slow down and turn into our driveway.

Finally, a Volvo station wagon pulled in and parked by the door to the studio. We had bought a beautiful, large, spring flower arrangement for the main entrance foyer. However, Mr. LeMar's entry to our house turned out to be through the cluttered studio. I rushed to the door, we exchanged brief hellos, he left his coat and umbrella in the studio and I guided him into the house proper. I had somehow expected a stiff, late middle-aged, formally dressed man in a Harris Tweed jacket, ascot and cavalry twill pants.

Instead, a boyish-looking younger man in jeans and flannel shirt appeared, as if straight from Little League practice. "Hi, I'm Dunc LeMar."

I returned his greeting and introduced myself and Hope. We led him through a short dog-leg corridor to the living room entrance and pointed proudly to the chairs against the far wall of the room about twenty feet away.

He stopped short, paused for about ten seconds and did not speak. Hope and I both looked expectantly at his face and watched in disbelief as he slowly but deliberately shook his head. "No, I'm sorry," he muttered, "They're not as represented."

Hope whispered in shock, "How can you know that at twenty feet?"

"I'm a professional and I am going to make a careful close inspection. But to respond to your question, the proportions of the chair and the ratio of its various dimensions are not correct for an original Chippendale chair. Incidentally, that aspect is best seen at a distance. Chairs by Chippendale, or attributed to him, are as well known for their balance and harmony as their carving."

I watched in stunned silence as he approached one chair and deftly flipped it over. I vaguely remember him describing areas of concern, including the carcass, the joinery, the condition and type of glue and, of course, the carving. He stated that these details and findings would be listed in his written evaluation. "My job is to render an opinion as to whether these chairs are by or attributed to Chippendale as represented in the Bill of Sale."

He added emphatically in a louder voice, "They are neither."

"Off the record, I'd say they are very good quality mid-Victorian reproductions of a generic Chippendale style, with a retail value of probably four to six thousand dollars."

Hope mumbled, "Do you think the seller was misled or was simply dealing in fake merchandise?"

"I can't say, but she is damned either way. If Mrs. Davidson did sell you fakes, she is a criminal. If she was duped, she shouldn't have been because she is supposed to be an expert in her field. I'm glad of course that you insisted on this appraisal as a condition of sale. One other thing—appraising is an art. Although it is sometimes based on hard, scientific evidence, appraisal is subject to individual interpretation. In other words, you are getting my expert opinion, as you would a medical evaluation. Carrying the analogy to its conclusion, another doctor might give you another opinion. I'll be sending you my report in the mail."

I wrote a check and thanked him as we walked out through Hope's studio to retrieve his coat and umbrella. As we passed the oak cabinet, he stopped and paused to look at the piece carefully. I remember my exact words: "Please, I've had my disappointment for the day. That's just a piece of junk I picked up on a Bronx corner last winter."

"Like hell it is!" he exclaimed in a loud voice that shocked me. "That is a very early Gustav Stickley piece and possibly very valuable. Please get those paint tubes out of there!"

LeMar went on to mention that a similar and he believed less important piece had recently sold at auction for $35,000. He showed me details that I had not noticed, including a large red mark and signature on the back of the cabinet.

He seemed very excited and said, "This may be the forerunner of that auction lot. It is smaller and in this instance possibly made by the master himself, because it is similar to the one that was made for his home at Craftsman Farms. The condition is excellent—don't touch it with anything."

He stepped back, admiring the cabinet. "Look how beautiful the copper patina is! Goodbye and good luck!" and he left the house and us in shock.

Hope and I headed back to the house and the liquor cabinet. "It's a good thing you insisted on the right of appraisal," Hope said, drink in hand, "and it's even better that you insisted we exercise that right."

"Well, I'm sorry it rained at Hilton Head," I quipped.

"And I'm glad it snowed in the Bronx," Hope replied with a grin. "I insist you call Anne Davidson now."

I picked up the phone, called Savannah and fortunately found her at the shop. Somehow I maintained my composure. Anne Davidson sounded stunned by the revelation, but was polite and very apologetic. Yes, of course, she would honor the warranty and would, upon receipt of the chairs, send us a check in refund, plus Duncan LeMar's fee.

Several drinks later, in a more mellow mood, Hope and I agreed after a long discussion that we would never know whether this had been an honest difference of opinion among experts or a crass attempt to bilk us. In any event, we decided to drop the subject of the chairs permanently. After all, no one had died and no money had been lost. Moreover, the Stickley cabinet would not have been validated without the chair purchase. Although the china closet appeared to be a real find, we certainly weren't going to celebrate yet.

The next day, we moved "Gus"—the cabinet—into the foyer and Hope filled the upper shelves with fine Minton china.

About a week later during dinner, Hope said, "I know it's a fine cabinet, but the Arts and Crafts style doesn't go with our other things. Let's put it up at auction and cash in our chips."

I concurred. Over the next week I called a number of galleries and auction houses to ascertain its value. Most sources requested photos before giving an estimate.

About ten days later, a woman named Elizabeth Gill called and identified herself as the expert in Arts and Crafts from Christie's. Gill stated that she had seen the photograph of our cabinet, which we had emailed to her, and was very interested in handling the sale. They had auctioned a similar piece that fetched $35,000. This was apparently the sale alluded to by Duncan LeMar. Gill mentioned in the conversation that she would be at a party in Westchester on Saturday evening and could examine the cabinet at that time if we were available. I replied truthfully that we had tentative plans, which we would cancel to accommodate her.

That Saturday evening we met Elizabeth Gill; we were in a subdued mood following our recent disappointment. Gill was upbeat and could best be described as an attractive former preppie trying to keep that look even as she approached middle age. She examined the cabinet carefully and professionally.

Her comments were concise. "This is indeed an important and very early example. It is unique because the dimensions are significantly smaller than the catalogued cabinet. The condition is pristine except for the panes of broken glass, which are easily replaced. I would estimate the cabinet conservatively at $25–35,000 in the sales catalogue. Unofficially, I would guess that it will bring well above the high estimate, perhaps in the area of $50,000."

She added, "Possibly more if the right people show up in person, online or on the phone and start bidding against each other. Conversely, bad weather and a lack of competition might have the opposite effect. Therefore, I would suggest a reserve price of $18,000 in order to protect you."

I asked several questions, the most significant relating to her belief that it was important and unique. Her answer was largely technical, but the gist was that, in her opinion, the cabinet might by its description be the one mentioned in an early article written by Gustav in the Craftsman Magazine and that he later built for his own home.

We thanked Gill for her advice and for making the trip. I told her we would think through the matter and call her the following week. Monday morning I contacted Ms. Gill, had a brief conversation and asked her to send the contract for the auction sale. Ten days later the cabinet left Scarsdale.

At the end of the week we received an email from Anne Davidson advising us that an expert from a museum in Atlanta was in town and had checked the chairs that had recently arrived. In his view, the chairs were genuine Chippendale rather than attributed to and thus far more valuable than the original sales price. In view of this, she inquired whether we would consider taking them back or at the very least getting a third opinion from another expert whose credentials we would all agree upon before the inspection.

I returned her email immediately. Tactfully, but in strong language, I rejected her suggestion and stated that I expected a full refund. Nevertheless, another ten days passed without a check from Savannah. I was too angry to call her and instead gave my attorney an account of the whole matter. He agreed to send his own letter that would fall just short of threatening a lawsuit. However, the next communication from *Huneycutt Antiques* was a copy of another appraisal attesting to the genuineness of the chairs. I calmly called my lawyer and told him to proceed with the lawsuit. I didn't ask the details of his correspondence, but was relieved when a short time later a check covering the sale and the appraisal fee arrived from Anne Davidson. There was no letter of apology for the delay, just the check and a formal release to any right or title to the chairs, which I promptly signed and returned.

Our Stickley cabinet just missed making the late spring auction and was held over until the fall. Elizabeth Gill assured us that the delay would give her extra time to generate formal and informal publicity for the cabinet and thus heighten interest for the fall sale.

During that summer, except for entertaining friends with the story of our wonderful luck, we concentrated on grooving our golf swings. About three weeks before the sale, we received a copy of the auction catalogue containing a full-page color photograph of the cabinet. The lighting and photography was superb, making that cabinet look even better than it did in life. It was at this point that our level of expectation and excitement began to rise.

Hope was too nervous to attend the sale. I sat by myself near the rear of the room in order to watch other bidders. Our lot was scheduled to be auctioned near the end. I noted happily that the majority of earlier lots sold near or above their high estimates; only two pieces failed to make their reserves. It seemed to take forever for the auctioneer to reach our lot and when he did, the whole thing was over very quickly. The first bid was $8,000 and they increased quickly by increments of $500 and then $1,000 to $12,000. The auctioneer glanced at the young woman holding the phone, gave a final warning and said softly, "Passed."

I couldn't believe it and didn't feel like rising from my seat at the end of the sale. I found Elizabeth Gill scurrying about and before I could say anything she blurted, "Do you want to sell it through us to the high bidder?"

Instead of responding, I inquired angrily, "What the hell happened?"

She glanced at me without expression and coolly remarked, "Oh, it was trashed by the cognoscenti. The word was that it was probably a later piece." She continued in a more vibrant tone, "I still think it's a great early piece—time may prove me right."

I left sadly without commenting further. Driving home in a depressed fog, I dreaded giving Hope the bad news. At the front door I grabbed the mail, stepped over the threshold and confronted Hope in the foyer.

"What happened, what's wrong?" she said.

I summarized the auction action or rather inaction, then offered weakly, "Well, we have an antique worth $12,000 that was found on the street."

Hope replied, "I'm terribly disappointed and it's much more than the money. I thought we had an historic piece by Gustav Stickley. In any case, we've certainly had an education these last nine months!"

Picking through the mail I tore open an envelope with *Huneycutt Antiques* printed in the corner. Inside, without any cover letter, was a copy of a fax from a London newspaper. The headline, over three columns wide, read, "Chairs by Chippendale Sell for Record Price!" The first paragraph reported that the price was just over 100,000 pounds.

I glanced through the rest of the article, which had a picture of "our" chairs. The buyer was a museum in Scotland and the seller was identified as *Huneycutt Antiques* of Savannah, Georgia, USA. Hope looked up at me as I handed her the fax. I said, "More of an expensive education than you could imagine!"

Well, this is the end of the story—for now. Will a future auction or time and research determine that our cabinet was the personal and seminal work of an American Thomas Chippendale: the gifted Gustav Stickley?

In the meantime, our treasure is still available.

My name is Sy Green and if you are interested in purchasing a rare Gustav Stickley cabinet in fine original condition, I can be reached at Southern Uniform Rental. You can Google us; we're in the Bronx.

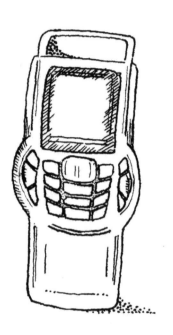

TWENTY FOUR

There's an App
for That!

L ong Island Antique Management or LIAM is located in tony
suburban Garden City, New York. They produce and manage
antique shows in the area extending from Brooklyn/Queens
to the eastern tip of Long Island.

Phyllis Rossi, the diminutive CEO of the group, had started her
career in a large public relations firm, *PR Publix*, and after twenty-
five years had risen to Vice President. The PR business, along with
many others, tanked with the downturn of the economy. Inspired by
her experience in the family-owned antique business, Phyllis changed
paths.

Throughout childhood, little redheaded Phyllis would always
stop by the antique store on her way home from school in Great
Neck, another affluent bedroom community of New York City. The
store, *Golden Treasures*, was a delight to visit with its fascinating array
of furniture, paintings, interesting objects and jewelry. Cute, person-
able Phyllis seemed to draw customers: they scheduled their visits to

coincide with her after-school routine and always made a fuss over her. This winning attitude was a factor in guiding Phyllis to her major in public relations at nearby Hofstra University.

LIAM's offices were bright with natural light from their southern exposure and surprisingly quiet considering they were on Stewart Avenue, a busy road leading into Garden City.

One Saturday morning, Phyllis sat at the round conference table between her daughter Karen and Donald LeBlanc, her longtime associate. Karen resembled her mom: petite and carrot-topped. Phyllis was now sixtyish, still energetic and trim, and wrinkle-free thanks to regular Botox. Her hair, now its natural gray, was arranged in a flattering pixie cut.

Donald's responsibility was to supervise set-up at the antique shows and look after the many details and dealer relations. The 240-pound, six-foot-four ex-football player had the appropriate presence to keep complainers in line. Karen was the "gal Friday" of the organization.

Facing the three key members of LIAM across the table was their invited guest, John Carroll, an Internet and media consultant.

Phyllis quipped, "Guess the GPS worked perfectly—you got here right on time!"

"Actually, I know the area well. I'm a New York Islander fan and I make this run many times during hockey season," he said, chuckling. "It's going to be a lot shorter trip for me when the Islanders move to the Barclay Center in Brooklyn."

Phyllis retorted, "But it's not going to be good for business out here."

She would never have pictured Carroll as a hockey fan on his way to a game. Late thirties, balding, with a curly, unkempt black beard and steel wire-framed glasses, he could easily have been cast as "Assistant Professor at a New England College." The slightly rumpled, out-of-date Brooks Brothers vested suit completed the look.

Phyllis addressed the visitor. "We've gone back and forth for weeks discussing your idea for an antique show app. John; let me summarize with you the problems of the antique industry, particularly as it applies to us at LIAM." Phyllis took a sip of coffee and cleared her throat. "Not in any particular order, here are the important factors that are negatively impacting the industry: Number one eBay. Collectors are looking there first for obvious reasons: cost, huge selection and ease of delivery from anywhere in the world.

"Number two—young people are more interested in spending their disposable income on electronic gadgets: Smartphones, laptops and pads. Ironically, these devices are more likely to link them to our competitors in the antique business, like eBay, Google and online sellers.

"Number three, finally, is the economy. The depressed housing sector has negatively influenced the home furnishing market. As a consequence, sales of vintage furniture have dried up. When young buyers are faced with the necessity and desire to purchase decorative items and furniture, they usually choose Target, Pier 1, Ikea and Macy's."

She paused for a moment and noted the others were nodding agreement. "John, I don't know if you've ever attended an antique show, but the crowd these days is preponderantly gray-topped. The bottom line is that all of the above is affecting attendance at antique shows. It is a vicious cycle: the customers don't come and the dealers don't make money, so they cancel, the shows become smaller and the show managers can't make it, especially since our expenses—rentals, labor costs and insurance—keep increasing. Bottom-bottom line: ten years ago, we had ten events a year. Now we're struggling to make it on the five we have left."

All eyes turned towards Carroll. "Well, that's why I'm here."

"I want to tell you why we reached out to you specifically," Phyllis said.

"The more I know, the better I can tailor a program to help address the problem."

"Well, our shows on Long Island are small—seventy dealers on average. Occasionally, we produce an event that will attract a hundred or more dealers. To be painfully honest, we're now operating on the edge of profitability. However, we are going to take a huge financial gamble next spring. We've made a deal with the new Barclay's Center in Brooklyn. The basketball season will be over for the Nets and I don't think the Islanders will have moved there yet. Management of the facility is anxious to fill some open dates and demonstrate novel uses for their arena floor layout. The available space is larger than the basketball court layout and uses the bigger dimensions of the hockey rink. The circus, ice follies and rock concerts are successful and fill some dates. However, that still leaves lots of down time for trade shows. They are putting our antique show in the latter category. I've been working on the floor plan. We have room for 200 dealers, including other arena space. We are going to call it the first *Brooklyn Antique Show Happening* or the BASH at Barclays."

"I like the sound of it!" was Carroll's enthusiastic response.

Phyllis continued, "Here's why we asked you to come. We are hoping that your Antique App will not only attract customers, but also be an added incentive for dealers to want to sign up for BASH. As it stands, I don't think we can attract 200 dealers otherwise. We need 150 signed up just to break even. Now the floor is yours!"

"Well, I'll summarize the materials I previously emailed to you. Each registered dealer will get a hard copy version as well as an email packet explaining our service and the fact that this is a first for the antique industry. We will lay out clearly the reasons we think this novel approach will work and go on to describe how they can list the items with photos for the customer to see. We'll charge a minimal fee of one dollar per listing up to a maximum of fifty items. The device will be pictured and we will loan the device free to each attendee to the show, along with instructions. Either by voice command or typing, the potential customer will be directed to a particular booth where the desired object is for sale. We are available online and by toll-free number to answer any questions about the listing procedure. Finally, our staff of excellent techies will be available at the show dressed in distinctive shirts with lightning bolts to explain, distribute and demonstrate the programmed devices."

"Incidentally, the hand held equipment will be similar in size to those offered by museums in their voice-guided tours. With your approval, I suggest we call this device, and the potential future app that can be installed on a Smartphone, the *Antique Finder*. The concept is already copyrighted."

Phyllis interrupted. "I'll give you an example of a listing and tell me if we're on the same page."

"Okay—go ahead."

"Vintage 18-karat Patek Phillippe wristwatch, circa 1930's: $3,200."

Carroll replied, "Yes, that sounds fine and I would suggest—if the dealers agree—that we make listing the price optional."

"That's a good point. I think flexibility is paramount at first. I'm sure that after the first run, we'll learn a lot and change many things. My other question to you is what is your long range goal in all of this? Antique shows alone would make a very small market for you."

"Yes, of course. Antique Finder is a test model for more sophisticated devices to follow. What we see happening is, of course, eventually eliminating the device and having an app for sale that could be downloaded to a Smartphone."

"Can you tell us how this will work, logistically, when you first hand the instrument to a customer?"

"One of our people will hand the attendee a device after they pay their admission. They will be shown how to access the first screen, which directs them either to typing or the voice-activated method. They make their request for a particular item and the device brings up a list of dealers who have this item, along with their booth number and directions to that location."

Carroll took a long drink of water. "Let me talk more about our longer-range goals. A large Internet company, *Virtual Ventures International*, is backing us. If this concept proves to be valid, we could easily program many apps for every conceivable trade show, convention or exhibit. Apps are important because of the advertising they generate. For example, the antique show app could have advertising from adjacent shops, restaurants and various entertainment venues in the area along with the show dealer information, so they could also draw customers after the show."

The group spent another half-hour familiarizing Carroll with various antique and collecting areas.

"My staff will give each participating dealer an opportunity to list his or her stuff," he told them. "With this background information, I'll be more attuned to the potential inventory. We will carefully check the descriptions and make sure we note everything correctly. If we have any questions about the listing, we'll contact the dealer directly and give everybody a chance to correct the listing before it is finally online on our website."

Phyllis Rossi stood to signal that the meeting was over. "Sounds good to me! It appears to be a win-win for the dealers, the customers and you guys, too."

"We'll see—and thanks for the opportunity to try this out. We'll see you all again at the show in six months and of course we'll speak in the interim. Goodbye!"...

Paul Grogan, Ph.D., stared at his computer in the office of his Long Island home. He had just enough time to check his email before the first of his three patients for that day was due. The semi-retired psychologist, in his late fifties, was running out the clock on a practice of almost 30 years. The income from this activity supported his three most significant interests: his daughter Suzanne; his seven-year-old granddaughter, Millie; and an antique business. Paul had been divorced from Suzanne's mother, Hilda, for almost eight years. A strong physical attraction and many common interests had not been enough to negate their insurmountable problem: in spite of both being successful psychologists, they would have screaming fights ten times a day, every day. After the insertion of Paul's second stent necessitated by severe coronary ischemia—certainly aggravated by the daily fights—he and Hilda had agreed to end their marriage.

Paul was resigned to the fact that he would probably live out his remaining years without the emotional companionship he craved. He looked more like a retired airline pilot than a psychologist. With his tall, spare body, accent-free articulate speech, buzz cut and aviator glasses, he would be considered a catch by the over-fifty crowd. Nevertheless, he had not had a relationship recently that lasted more than two dates. Ironically, his daughter, 30-year-old Suzanne, was currently going through a divorce, but her home-based computer business allowed her to care for Millie and help her father at antique shows.

Grogan regularly participated in the LIAM shows. *Paul's Pleasures* specialized in historic medals and New York City memorabilia. Rare World's Fair collectibles and Olympic material were other specialties.

Paul was about to delete an email headed "Enhanced sales for your next show" thinking it looked like spam or maybe a Viagra solicitation. He noted the sender was *Virtual Ventures International.*

He decided to open it anyway. It announced a new sales aid, The Antique Finder, which would first be used at the BASH show. A detailed examination would have to wait, as the office bell announced the arrival of his first patient...

Several months later, in Manhattan, John Carroll watched his two programmers entering the inventories provided by the BASH dealers onto the Antique Finder site.

Jenny, one of the young programmers, asked John, "What the devil is this entry describing Persian carpets? He lists Kirman, Bijar, Tabriz and Sarouk."

John replied, "That's one I can answer. They're cities in Persia, or Iran as it is known today, where the carpets were made."

The other programmer, Jimmy, piped up, "What's a Rookwood rook?"

"Well, Rookwood was a pottery manufacturer in Cincinnati in the early 20th century. A rook is another name for a crow. This entry is definitely not describing the 'castle' in chess."

It took several more days to complete the listings. In many cases, they had to call the dealers to clarify the descriptions. On the last afternoon, John was helping Jenny and Jimmy complete the programming.

Jenny moaned, "Ready for this? I'm so tired of doing this, I'd rather process a listing for used toilet paper samples, but this is really weird. This is an entry from a dealer, Paul Grogan, who calls his business *Paul's Pleasures*. First he has what looks like a legitimate entry for the participant medal for the 1936 Berlin Olympics for $300. That was the most famous Olympics and it has historical and political significance. Then he adds several more legitimate-looking entries. But this is the last one, all capitalized:

FIFTYISH MALE ANTIQUE LOVER. VINTAGE BUT STILL IN GOOD SHAPE—ACQUIRING A SECOND PATINA. WOULD LIKE TO HANG TOGETHER WITH COMPATIBLE FEMALE EXAMPLE. CLOSE PROXIMITY OF THE PAIR WOULD ENHANCE THE TOTAL EFFECT."

"I think we'd better call him," John said.

That evening, Carroll called Paul Grogan. "Hi, Mr. Grogan, this is John Carroll from the firm that is programming your inventory into the website for the *Brooklyn Antique Show Happening* at the Barclay Center."

Paul laughed. "Yeah, I expected your call. I hope you chuckled when you read my entry."

"Very funny! But I must ask—are you serious?"

"Absolutely. What harm can it do? Maybe I'll end up with a coffee-break date at the show or even better—a sale!"

"Okay, let's go for it. I won't mention this to the LIAM people; however, promise you will get back to me if there are any positive results."

"You're on!"…

All 202 booths at the Barclay's BASH were rented at an average of $1,200 per space. The paid attendance was excellent. There were some minor glitches in the *Antique Finder* device: some of the customers were in too much of a hurry even for the brief time required to distribute and explain the device's operation. However, many who initially rushed by the *Virtual Ventures International* counter returned later for a chance to explore the new toy.

Later, Phyllis Rossi calculated that over two-thirds of the attendees tried out the novel device. The following week, she called John Carroll and had a lengthy discussion with him about the feedback she had received from customers and dealers.

"I think the furniture and lighting dealers did best with it. I'll tell you why: people who are looking for a dining table, sofa, desk, bookcase, lamp, etcetera, have a real need and desire to make that purchase. They may have a place in a new home or are redecorating and have a space to fill. There are also certain customers who are looking for items missing from their collections. It might be a specific book, beer mug or commemorative silver spoon. On the other hand, the jewelry people did less well with the *Antique Finder*. Jewelry sales are mostly impulse-driven. The *Antique Finder* works best for those who have something specific in mind.

"Our corporate bosses, *Virtual Ventures International*, are always a step ahead. If we are involved in future shows, we will be able to program customers' Smartphones prior to the show or more quickly than we were able to do with this system at the event."

A few days later, Paul Grogan called John Carroll. After exchanging brief greetings, Paul recounted his experiences. "Well, first, I can happily inform you that there was one strong sale as a direct consequence of the *Antique Finder*. I sold a rare Lake Placid 1932 Winter Games bronze medal for speed skating. The sale price was $2,800 and I hadn't even listed it—but the Berlin Olympic listing brought the buyer in."

"Great!"

"However, before you even think of asking, I can report that I didn't succeed in selling myself!"

They both laughed and he continued, "Two women stopped by and we all had a good laugh while coming up with new metaphors for mature people. One gal asked if my finish was original. I answered that I had had minor plastic surgery but was acquiring a new look."

John answered, "With your sense of humor maybe we should have an auction—the ladies would be trying to outbid each other!"

"Actually, I'm a psychologist and I have a terrific idea in the social networking area that would involve a device like the *Antique Finder*."

"Well, Doc, we're located in Midtown. Make a trip to the city on your day off. I'll buy you lunch and we can talk."

During lunch at *Corfu* a couple of weeks later, the good food and drink permitted only a brief introduction of Dr. Grogan's concept. "Here's the setting for my idea. Picture a weekend singles cruise from New York. Each participant will, in advance, get a questionnaire similar to the one sent for BASH, except that the individuals will be asked about fifty questions relating to themselves, including age, religion, education, income, occupation, vacation preferences, marital status, entertainment preferences, hobbies, attitudes about children, sex, etcetera. Then they will be asked what they seek in a partner."

"I'm interested," John said. "Let's continue this discussion at my office. It's just down the block."

The conversation resumed once they were comfortably seated in Carroll's office.

"John, here is how I envision this might work aboard a cruise ship. Each person would carry a device similar to the one at the antique show. However, this would be much more sophisticated in its operation. Before the cruise, as I suggested, the questionnaires would be filled out. *Virtual Ventures International* would give the recruits an added incentive by handing out the devices free."

"So far this all sounds feasible."

"This is how I picture the operation. The participants on the cruise would carry the programmed devices whenever they come out of their cabins for all the activities: eating, dancing, exercising, and drinking, and so on. Incidentally, I've even thought of a good name for it: *Smartconnection*, because I'm guessing that at some point it will become available as an app for Smartphones also. Each device will have a number whose importance I will explain later. If two people meet, pass each other or are sitting near each other at a bar or restaurant and find the other party attractive, they unobtrusively press a button on the device. In a matter of seconds, the two devices electronically review the programmed entries on the other's device. If there is a pre-set degree of compatibility, the device vibrates and the number of the other party's Smartphone is printed out like a text message, along with the percentage of compatibility—up to 100 percent if that's possible. The two people confront each other and go off to further explore their compatibility. "

John responded, "Just to make this clear—the fact that the devices are numbered avoids embarrassing mistakes. I love it!"

"Do you really think this is doable? You're the technical guy," Paul said.

"Actually, I'm not that technical, but I know the IT people would certainly have the capability of making it work. There would be an even bigger audience for this than the antique app. Singles would all have this app on the Smartphones they already carry everywhere. The cruise ship would make an excellent pilot study!"

The two men parted, but agreed to stay in touch...

Less than a year later, the first *Smartconnection Cruise* was advertised. The IT engineers had easily figured out how to get the technology packaged into a handheld device. A Smartphone app was also available for that first sailing and would undoubtedly be the preferred technique for the increasing Smartphone-carrying public.

Paul Grogan was rewarded for his idea with a free cruise and the potential for some significant earnings, as he was to be paid one dollar for each app sold in the future after the pilot program. He would also serve as an informal consultant for the company and help out with any problems on board with the "Smart Cruisers."

Paul's first observation when he joined the cruise was that everyone aboard was having fun! Liquor sales were booming and a second cruise was already planned. The number of cabins shared after the first night was, of course, very difficult to quantify. The success of relationships that continued beyond the cruise and became more serious would require much additional assessment to gauge accurately.

The first night at sea, after vigorous vibration of their individual devices, Paul got together with Lily, an attractive woman about his age. Their meeting and somewhat brief conversation led to an amorous night in his cabin.

Next morning, when they were both sober and more awake, he queried her. "I bet you're into antiques, biking, the theater and mystery novels or at least many of my interests—that device certainly vibrated!"

Lily replied as she was dressing, "Not really. I just checked everything on the list, because I wanted to have a good time on the cruise."

They both laughed as they walked towards the dining room for a late breakfast…

The ship had passed under the Verrazano Bridge and was less than a half-hour from docking. Paul noticed a woman standing about forty feet away, staring at the Statue of Liberty. He could not see her face, but she had attractive hair and a slim, upright figure.

He called out, "Don't turn around! We have to give these devices back in a few minutes. Just for fun, press the button and I will press mine to see if we're compatible. "

The instruments vibrated at maximum strength as the woman turned and faced him. He was shocked at first and then laughed.

"You see, Hilda, we are still compatible—the device works!"

His ex-wife did not laugh. "No, it proves just the opposite. We've already tried and we are definitely not compatible. The *Smartconnection* app is not so smart after all!"

ABOUT THE AUTHORS

Avid collectors, dealers and writers in the antique field for more than thirty years, our particular focus in collecting is in Arts & Crafts. The experiences we have had in the trade and our imaginations inspired these stories. The authors hope you enjoyed their tales—we are hard at work on our next anthology.

Arthur Cobin and Vivien Boniuk are married and live in New York City surrounded by their various collections.

Made in the USA
Middletown, DE
29 April 2019